Light through the Cracks

How God Breaks In When Life Turns Tough

Ten True Stories

By Joanna Watson

PUBLISHING

Endorsements

"I defy you to put this book down once you have started reading it! It is a fascinating collection of 21st century true stories that Joanna has carefully researched and recorded. She writes fluently and appealingly. Is God still active today and does he listen and respond to our prayers? If you are in any doubt then you must read this book! I felt faith in a loving God rising as I read the narratives, and I also found myself learning how to pray more consistently as I read about the effects of persistent prayers for those in trouble of any kind. It is intensely personal, clearly authentic and gloriously uplifting. Read it yourself and then buy copies for all your friends and family!"

Anne Coles
Author, speaker, and former leader of New Wine Conferences

"In *Light Through the Cracks*, Joanna Watson takes us on a faith-building journey through her beautiful storytelling. Each chapter is a self-contained story of God's grace, intervention and sovereignty over all of life's diverse circumstances. Read them and celebrate the goodness of God, and your own faith will be enlarged and sharpened."

Simon Guillebaud
Author, speaker, and founder of Great Lakes Outreach

"I devoured this book! Written from her experience of a terrifying accident as her car plunged down a mountainside, and the amazing series of co-incidences – or 'God-incidences' as she calls them – that followed, Joanna seeks to show that God's hand is at work in life's events far more than we realise. Since that accident, she has carefully gathered, and beautifully written, other stories of ordinary people who encountered God in extraordinary ways in tough times as he broke into their situations, sometimes miraculously, sometimes through the seemingly mundane, to turn things around. Her encouragement to us is that God is still real and still does miracles, though we may have to battle in faith and persistence in prayer, and cling on to his promises to see them. Each story, deeply moving in its own way, certainly provoked me to stir up once again my belief in the God of miracles."

Revd Mike Beaumont
Author, pastor, Bible teacher, and broadcaster

"Not only does this book engage the reader through brilliant, page-turning storytelling, but Joanna Watson's *Light Through the Cracks* is a reminder to us all that, in the rollercoaster of life, God's hand is always at work, comforting, guiding, ordering. These deeply personal stories draw us in and remind us of the times when we, too, have seen and felt God's presence, even at those times when such hope feels impossible. Everyone should read this book and take from it a message of profound hope."

Chine McDonald
Writer, author, and broadcaster

"This is a book about God's activity. Sometimes that activity is instantaneous, like the teenage woman released from years of chronic pain. Sometimes it's mysterious, like the struggling church that finds a bin bag of cash by its front door. Sometimes it comes as dramatic intervention, other times as a quiet work in the heart, yet always is it miraculous. Through careful interviewing and compelling storytelling, *Light Through the Cracks* will have you expecting God's powerful touch in your life and circumstances too."

Sheridan Voysey
Presenter of *Pause for Thought* on BBC Radio 2, and author of *The Making of Us* and *Resurrection Year*

"In *Light Through the Cracks,* Joanna Watson primes the pump of our expectation for the supernatural to invade our everyday lives. Through ten true stories of ordinary people encountering an extraordinary God in the toughest of circumstances, we are left in no doubt: that the God of miracles is HERE. Right now. In the West. Powerfully at work. It's in the retelling of these good-news stories that the light shines all the brighter. So this is a book to read and then pass on, so that many more people can experience how life's unwelcome 'suddenlies' can be transformed into moments of deep encounter with the God of hope."

Helen Azer
International teacher, pastor, and Director of Ministry with Heartcry for Change

"Does God hear our prayers? Does God care? Does God involve himself in the details of our lives? Does God ever intervene? Really? Joanna Watson's exciting new book exclaims a resounding 'YES!' God is with us; God is for us. This book begs important questions of, 'Why them? Why there? Why not here?' But it will also raise faith in us to believe, and seek, and expect to see more of God's gracious and miraculous intervention."

Revd Simon Ponsonby
International author, speaker, teacher, and Pastor of Theology at St Aldates Church, Oxford

"*Light Through the Cracks* is an engaging collection of real-life stories, documenting the work of God within brokenness, suffering and significant challenge, in accounts of ordinary people encountering an extraordinary God. As someone who lives with chronic illness, it's an encouragement for me to read these stories of healing and provision against the backdrop of broken, messy people and situations. This is not a book of perfect endings, but it is a book that leads us into hope and reminds us that God does, sometimes, break through in great power. It is vital that Christians find ways to keep telling the stories of God, and this book is one that celebrates God's work, increases our faith, and helps us remember and share our own stories. Readers will come away encouraged, consoled and expectant."

Liz Carter
Author of *Catching Contentment* and *Treasure in Dark Places*

"The question of why God would allow suffering is one that many have asked. While there are no easy answers, Joanna Watson, in her beautifully written book *Light Through the Cracks*, shows us that God is far from absent, even in the most heart-wrenching of circumstances. In story after story, we learn that prayer changes lives, that friends make all the difference, and that God is able to do extraordinary things in situations that ordinarily might sink us. Even if you are not sure what you believe, I encourage you to read this book. You will have a glimpse of what could be possible if it's true that God is real."

Sharon Dirckx
Lecturer, speaker, and author of *Why? Looking at God, Evil and Personal Suffering*

Dedication

For my parents

Contents

	Introduction	11
Chapter 1	**Synchronisation is his watchword** Siblings in a car accident in the USA	17
Chapter 2	**X-rays never lie** A man with a stroke and a tumour	43
Chapter 3	**Beautiful inside and out** A complicated birth	71
Chapter 4	**Power in the name of Jesus** A woman with stomach cancer	103
Chapter 5	**All it takes is one split second** A married couple in a car accident in the UK	131
Chapter 6	**Hard pressed but not crushed** Twins born prematurely	165
Chapter 7	**Building on God's grace** A church threatened with closure	197
Chapter 8	**Nothing can separate us** A boy in a hammock accident	225
Chapter 9	**Holding onto a prophetic promise** A man with blood cancer	255
Chapter 10	**Release from a prison of darkness** A teenager ill with ME	289
	Acknowledgements	323
	Making contact	327
	Further help	327
	Further reading	327
	About the author	329

Introduction

*"The light shines in the darkness,
and the darkness has not overcome it."*
John 1:5

Strictly speaking, I could be dead.

The fact I'm not is because God saved my life.

Leonard Cohen once famously sang, "There is a crack, a crack in everything. That's how the light gets in."[1]

As a Christian, I believe that "the light" comes through Jesus, because the Bible says: *"The light shines in the darkness, and the darkness has not overcome it,"* referring to Jesus.

The story of what happened to me is one of ten true stories contained in this book, united by a common theme. They all reveal how God has broken into some very dark and difficult situations; how he has brought *"light through the cracks"*.

What binds this book together?

Whether it is cancer disappearing without trace; a man defying death, multiple times, following life-threatening injuries incurred in a head-on road collision; a baby born prematurely, only to confound the medical predictions about his prognosis; cash appearing out of nowhere to keep a church from closing; or a teenager seeing her long-term debilitating illness disappear

---

1. From the song "Anthem" on his 1992 album, 'The Future'.

in an instant, these and all the other stories in this book are ones that need to be told.

They are stories of ordinary people who have encountered God in extraordinary ways. Stories in which life turned tough. Stories in which God broke in – sometimes miraculously, other times in the seemingly mundane – to turn things around. Stories in which God shone into the darkness, resided in the midst of the darkness, dispelled the darkness – and made his voice heard and his presence felt.

Why has this book been written?

I have written this book with three main purposes in mind:

1. To generate faith for miracles

We live in a world that is saturated with cynicism, hopelessness and despair. It permeates the media, influences our prevailing culture, and drip-feeds negativity. It can be hard to be joyful, hopeful and optimistic – even for people of faith.

Christians believe that prayer has power; that God intervenes when we pray; and that miracles can happen when we pray. They are relatively rare, but they occur more often than we realise.

Miracles are possible because God is at work in the spiritual realm, as well as the physical realm; in the extraordinary, as well as the ordinary. He heals through medicine, but also supernaturally. He provides financially through a steady income, but also out of thin air. He expects us to heed warning signs, but also sends angels to protect us from danger. He speaks through the Bible, but also through dreams and visions. The Bible is packed with miracle stories.

This book spans two decades and contains ten modern-day-miracle stories. They reveal God at work, not just in the dim and distant past, or in some far-flung part of the world – but here at home, in the 21st century. They will inspire you for what is possible through prayer in the name of Jesus; stir you up to be bold in asking God for breakthrough in your own situations; and encourage you to cultivate faith for miracles.

2. To celebrate what God has done

We live in an age that is constantly changing and relentlessly future-facing. Our social media feeds provide a continuous scroll. Boxsets mean we binge-watch without waiting. News headlines are never the same on simultaneous days. Once something has happened, we quickly forget it and move on.

In the Bible, the word "remember" occurs over 230 times, and frequently in conjunction with a call to celebrate. It is clear that God wants people to remember and celebrate what he has done.

At Christmas, Christians remember and celebrate the birth of Jesus. At Pentecost, they remember and celebrate the outpouring of the Holy Spirit. At Easter, and whenever Christians break bread and wine together, they remember and celebrate the central events of world history – the death and resurrection of Jesus.

When God performed miracles in the Bible, the people built piles of stones and gave the places new names. Each time the people passed by, as they wandered through the land, they would remember and celebrate what God had done – with each generation passing the stories down to the next, until they were written down.

In the 21st century, we need a modern-day equivalent of piles of stones and new place names. We need to share and record the stories. We need to remember and celebrate, rather than forget.

This book seeks to do this. As you read these accounts of God breaking into seemingly impossible situations, they will encourage you to celebrate what God has done.

3. To activate an invitation to write

A few years ago, within the space of eighteen months, three different Christians, all unknown to me, spoke prophetically into my life, inviting me to write. The first was a Costa Rican in London; the second, an Australian in Oxford; the third, a South African in Johannesburg.

On each occasion, the message was clear: I needed to write down my stories and the stories of those around me, because God was going to use them to impact many people. On each occasion, the way it happened was consistent: I was in a public Christian meeting, the worship and teaching had ended, and the words were spoken over me in front of other people. (God probably knew I would need witnesses to hold me accountable!)

In the years since, I have sought to activate this invitation, initially in setting up a blog, and now through writing this book. I have many more stories than those you will read here. This is just the beginning!

How should this book be read?

This book contains ten true stories, each in a separate chapter. This means, if you so desire, you can read them in any order you like. However, the chapters are set out in chronological order because several of them include snippets of my own story which will make most sense if read in sequence[2].

The content for these stories has come from a variety of sources. With each one, I interviewed the people involved and

---

2. The only exception is Chapter 3. The context for how I know the friend in this story is chronological. However, the story itself occurred later.

transcribed the recordings before incorporating journal entries, notes from letters and cards, and prayer emails and texts – plus, where applicable, blog posts, newspaper cuttings, song lyrics and Bible verses. Everyone named has given their permission to be included.

All the stories are accurate, as far as those involved are concerned, and I am grateful for all the fact-checking they have provided. In sharing them, I have tried my best to get a good balance. These are not journalistic reports, nor are they novellas. They are, at their heart, stories, and I have tried to write them in as accessible a way as possible.

Where I have inserted conversations, often these are approximations. A few of them were recorded or recalled word for word, but many were not. In some cases, where it brings clarity, people have been deliberately left out of the narrative, even though they were present during the dialogue.

In conveying the highs and lows of these stories, you need to know, up front, that not all of them have happy endings. However, that does not diminish the ways in which God broke in along the way. So if you want a book that addresses theological issues – such as why God allows suffering, or how he answers prayer, or what evidence there is for miracles – you are reading the wrong book! There are plenty of other books out there which will help you consider those things, but it is not the aim of this one[3].

One final thought …

All of us are narrative creatures, hardwired for stories. Stories transcend time, span generations, and cross cultures. True stories are particularly powerful, especially when God is involved, doing extraordinary things for ordinary people. But

---

3. Further reading suggestions are provided at the end of this book.

telling these stories makes us vulnerable as we have no say over who will read them, and no guarantee of their response.

As you read this book, I hope you will appreciate the courage of those who have stepped outside their comfort zones to share from their hearts, through my words on the page. But I also hope you will encounter Jesus, without whom these stories would not exist.

Joanna Watson

CHAPTER 1

Synchronisation is his watchword

Siblings in a car accident in the USA (1999)

"For he will command his angels concerning you
to guard you in all your ways;
they will lift you up in their hands,
so that you will not strike your foot against a stone."

Psalm 91:11-12

This story is my own. It's about a car accident that I had while on holiday in the USA. I was with my brother, Adrian, who is two years my junior, and we were both in our twenties at the time. It also features my friends William and Stella, who I knew when they lived in the UK, but are now in the USA.

"Looord Jeeesuuus!" I scream from inside the car, as it hurtles over the edge of the road, plunging down the side of the mountain, into pitch-black darkness.

A huge dust cloud billows up as the wheels tear over the steep, uneven ground. Thud, thud, thud.

The car seems to pick up speed in the descent, only prevented from careering completely out of control by the gigantic conifer trees clinging to the slope. The nauseating sound of the needle-filled branches scraping against the windows is a stark reminder of the forested wilderness we are driving through.

It is totally terrifying.

Somehow I find the brake. Slamming my foot against it, unable to see anything around me, I can feel the car flipping. Spinning over on itself, the back wheels rise into the air, the boot tumbling over towards the bonnet, until it crashes to a stop, finally coming to a rest on its roof.

Upside down and held in by my seatbelt, the car has plummeted about fifty metres over the side of the mountain, and I am in agony.

I know I have injured my back.

Making plans for a holiday of a lifetime in the United States has been an exciting adventure.

At the time, I'm working as a solicitor for a large and busy law firm based in south-east England. Most of my clients live in social housing, their legal fees covered by a means-tested, government-funded scheme. My role is to help them navigate every aspect of the breakdown of family relationships, between spouses, between parents and children, between siblings. It's an emotionally messy business.

The previous year, within a year of qualifying as a solicitor, I successfully fought and won a case that went to the Court of

Appeal and made law, securing the rights of unmarried fathers to see their children after the parental relationship breaks down. My colleagues keep telling me to milk the fame and prestige, jealous that I managed to land such a once-in-a-career case so early on. But I am restless and yearning for more.

Regardless of whether I'm facing perceived "success" or "failure" in my work, my clients' capacity to cause each other so much pain, hurt and disappointment never ceases to amaze me, and I regularly feel drained as I leave the office or the court room.

I'm more than ready for a holiday.

My brother Adrian has been keen to come with me. He works with an organisation, serving and supporting adults with learning disabilities. A gentle giant, caring and compassionate, his job, like mine, absorbs significant emotional reserves.

The United States is somewhere we've always wanted to explore and we're both feeling excited.

Adrian and I spend many hours reading our guide book cover to cover, and flicking through the alluring glossy photos that fill the travel agents' brochures – the choices are immense. Iconic buildings and city streets made famous by American movies. Historic monuments and museums. National Parks brimming with mountains, forests, lakes and waterfalls. Vineyards set in rolling hills. Deserts stretching for miles. The whole area is portrayed as a tourist's paradise, a photographer's dream, an idyll for those, like us, who love the great outdoors. We know it isn't going to disappoint.

One thing is clear: we want to make the most of such an amazing opportunity, to visit all the highlights, to see all that we can in the time we have available. Along the way, we want to weave in a visit to my friends from church, William and Stella, who recently relocated from the UK to the USA.

As we look at a map and register the sheer scale of travel involved, we quickly calculate that public transport isn't going to be an option for the amount of mileage we will be covering. The states in this part of the world are vast and, even navigating a relatively compact set of sites will be complicated without a vehicle. When we book our flights, we also book an economy car, more than sufficient for our needs, to be collected upon arrival at the airport.

❖

Arriving at the airport, jetlagged and bleary-eyed after our night flight and keenly aware of the not insignificant time difference with home, we make our way to the car hire desk.

"I'm afraid we don't have any economy cars," the convivial young man at the desk tells us, far too bright and sparkly for such an early hour. He shakes his head as he studies the computer screen in front of him, before turning to the paperwork spread out on his desk, and then back to the screen again. Watching him work is keeping us awake.

"I tell you what," he says after what feels like an eternity, bursting into a smile, his pristine white teeth in perfect proportion, "how about we give you a big car for the exact same price?" He speaks persuasively, willing us to accept his solution.

"Umm, err, yes, that's fine," I reply, realising we don't really have a choice. "That sounds great, thanks."

Paperwork complete, keys in hand, he helps us locate the car in the midst of the immense number of bays in the multi-storey subterranean airport carpark, and runs us through its safety features.

Before we know it, we are on our way, and our first stop, in our huge new hire car, is William and Stella's apartment, not far from the airport.

William and Stella know how to extend hospitality. Kind and friendly in personality, I've got to know them through being in the same church, and it's so lovely to see their familiar faces and experience such a warm welcome. No matter what the travel guidebooks say, staying with friends always beats anonymous hotels and guest houses.

We're fed and watered, and fall into a deep sleep that first night on American soil. The following morning, over coffee and pancakes, we are eager to hear their recommendations of places to see and things to do while we're staying with them.

Over the following few days, Adrian and I enjoy many of the best-loved local tourist destinations, and our cameras are full to overflowing with photos of all that we've seen and done.

By the time we start our onward journey, hope is riding high. The scenery is stunning. The people are consistently friendly. There's a sense of certainty that this holiday is going to be good.

The night before the accident, we arrive at the youth hostel on the edge of the National Park, checking in at exactly the same time as a young American backpacker. Travelling and hitchhiking solo, we get chatting with him in the sociable communal kitchen while preparing our evening meal.

"Are you guys driving into the park tomorrow?" he asks us, having established already that we're in a hire car. "If so, can I catch a ride with you?" His voice rises with the inflection of the question as he studies our faces for a response. He pauses a moment. "I can help pay the entrance fee," he adds.

It doesn't take long for a deal to be brokered.

Hiking around the National Park is fun. Our newfound friend is spontaneous and easy-going. For one so young, he's mature beyond his years and we spend all day together, surrounded by the vast scenery of huge mountains, spectacular lakes and dense forests, full of towering evergreen conifer trees.

There is excitement when we stumble upon new trails, gasps of delight when the awe-inspiring views demand yet another photo, and the encouragement of stimulating conversation. After a full day of hiking and exploring, just as the sunlight is turning towards dusk, we make an impromptu decision. Our travel guidebook is suggesting that if we drive to one of the highest vantage points in the National Park, renowned for its panoramic vista, we will be able to watch the sun setting over the horizon. We agree to seize the opportunity and are quickly following the route that will take us to the viewing point, aware that we need to time it just right.

We are not disappointed.

It's stunningly beautiful to see the sun set from such a special place, with the changing colour of the light reflecting across the mountain range, and we're not the only ones with the same idea. Quite a crowd of tourists and travellers have gathered alongside us to share the moment, all of us whispering with hushed voices, trying to take in the glorious splendour of what's unfolding in front of us.

Afterwards, driving down the winding mountain road, I am concentrating hard. Darkness is rapidly rolling in, and I'm still adjusting to an unfamiliar car, sitting on the "wrong" side of the car, driving on the "wrong" side of the road, and operating in a different time zone.

There are two or three other cars in front of me, illuminating the road, and I'm trying to keep up with their tail lights. Without any warning, a mountain tunnel appears up ahead, flooded with artificial light. It's only short and the road soon emerges out the other side – into thick pitch blackness. My eyes have to make a rapid adjustment; there are no cats' eyes or street lights to help my navigation.

Suddenly, there's a sharp and unexpected hairpin bend, lacking any arrows or other signs or markers to indicate its presence. The road is curving around to the right, and I'm turning the wheel, conscious of the unfamiliarity of the car's power steering. I can no longer see the tail lights of the other cars in front of me, which have sped off into the night.

Slightly oversteering to the right, and then to the left to compensate, my eyes still struggling with the depths of the darkness, before I know it we're hurtling over the edge of the road and I'm screaming, "Looord Jeeesuuus!"

It all happens so quickly.

For a split second there's a disconcerting silence in the darkness of the car as the dust clouds start to settle and I try to take in what is happening.

"My back, my back. Lord Jesus, my back. My back, my back. Lord Jesus, my back."

A cry of prayer is coming out of my mouth, barely audible, an in-built instinct kicking in. I'm repeating the same phrase over and over, willing the intensity of the pain in my spine to disappear. I should be feeling panicky. Instead, I feel a strange sense of peace.

"Are you alright?" my brother asks me from the passenger seat where his seatbelt is holding him in and upside down, just like me.

"I think so," I whisper, "but I've hurt my back. I know I've hurt my back."

"Don't move," he responds, reassuringly calm. "Are you paralysed? Can you feel your feet?"

I try to press the soles of my feet into the insoles of my sneakers, but it's not straightforward being suspended in mid-air, as I am right now, and I'm unsure whether the messages from my brain are reaching that far. Slowly, it occurs to me that I might be paralysed, and I can feel the fear. But I keep on praying, deliberately, intentionally, and calm continues to fill the car.

It slowly registers that I am alive. I could so easily have been killed.

I also feel relief and gratitude that I've removed my purse belt, in which I have been carrying around my house keys, passport and credit card, as it dawns on me that the seatbelt strap is sitting tight across my stomach.

"Are you OK?" I dread the answer, knowing any injury would be my fault, given I'm the driver.

"Yes, I'm alright," he replies. "I held my hands over my head to protect myself. The airbag went off. I'm alive. So are you. We're both alive."

And then he prays out loud in an unbelievable act of surrender, upside down, in the darkness, suspended on the edge of the mountain.

He tests the passenger door but it won't budge. I reach out to the driver's door to do likewise, but I jar my back and let out a yelp of pain. "Be careful," Adrian cautions me. It quickly becomes apparent that the impact has caused the car bonnet to shunt backward, jamming the doors. *How on earth are we going to get out?*

Suddenly a voice, strong and secure, comes from the backseat. We've been so absorbed in the moment that we've temporarily forgotten there's a guest in the car.

"It's OK," our backpacker friend says, his American accent projecting into the black stillness of the night, totally unfazed and unhurt. "I'll go and get help."

Before we know it, he's scrambling somehow out of the car wreckage. Momentarily orientating himself in the darkness, he's heading up the side of the mountain, through the forest wilderness, back to the road we've just tumbled off, while Adrian stays with me in the car.

Adrian later tells me that, unwittingly, he has been saved from a difficult choice: *Should he stay with me in the car, knowing I have badly hurt my back? Or should he clamber up to the road to flag down cars and seek help?*

Our newfound friend's presence in the car means the decision is taken out of his hands.

There's a steady trickle of traffic coming from the right, the main route for cars heading home from the viewing platform. Each one contains passengers who, moments earlier, were our companions in watching the sunset. Each one is driving through the huge dust cloud that's been generated by our car as it plunged over the edge. *Are they aware? Have they noticed? Do they care?*

Standing on the side of the road, somewhat bedraggled, the young American backpacker tries to get the attention of any drivers or passengers that see him. There are no cats' eyes or street lights to illuminate him. He doesn't even have a torch. All he has is courage and conviction. His new-found British friends need his help.

In quick succession, three cars stop.

The first car has a doctor in it. A huge, hulking, six-foot-six giant of a man, a French doctor who's on holiday with his family. It's he who gives my back an initial medical assessment.

The second car contains a man with a mobile phone, a rarity in 1999. What's more, his phone is connected to a network that has reception, so he's got a signal even in this remote mountain range. It's he who calls the emergency services for an ambulance.

The third car has three sisters in it, one of whom turns out to be a Christian. It's she who clambers down the mountain, kneels by my side, holds my hand and prays with me.

Coincidences? I don't believe in them.
God-incidences? Most definitely.
Synchronisation is, after all, God's watchword.

It's 1999 and these are the halcyon days when home landlines are the norm for making and receiving phone calls. But here's a generous American man who "just so happens" to be in the National Park, with a functioning mobile phone, driving past the scene of the accident when he spots a young man standing on the side of the road, flagging down cars to come and help us. He didn't have to stop; he chose to do so.

"Please use it to make emergency calls to your family," he offers, handing the phone to Adrian. Before he can have a chance to protest, "The cost doesn't matter," he reassures him. *How can a stranger be so generous?* Adrian wonders.

The problem is that our parents are on holiday on a caravan site in Cornwall, and neither Adrian nor I have a phone number that we can use to reach them. All we have are home landline numbers, memorised by heart.

One of the memorised numbers is for our sister who's due to stay with our parents at the caravan site that weekend, leaving on the Friday. The accident has happened on a Wednesday night, local time in the States. This means that Adrian is able to get hold of her, on her home phone, before she heads into work on the Thursday, and travels down to Cornwall on the Friday. For obvious reasons, she has the caravan site number, which she passes on, enabling Adrian to call our parents.

At the same time on that Thursday morning, she calls the house I share with three friends, hoping and praying that one of my housemates will be at home.

Amazingly, the most unlikely candidate amongst my housemates is the one to pick up the phone. Ordinarily she works long hours as a project manager for a logistics company, commuting into central London every day, leaving at the crack of dawn and returning well into the evening. But this day is different.

The day before, she quit her job so she can take a year's sabbatical. The day my sister makes the call to the house landline, she's at home, packing. The following week, she's heading abroad to work in logistics for an international aid agency.

Once again, God's timing is impeccably perfect.

Her reaction to the news is typical of her generosity of spirit. Unbeknown to me at the time, she immediately phones around my core local Christian friends, urging them to pray for us. She also organises a spontaneous gathering for people to come together to pray after work that evening, in the living room of our house. She doesn't know where I am, how I am or what's happening. She just knows she has to mobilise people to pray.

My parents are in Cornwall, sitting at the caravan table, when the owner of the caravan site strides across the grass and knocks on the clear plastic window to get their attention. "There's a phone call for you from America," he says breathlessly as my parents exchange anxious glances, and my dad sprints to where the owner's wife holds out the phone receiver, the cord of the landline looping out behind her into the hallway of their house.

As my mum absorbs the news, she's standing, in shock, outside the caravan. In front of her is a beautiful view. Inside, she's in turmoil. Anger wells up as she rants at God, "Why has this happened? Why, when I've been praying daily for their safety on this holiday?"

As she prays, she senses God whisper in a still, small voice, "But they *are* safe, aren't they? Why are you worrying?" Out of nowhere, she experiences an overwhelming sense of peace.

The French doctor keeps asking me, "Can you feel your feet? Can you feel your legs? Do you have any sensation below your waist?" Even though he's shining a torch into the well of the car, which means I can only see his silhouette, his manner and tone are reassuringly calming and he puts me instantly at ease.

He's clearly in a dilemma. Mindful that back injury patients shouldn't be moved, he can see that the car, in its upside-down state, is leaking fuel, causing concern that it might combust and go up in flames.

"Try pressing the soles of your feet into the insoles of your sneakers," he suggests.

"I've already tried that once, and I couldn't really tell whether it worked," I inform him, thinking of my brother's request to do the same only a short while earlier. Nevertheless, I try.

It's hard to tell whether I can fully feel my feet, suspended mid-air as I am at this moment. But it's enough to convince the doctor that I'm not paralysed and, because he remains fearful of the fuel leak, he takes the full weight of my body upon his strong and sturdy frame, assists me out of the car, and gently lays me down on the scrubland of the forest floor.

I'm acutely aware of a lot of American accents in every direction, over and above my head. "She's lucky to be alive," is a repeated refrain. "Don't move," I'm cautioned. I can hear the park rangers using their intercom radios to explain the situation, over and over, as they seek to garner appropriate help. Torches are flashing as people peer on to the scene, trying to make out what's going on in the dark.

Lying on the ground, Adrian sitting beside me, one of the three sisters, a blonde-haired lady in her thirties, kneels down and holds my hand. "Everything is going to be OK," she says, in a calm and gentle voice. I appreciate her reassuring optimism, and then, "Looking at that car, Jo," she says, reflectively, "someone or something has watched over you tonight."

"I'm a Christian," I reply. "I really believe that was God." And then I continue, without hesitation, "Whatever God's got in store for me hasn't yet happened. It's obviously not my time yet." Even as I say it, these sentences are seared into my memory by a red-hot iron.

"I'm a Christian too," she replies, kindness evident in her tone. "I'd really like to pray for you."

Just as she finishes praying, one of the park rangers comes over. "You were lucky you were in a big car," he informs me, looking over at the wreckage. "It might look messy, but it's retained its shape, and the airbags will have helped save your lives."

I reflect, ruefully, from my vantage point on the forest floor: *We had ordered an economy car, and we wouldn't have been driving a big car if it hadn't been for the persuasion of the convivial hire car company executive at the airport.*

"An economy car would have crumpled when it crashed," the park ranger tells me, gently and firmly. "It wouldn't have retained its shape." He pauses a moment, before adding, "It also wouldn't have had any airbags."

As his sobering words start to sink in, I'm acutely aware of how many tiny details God has synchronised ahead of time. The crumpled car is near enough but far enough away in the event of an explosion. A doctor is tending to my medical needs, having just determined I'm not paralysed. An ambulance is coming to take me to hospital. A fellow Christian is holding my hand and has just finished praying for me. And now I'm discovering that the spec of the car itself has helped preserve and protect us.

There's no room for doubt that God's looking after me.

The first I'm aware of the ambulance is when I see paramedics bringing a stretcher down the mountain, weaving and rustling in between the huge conifer trees, their head torches beaming out, announcing their arrival. They then proceed to strap me, quite literally, to the stretcher, while simultaneously asking if I have medical insurance. It feels surreal.

Coming from the UK with its "free at the point of need" National Health Service, I'm shocked that I'm being questioned up front about my ability to pay for the medical care I'm about to receive. *What if I say "no"? What if my insurance cover is inadequate? Will they abandon me here on this mountain?* I feel at a distinct disadvantage, answering their questions whilst being strapped so tightly, flat-pack style, to the stretcher. Irrespective of the pain, I can barely move.

When a discussion ensues about whether or not to helicopter me out, how much that will cost, and whether the insurance will cover it, I feel grateful that Adrian and I have read the small print and ticked the box that gives us the additional medical cover that I'm about to discover I need.

As it turns out, there's no helicopter available. So, instead, the paramedics decide to carry me, strapped to the stretcher, up to the waiting ambulance. Despite their best efforts, conifer tree roots are protruding at inconvenient junctures, making the ground uneven and bumpy. They struggle to see them in the night, and each jolt pierces straight through my spine. So I'm glad when we reach the road. I'm also glad for a double shot of morphine to numb the pain.

At the edge of the National Park, I'm transitioned from one ambulance to another. The morphine has kicked in and it's making me woozy. A swirl of voices is circling in slow motion above my head, debating between two different hospitals. Both are in places whose names and locations mean little to me. *I honestly don't care*, I think, *as long as it's one where the back pain can be stopped.*

By the time I check in, morphine is combining with tiredness and I'm drifting in and out of consciousness as I'm taken off for X-rays. A member of staff prays, out loud, over the intercom, following a brief announcement, and it dawns on me that it's a Christian hospital. *Did God ordain even the choice of which hospital I was taken to?*

Everyone on shift this evening is kind and friendly, warm and welcoming, despite the anti-social early morning hour. They epitomise American "service with a smile" and I feel blessed.

Striding into the waiting area comes the spinal consultant. "Your X-rays are inconclusive," he informs me. Then, responding to my look of shock, "There are no obvious fractures, so I'm going to write you a prescription for extra-strong painkillers, and then you'll be discharged."

How can this be? I think. *Why am I experiencing such excruciating pain? If there's nothing on the X-rays, what on earth have I done?*

It's not long later that, confused, desperately tired, still in pain despite the morphine, and not more than a little disorientated, I'm told I'm being discharged.

Fighting off sleep deprivation, I suddenly hear my brother's familiar voice, and we delightedly greet each other.

"I'm so glad to see you," I say. "What happened after I left?"

"I was standing on the side of the road watching the ambulance head into the distance, its wheels stirring up dust as it disappeared from view around a bend in the road," he explains to me, "and all I kept wondering was whether I should have insisted I go with you."

I reach out my hand to reassure him.

"But then the three sisters took me under their wing," he continues. "It turns out they are on vacation, but they gave us a lift to the youth hostel, and helped me pack our bags. I said goodbye to our backpacker friend, and then they drove me here."

"That's so kind," I say, feeling humbled. "Where are they now?"

"They said they were going to check into a local hotel for the night," he tells me, "so I assume that's what's happened."

We locate some seats in the crisp and clinical hospital waiting area, huddle with our bags, and wonder what to do, given the early hour of the morning. We are a sorry sight, Adrian slumped in his chair and me lying flat on several chairs pulled together, both of us fending off sleep and, in my case, the effects of the morphine.

But God already has our next steps planned.

Shortly before dawn, from our seats near the entrance we observe a change of shift. The medical team who have seen and assessed me are leaving, while a new team are coming on duty. As both sets of people pass us sitting in the waiting area, it reminds them that we're still there.

Not long later, a new duty doctor, a grey-haired elderly statesman type, dressed in a freshly ironed white coat, emerges from the radiography room, clutching hold of what turns out to be my X-rays.

"Are you Joanna?" he asks, as he approaches me and my brother.

"Yes," I reply, a little perplexed. "Why?"

"We, the radiographer and I, have just re-examined your X-rays," he says, pausing to look me in the eye. "I know my colleagues on the last shift discharged you, but I'm now readmitting you." Adrian and I struggle to grasp what he's telling us.

Taking each X-ray in turn, he sits beside me and proceeds to point out what he and the radiographer have spotted.

"You've actually fractured two of the vertebrae in your spine: T12 and L1," he explains gently and slowly. "They are stable compression fractures, so there's nothing to be alarmed about," he reassures me, responding to my audible gasp. "You'll need an MRI scan so we can check the detail. But you'll likely need a back brace or you could inadvertently do permanent damage to your back."

"Will I be paralysed?" I ask, panic rising.

His response is kind, clearly aware of my unarticulated fear. "If the bones had compressed in the other direction, towards your spinal cord, we'd be looking at a different scenario," he says. "But God has watched over you, and you're not going to be paralysed."

As I'm taken to a side room for observation, relief pierces the fog of sleep deprivation and pain-killer medication. At last, there's an explanation for the agonising pain in my spine.

"You guys! How are you?" William's deep friendly voice booms into the room, his figure filling the doorway as he leans into the frame, Stella peeking over his shoulder, surveying the scene. Dressed in a pale cotton hospital gown, I'm lying flat on my back in bed, snatching naps. Adrian occupies the bedside easy chair, silhouetted by the daylight pouring through the huge window behind him.

Gratitude swells up within me as they scoop us up with huge hugs. "Thank you for coming," I smile through my sleep-deprived haze. "We're OK, all things considering, but I'm just waiting for a back brace to be made."

"We'd gone to bed early when Adrian rang," Stella explains. "We weren't expecting any calls and it was late in the evening, so we knew it must be an emergency."

"Adrian sounded so distressed that, as soon as we heard what had happened, we looked at each other and knew immediately what we needed to do," William interjects.

"We leapt out of bed, got dressed, threw things into an overnight bag," Stella continues, "and left voicemail messages for our employers, apologising for our absence from work today."

"We've driven non-stop to get here, praying all the way," William adds.

Their kindness overwhelms me; even more so when he takes charge. "Let me and Adrian head into the National Park and liaise with the police and accident investigators," he says. "We can collect your belongings from the car and sort out the insurance claim."

"I'll stay with you while you rest," Stella says with a smile. "I can keep you company when you want to talk, and pray and read when you don't." Her care envelops me as she muses, "What a blessing you didn't leave the hospital when you were discharged."

Her comment resonates. *What if the radiographer, who arrived at the change of shift, hadn't bothered to re-examine my X-rays? What if I'd done permanent damage to my back, aware of the pain but ignorant about the reason why? How would they have contacted me to inform me of the initial oversight and subsequent diagnosis?*

I sense God's still, small voice as I drift in and out of sleep. *I am in control, Jo,* he reminds me, *and I have synchronised all the seeming "coincidences".*

A gentle knocking on the door wakes me from my slumber and I open my eyes to see the blonde-haired lady from the scene of the accident peering into the room, her hand clasping the door, uncertain about entering.

"Do you remember me?" she tentatively asks.

"Sure, I do," I respond, gesturing an invitation in. "This lady prayed for me by the car, in the dark of the mountainside, late last night," I inform Stella.

"I thought you could use these," she says, crouching down by the side of my hospital bed and handing over a set of keys. "They're for the hotel room where my sisters and I stayed last night. It's just around the corner from here." I open my mouth to speak and she gestures for me to be quiet. "We're checking out now, but we've paid for the next twenty-four hours because we figured Adrian could use it. You, too, if you're discharged today."

Amazed at such undeserved generosity, tears trickle down my cheeks.

"There, there," she says, grabbing a box of tissues from the top of the bedside cabinet and thrusting one into my hand. "You've gone through so much these last few hours. It's the least we can do."

I struggle to say thank you and Stella steps in when words fail me.

When the door bursts open, I'm greeted by the broad grin of a middle-aged nurse, clearly comfortable in her own skin. "I've got you your back brace," she announces, in a strong Caribbean accent, holding forth the contraption she's clasping. Chattering as she works, she takes great delight in helping me swing my legs over the side of the bed and into a sitting position. "Here you go," she says, as she shows me how to rest the padding on my chest and hip bones, straps me in, and lets the metal side poles do their work.

"Ouch!" I exclaim, as it forces me into a ramrod pose. "I'm not used to sitting so upright."

"It looks stylish," Stella says, and the nurse nods agreement.

"You'll soon get used to it," she smiles, showing me how to take it off, and put it on again.

Returning me to lying flat on my back again, she leaves a sense of positivity in the room, and I turn to Stella, feeling reflective. "Stella," I say, "I feel as though I'm being carried by kindness at the moment. Every time I stop to take in what's happening, I can see God's imprint. It feels like people are praying for me."

"They probably are," she replies, squeezing my hand.

It's only later that Stella and I realise – allowing for the time difference between the USA and UK – it's then when my friends back home have gathered to pray for me.

William and Adrian are clearly shaken when they return from the National Park. Standing at the end of my hospital bed, they can't stop commenting on the state of the car.

"It was a mess," William says. "I honestly don't know how you guys came out alive, or how you came out unparalysed, Jo. You sure had guardian angels watching over you last night."

37

"In the daylight it looked terrible, especially now it's been turned over, right-side up," Adrian whispers, visibly trying to process what he's witnessed. "It was a tangled heap of metal," William adds. "The windscreen was shattered. The roof was crushed." We all fall silent. "We've activated the car insurance policy," he adds, "so that's one less thing to think about."

"Thank you for going with Adrian," I say to William, knowing how daunting it would have been to deal with the administrative aftermath on his own.

William smiles and shrugs. "That's what friends are for," he says.

When I'm discharged from hospital for the second time, about twenty-four hours have passed since the accident, and I'm surprised to be invited to sign a disclaimer.

"What's this for?" I ask.

"It's to confirm you won't sue us for our initial oversight in missing your two spinal fractures," the receptionist informs me. Amazed at the cultural differences in public healthcare provision between here and home, I sign without hesitation.

Never have a hot shower, change of clothes and dinner been so welcome as in the hotel room that the three sisters have so generously funded for us. All of us indulge this luxury with delight, before William drives us back to his and Stella's apartment, our conversation mostly revolving around the vagaries of healthcare delivery.

The doctors have advised me to rest, recuperate and wear the back brace as often as I can for the next couple of months, and Adrian and I are deeply appreciative of William's and Stella's offer of hospitality. We both sleep deeply, but the following morning, Adrian is clearly in pain and discomfort.

While the focus has been on me and my back, he's neglected to mention how his little finger is throbbing. "In the scale of injuries, I figured it was pretty insignificant," he says. When he seeks medical attention at the local health clinic, he discovers his little finger has a hairline fracture. "It's a typical 'boxer's injury'," he's told. Holding his hands up to his head, balled into fists, at the point of impact in the accident, the airbag went off, cracking his little finger in a barely perceptible way. "I'd never have known it was fractured," he ruminates. "I'm glad it's been seen."

Within a few days, Adrian and I visit the young American backpacker who, after helping us at the scene of the accident, returned home immediately.

"We pray for him every day," his mom tells us, "and we were praying especially for him during his trip."

"We kept asking God to bring Christian young people across his path," his stepdad adds. "We just never anticipated it would involve such a serious car accident!"

"When the three sisters returned me to the youth hostel," our friend explains, "I was in a state of shock and couldn't believe I wasn't injured. But I couldn't continue with my travels. I just wanted to get home and see my mom."

"You were so key in our rescue," Adrian says. "If you hadn't gone to get help, I'd have been facing a dilemma about whether or not to leave Jo on her own in the car. We couldn't have done it without you."

"Thank you so much," I quickly concur.

"From the moment he told us what happened, we've not stopped praising Jesus," his mom says. "We're sure you had guardian angels watching over you that night."

"We keep being reminded of God's promise in Psalm 91 verses 11 and 12," her husband tells us, grabbing his Bible and reading, "For he will command his angels concerning you, to guard you in all your ways; they will lift you up in their hands, so that you will not strike your foot against a stone."

I couldn't agree more.

"We called your old flatmate and told her what's happened," Stella tells me one evening during our stay. "She's asked the church office to put a prayer request notice in this Sunday's news bulletin."

Later, back in the UK, I discover that my one Christian colleague "just so happens" to be at church that Sunday, reads the news bulletin, sees the prayer request, and informs our employer.

This turns out to be a godsend.

His prescience enables me to secure a week's leave immediately after returning home, because he's enabled our employer to negotiate an extension with the person who's providing holiday cover for my workload. It also means that, upon arriving home, I've already received a letter in the post informing me that I'm covered by my employer's private healthcare plan, which enables my family doctor to expedite a referral to a spinal consultant. Even in this, God is dovetailing the details.

Some people believe in coincidences, but I'm not one of them. Before, during and after the accident, I'm convinced that God's coordinated the specifics.

During the six months I'm encased in a back brace, I have multiple opportunities to share the story of the accident and how God intervened in it; conversations that wouldn't otherwise have taken place. "It makes you believe in guardian angels, doesn't it?" suggests one colleague. "It sounds like someone or something was watching over you," remarks another.

Unable to sit at a desk for extended periods of time, I work reduced hours, spending the remainder of each day lying flat on my back, staring at the ceiling.

Sobered by the awareness that I could have been killed or paralysed, I keep returning to the words I uttered on the mountainside: "Whatever God's got in store for me hasn't yet happened. It's obviously not my time yet." *But what still needs to happen? Where's my life heading? What does God have in store for me? Why am I working in a law firm when I've always seen my legal training as a means to an end, not the end in itself? How can I use this experience for good?*

It doesn't take long before I sense God moving me into a new season.

Despite my colleagues' protestations, the accident becomes the launch pad to leave law behind, and forge a new career in a new sector, to change location, and take a different direction in life.

As I recorded in my prayer journal just days after the accident: "Today, as I write this, I'm thanking God I'm alive. I could so easily have been killed or paralysed, and that reality is only just hitting home. All I know, in the depths of my being, is that it wasn't my time. God has graciously saved my life. Instead, I'm here and I'm alive. I may have fractures in my spine, but they are healing and I'm walking. I'm a living testimony to God's protection, provision and preservation. Nothing has been a mere 'coincidence'. He has coordinated everything."

CHAPTER 2

X-rays never lie

A man with a stroke and a tumour (2000)

*"For I am the Lord your God,
who takes hold of your right hand and says to you,
Do not fear; I will help you."*

Isaiah 41:13

This story is about my dad, Keith, and it tells of what happened when he had a stroke and a tumour on his adrenal gland. At the time, he was working as a university professor. It also features my mum, Sheila, and other family members, including me.

"I'm sorry to have to say this, but I don't think you'll ever be able to write again."

Such a simple sentence. Uttered in a well-meaning way yet it penetrates deeply, delivering the most devastating prognosis to a man who is constantly using his right hand to write; whose career has been carved around reading, writing and research.

The words are being pronounced over my dad by a petite-framed registrar, a middle-aged man originally from Myanmar, his face sincere and earnest. He stands at the side of a British hospital bed in a bright white, high-ceiling ward, a large window looking out over minimalist manicured greenery towards buildings beyond. His patient, my dad, lying motionless on his back, propped up by pillows, wears metal-rimmed spectacles perched on his nose, his head of wavy, thick, dark-brown hair belying his age; at sixty years old, many men younger than him have already gone thinner and greyer.

The stroke has been sudden and unexpected. It stole into Dad's sleep, at home, in the night, and now the entire right side of his tall, well-built frame feels like a dead weight. His limbs are leaden, his head befuddled, his speech slightly slurred. It's difficult to focus on what he's being told.

"There are some things you may be able to do again," the registrar continues slowly, trying to be upbeat, watching as his words sink in. "You may be able to stand again. You may be able to walk again. But I'm telling you now, I don't think you're ever going to be able to write again."

As his future heads into the unchartered territory of stormy seas, the shock sinks in, and Dad starts to cry.

Growing up, Dad would often recount stories from his past for me and my siblings. Each snippet would unfold another page from the narrative of his life, helping us understand him a little bit better.

Following the stroke, I would often find myself reflecting on two particular facets of Dad's life – how he found faith in Jesus, and the journey that led him into academia – because both felt integral to this particular part of his story.

One Sunday afternoon, I decide to elicit Dad's thoughts on this. We are sitting at opposite ends of a comfortable soft-cushioned sofa, in the spacious living-room of our Edwardian family home. An open-hearth fireplace is to our right, a bay window at the opposite end of the room, looking out over a small patio and, beyond that, the garden. The leaves are changing colour and starting to fall from the trees; it's a dull, grey autumnal day.

As we discuss the story of his stroke and what followed afterwards, I raise the issues uppermost in my mind. "What do you remember about how you became a Christian," I ask him, "and how did you end up in a career for which writing has been so central?" I pause a moment before continuing. "I realise that's two questions in one, but the answers feel important to the story."

"I agree," he says, nodding, and then he takes me back to the beginning.

My paternal grandpa was a mechanical engineer. Momentary fame came when he received awards for designing the gear box, still used today, in Aston Martin cars. His salary was modest and, with three children to educate, Dad was encouraged to apply for, and was successful in gaining, the top open scholarship to an Anglo-Catholic school in northern England. Some forty miles from his home town, he reluctantly became a boarder.

School included attending chapel services, singing in the chapel choir, lengthy discussions about philosophy and religion, and getting confirmed. School holidays included attending a local Methodist church Sunday school with his brother and a friend in a pony and trap.

What none of it included was conversion, which only came later.

"Are you a Christian, Keith? Do you know where you're going when you die?"

John was a friend who studied history with Dad when they were undergraduate students at university in Scotland. His dramatic conversion to Christianity had left him exuding evangelistic zeal, and he would frequently be found standing in the university quadrangle, preaching the gospel to whoever would give him the time of day.

Dad was taken aback. He had always assumed he *was* a Christian. But he soon realised that, when confronted with John's provocations, he was unable to defend the faith he thought he had, despite having read many of C.S. Lewis's books.

One evening in their third year, while living in digs, John invited him to a guest service in the local Anglican church. The preacher's message was based on the Bible passage in 1 Corinthians 15: "If Christ be not risen, our faith is in vain." Without hesitation, Dad felt the Holy Spirit prompt him to respond as he realised that Christ, indeed, was risen. During the altar call, he went forward in floods of tears and committed his life to Christ.

This decision changed everything. His identity. His outlook. His direction. His perspective. His decisions. Our family tree.

Prayer and Bible study became the bedrock of his being. Church services started resonating. Even his family noticed a difference, although his parents initially failed to understand what he meant when he wrote home to tell them he had become a Christian. It was only when they saw him in person, a short while later, that they recognised the transformation that had taken place.

It was never Dad's intention to become a university professor. But he inadvertently started, from scratch, a highly popular post-graduate course, which is regularly oversubscribed, and he has taken the course into pioneering new areas, not covered by other universities in the same way. His students are teachers from all over the world, particularly Sub-Saharan Africa and South Asia, and all of them comment on his pastoral care, not just his academic credibility and expertise.

Hindsight helps him see God's leading into the role he now holds at a red-brick university in the south of England.

Back in the 1960s, after completing university in Scotland, he took up a graduate management traineeship with a large British company in South Wales. But two years of working in the largest can-making factory in Europe helped him realise he was not cut out for looking after a production line of people packing cans into cartons. Instead, he applied, and was accepted, to join the British Council.

As a result, Dad found himself not just training to teach English as a Foreign Language (TEFL) but putting it into practice with various placements, teaching English to the Polish in Poland. Not long later, exciting opportunities came up to relocate to Bangladesh, and then Thailand, where part of his role included teaching English to two of the princesses in the revered royal family while he was based in Bangkok. By then, he had met and married my mum, Sheila, who accompanied him.

By the early 1970s, his work with the British Council returned him to the UK while he completed a part-time PhD, funded by an award from the UK Government Department for International Development. Commended for the "Rolls-Royce" quality of his thesis, he used it to set up a new department in the British Council, jointly with a colleague, focusing on comparative and multi-cultural education. A few years later, while considering the offer of an opportunity to be posted to Iran, Dad received a letter from a professor in his field at a red-brick university in the south of England. "My retirement is imminent," he read, "and I'd encourage you to apply to be my replacement." After prayer and reflection, he successfully applied for and accepted the offer of a position as a lecturer.

It is only during, and after, the 1979 Iranian Revolution that he appreciated how God protected him and his family. Watching the news unfold from afar, he realised they could so easily have been caught up in the traumatic transition and turmoil in Iran, and he wept at the exile of so many Iranians.

Under Dad's leadership, his university department experiences significant growth and welcomes large numbers of post-graduate students. He loves the variety that the role affords him – visiting different types of educational institutions, speaking at various conferences, acting as an external examiner for other universities, and researching and writing books and articles.

In every sense, he is flourishing.

The turn of the century, a little over two months ago, is fast fading from memory, and we are now in early March. Green shoots are piercing the ground. Parks and gardens are full to bursting with daffodils and tulips. Trees are heavy-laden with the scent of pink and white blossom. Temperatures are rising. Sunshine and blue skies are returning. Everywhere there are signs of new life.

It's a weekend and Dad should be feeling optimistic and buoyant. Instead, he is feeling stressed, burdened and extraordinarily tired.

As a respected professor in his niche field of expertise, he works hard and travels regularly, training university students and academics across the UK. Monday morning saw him deliver lectures on the university campus near home, before cycling to catch a train into London to lecture a group of American students in the afternoon. Tuesday involved more lectures in the morning, research seminars in the afternoon, and an evening lecture for an international programme he's running as Chair. Wednesday was a day for writing a chapter for his latest book with a colleague at a university in the west of England. Thursday saw him mark exams and then travel to a city in the north of England and stay overnight in order to do a PhD student's oral "viva" exam at the university there, before returning home on Friday evening and cycling home from the train station.

By anyone's standards, it's been an exceptionally busy week. But it's also quite normal for a fit and active sixty-year-old. Yet today's inexplicable exhaustion is permeating every cell of Dad's body, sapping all his reserves of energy.

On the Saturday, a family friend came over with her university dissertation for him to look over as a favour and, after she left, he struggled to walk down the garden. His limbs felt like lead. He went to bed early and slept through the night undisturbed.

Now he's woken on Sunday morning, acutely aware that something isn't right. His arms and legs feel like dead weights and his right leg isn't working properly. He can't seem to move it, let alone get out of bed and balance on it.

That weekend, I am with my parents for a long overdue catch up, staying in my old bedroom at our family home.

Ordinarily, I'm sharing a house with a group of friends and working as a family solicitor for a large Legal Aid firm based in south east England. I recently unexpectedly won a Court of Appeal case about the rights of an unmarried father to see his son, which has received widespread media coverage. "It could be the pinnacle of your career," my colleagues keep telling me. Everything seems to be rosy. But the last forty-eight hours have felt anything but.

Two days ago, I was told I no longer need to wear the back brace that has been supporting my spine since it fractured in a car accident in the USA, six months ago. Seemingly a small step towards recovery, to me it's significant.

Last year I was contacted by friends at an international charity working with children at risk around the world. "We're looking for advocates to come and work with us," they told me excitedly, "and you'd have all the right skills for it." Won over by their enthusiasm, I agreed to consider it. "But only once my back brace is removed," I told them.

Last night, recalling my promise, I emailed my friends. "My back brace is off," I typed enthusiastically, "so please can you let me know whether your charity still needs advocates." The computer promptly crashed and, email – still being a relatively new invention, the words I typed seemed to disappear into the ether.

I should have heeded it as a warning of things to come.

This morning, before I set off to visit my parents, sitting in the spring sunshine at the table, enjoying a lazy Saturday morning breakfast with my housemates, the postman delivered two unexpected letters.

One was a registered letter from our landlady, addressed to all of us in the house, telling us she wants to sell up, and giving us two months' notice. None of us could quite compute this news. Ours has been a stalwart house-share in the local Christian community, combining various housemates over many years. Our friends have affectionately nicknamed us after the name of the road that the house is in, such is the reputation of anyone who lives there.

The other letter was from an American debt-collection agency, informing me of the outstanding amount owing for the medical care I received after the car accident last summer. It seems my travel insurance company is refusing to pay the full sum, so they have approached me directly, threatening me with court action unless I take immediate steps to clear the debt.

I'm still in shock when I arrive at my parents' in time for lunch that Saturday, and pour out my heart over all that's been happening. But we barely have time to process, before Dad starts complaining of an abnormal tiredness. The following morning, despite an early night and although he's slept well, it doesn't seem to have dissipated. If anything, it's worse.

Peeking my head around my parents' bedroom door, I can see, over on the far side of the bed, beneath the window, he is struggling to move his right leg.

"Do you think you've had a stroke, Dad?" I ask, speaking out my suspicions, "Should we get medical advice?"

Initially reticent, he soon relents, and Mum dials the number for the emergency doctor. There's a cursory diagnosis over the phone, and an ambulance is immediately dispatched.

Unfortunately, today is the day of this year's half-marathon in the town. Starting and ending at a local sports centre, many of the main roads and the bridges across the river are closed until the race is over. The ambulance has to take an enormous detour to reach us, turning the normal fifteen-minute journey into three long hours.

When the paramedics finally arrive, they are apologetic about the delays and clear about the diagnosis. "You've had a

Transient Ischaemic Attack, a TIA," they tell Dad. "It's like a mini-stroke." They recommend bedrest and a watching brief. "If you're not feeling better by tomorrow morning, and if your right leg doesn't improve, you should call your family doctor."

The tone of the day becomes muted.

When movement starts to return, he heads downstairs to sit on the sofa.

"Try to rest, Dad," I encourage, but rest evades him.

"It's not easy when I'm used to being so active," he says. "Today's tiredness seems to be taking over, dictating what I can and can't do."

Keen to distract his focus away from his feelings of exhaustion, I encourage him to change tack. "Please will you tell me about your overland adventure?" I ask, sitting by his side on the sofa.

I am referring to part of our family folklore when, in 1966, he and a friend travelled overland back to the UK from where they were working in what is now Bangladesh. Delighted to recount his adventures, he disappears to retrieve a slide projector, which he uses to show me the stunning variety of scenery they passed through on their 14,000-mile journey in their sturdy old cream wooden-framed Morris Minor Traveller, much of it via territory that would be utterly impassable in the modern era.

The diversion works, but only temporarily. When the slideshow is over, he slumps back on the sofa, his energy spent.

Later that evening I hover in the hallway and leave reluctantly. It's not easy seeing Dad, who is usually such a rock, looking so weak and fragile – I pray for him as I drive home.

The following morning, Monday, I am sitting at my desk in the office where I work, opening up my diary for the week, and I feel inundated.

My car exhaust fell off as I drove in today, making the noise of a tractor. My secretary has just unexpectedly announced she's resigning. I'm apprehensive about the demands of the American debt-collection agency. I'm still coming to terms with my home being sold and what that will mean for me and my housemates. And at the back of my mind, I am adjusting to the shock of Dad having had a TIA.

When the phone rings, I hesitantly pick up the handset to hear Mum's tearful voice. "Your dad's had a stroke in the night," she tells me. "The family doctor did an emergency home visit this morning. His blood pressure is dangerously high and he's getting chest pains, so an ambulance is taking him to hospital." She barely takes a breath. "Please can you come as soon as you can?"

My boss releases me without hesitation and I drive the familiar route as fast as I can, as safely as I can, despite the din of the broken exhaust. It's difficult to focus; I'm sobbing and praying, gulping air in between.

When I eventually reach the hospital, a car park attendant turns me away. "Sorry, ma'am," he says, "but I can't let you park without paying," stubbornly refusing to budge. "I have no change," I protest, "and I just want to see my dad." But he is adamant. "The rules are the rules," he says, and I have no option but to drive away, find a cash machine, spend some of the notes, get some coins in exchange, and return to the hospital car park. The tears have been flowing constantly, but I push on through, giving the car park attendant a glimmer of a smile, and forgiving him through gritted teeth.

Everything seems to be operating in slow motion. *How can so much have changed in just forty-eight hours?*

I find Dad sitting up in an old-fashioned, metal-framed hospital bed, wearing his well-worn plaid pyjamas. The ward's large window lies above his bedhead, and I'm greeted by the sterile smell of disinfectant. He tries to greet me, and I reach down for a hug, but he can't lift his right arm so I give him a lopsided squeeze, and he smiles with his eyes.

It's obvious that he's overwhelmed by absolute exhaustion, even more pronounced than the tiredness I've seen in him over the past two days. "It's unlike anything I've ever experienced before," he tells me, his speech slightly slurred. "All I want to do is sleep."

In a state of shock, I perch on a chair by the side of the bed, take hold of his hand, and pray out loud, asking God to heal him, in Jesus' name. I also help him get into a wheelchair to use the loo.

Literally overnight, there's been a role reversal in the generations, and I fight it: *It's not meant to be like this. It's happening too soon.* I'm only in my twenties.

The doctors, none of whom have a good bedside manner, are speaking an indecipherable language as they debate and discuss the cause of the stroke. They want to find the clot or bleed so they can dispel it before it causes more damage. But does the conversation have to take place within earshot?

The physiotherapist, a young blonde-haired woman in her twenties, is keen to understand Dad's medical history: "Have you ever had a DVT, a deep vein thrombosis?" she asks.

"No, not me personally," he replies. "But there's a history in my family. My father had a DVT. My mother had a stroke." He pauses, unsettled by the memories.

"We'll need to run some tests," she explains gently. "The doctors just want to try and figure out what caused it so they can prevent it happening again."

The test results leave no room for doubt: Dad has had a DVT. There's evidence of a clot in his right leg, but the medication he's given to treat it, unfortunately, makes matters worse rather than better.

"It feels like a battle," he tells me, struggling to slowly enunciate each word. "My body is fighting lethargy. My immune system is fighting infection. My mind is fighting depressive thoughts."

"Try to conserve your energy, Dad," I say. "Expend it on getting better, not on speaking to me." I squeeze his hand, "I know you're trying desperately to stay positive for the sake of the family," I reassure him, "but all we want is for you to be well."

His smile is wonky, droopy to one side, and it breaks my heart.

The doctors decide there's no need for Dad to remain in the Cardiac Unit as he no longer has the severe chest pain and high blood pressure he was experiencing at home and in the ambulance. He is moved to the Stroke Unit, where he is sent for scans before being taken to an all-male ward, three beds running along each long side of the rectangular room. The other five occupants range widely in age and severity of stroke.

By day, the physio and occupational therapists put him through intensive neurorehabilitation as they train new parts of his brain to learn the things he has been doing instinctively for decades. By night, he is kept awake by a delightful but delirious elderly man in the opposite bed and, when sleep evades him, he prays silently, conscious he's being carried by the prayers of others.

The registrar from Myanmar suggests a game of Solitaire. "It will test your dexterity, Keith," he says. "It will show me how your right hand has been affected."

He places a wooden Solitaire board on top of a shiny white plastic wheeled table, and swizzles it round and over the hospital bed. Out pops his stopwatch. "This makes me feel stressed," Dad slowly slurs.

Lifting the cold metal balls is painfully difficult. It takes all the muscle he can muster to manoeuvre his arm into the right place. Ever so slowly and gently, he moves his right thumb and forefinger together, forming a not-quite-complete circle around one ball at a time. Dropping them into different holes is even harder. Lifting his limbs is laboured; they simply won't do what they should do. Every movement is slow and sluggish.

He tries with his left hand, but it's just as much a struggle. "I'm not left-handed, and never have been," he tells the registrar, enunciating his words.

That is when the registrar issues his shocking prognosis: "You may be able to stand again. You may be able to walk again. But I'm telling you now, I don't think you're ever going to be able to write again." And Dad starts to cry.

He has never experienced such a low ebb in all his life. Books. Articles. Papers. Editorials. Letters. He writes all of them longhand, pen on paper, with his right hand. Writing is integral to who he is.

He knows he has a choice. He can walk by sight – believing what he has been told and what circumstances are telling him – or he can walk by faith – believing that God can heal him if he chooses to do so. Lying in his hospital bed, he starts to pray, in Jesus' name, asking God to restore his ability to stand and walk and write again.

Mum is visiting the ward every day, bringing a fresh stash of cards and letters with her each time. "Here's today's post," she announces, opening each envelope and reading out the messages inside. Both of them are moved to tears; the sentiments expressed are frequently the kind normally reserved for funerals.

When there are no more surface spaces to put them on, the nurses stick them to the wall around the window above the bed. "Aren't you popular?" they tease him. "They cheer up the ward though!"

Over the course of a few days, Dad notices a pattern as he ploughs through his post. In message after message, his Christian friends and acquaintances are pointing him towards Isaiah 41:13 in the Bible: "For I am the LORD your God, who takes hold of your right hand and says to you, Do not fear; I will help you."

"I feel sure this is God speaking," he confides in Mum and, later, in me and my siblings. "He's giving me a promise and, deep in my spirit, I'm going to hold onto it, trusting that God is going to take hold of my right hand and help me, so I'm not going to fear."

It's not new news that Dad has high blood pressure; he's been on medication for nearly twenty years to try and keep it in tow. What's changed is that he has low potassium levels; his heart isn't regulating his blood pressure properly, and the medical team are suspicious.

When the X-rays and test results are back, he's visited by a middle-aged consultant neurologist, her Scottish accent soft. "We've found a tumour on your adrenal gland," she announces, catching him completely unawares. "It indicates you've got a highly unusual disease called Conn's syndrome." She holds the X-ray up to the window, and points to the silhouette of a clearly defined lump.

"What does it mean?" he asks, bewildered. "Is the tumour cancerous?"

"It means that one of your hormones is secreting too much into your adrenal gland, so it's retaining sodium and losing potassium," she explains, "which is why your blood pressure is so high and your potassium levels so low." She pauses a moment. "The tumour should be benign, but we can't be sure unless and until we remove and test it. It's a relatively straightforward operation, but it will need to be done at a specialist hospital."

Dad nods to indicate he understands, trying to take in what she's telling him, and what the X-ray is showing.

Then she rubs her hands together in glee. "It's so rare," she pronounces, "you're the first patient I've ever come across with Conn's syndrome in all my years of practising medicine."

Dad's heart sinks. "I don't particularly relish the prospect of becoming a pilot project case study," he tells her, speaking slowly to minimise the slurring.

"I'll guide you through the process," she reassures him.

As she leaves the ward, he starts to pray, feeling convinced that the tumour is not of God. As he does so, he feels faith rising and fear subsiding.

"Your workload's been too large for too long," a well-meaning colleague pronounces. "It's a terrible tragedy that it's taken something like this for us all to realise."

Dad nods, fully aware of all he's been carrying.

When a close colleague passed away after a short, sharp battle with motor neurone disease, Dad was expected to pick up his workload, on top of his own, while the university found a replacement, who never came. This gave him a teaching load on a par with that of all his colleagues combined, plus more PhD research students than anyone else.

In addition, a couple of months ago he was persuaded to take on responsibility for his department's contribution to the process in which the university's academic research and publications are externally examined. He also remains editor for a popular international education journal.

Despite protestations, his pleas for help have not been heard; his workload has remained unwieldy.

When the vice chancellor for the university comes to the hospital for a visit, he looks sheepish. He's been made aware of just how much Dad is carrying and he's apologetic. He's joined, soon after, by Dad's head of department, who also acknowledges he's been carrying too big a workload for far too long.

"We've decided to split your workload into three," the vice chancellor says, "so that it's more manageable for those who will cover for you."

"It feels too little, too late, if I'm honest," Dad responds softly and slowly.

Besides, he's aware of other stresses and strains in recent months.

There's been immense pressure from the lodger in the family home, a man who likes to process his thoughts out loud. He and his estranged wife are divorcing, so he's been regularly coming in from work, sitting at the bottom of the stairs, opening his mail, reading out the letters from his solicitors, and lamenting his lot in life. Dad has been unable to escape because his book-lined home study is located at the bottom of the stairs, with a large window looking out to the driveway, and he's usually to be found at his desk, door ajar. Although the lodger moved out three weeks ago, the stress has been cumulative over several years.

Concerns about my youngest sister, who has severe learning difficulties, have been rising to the surface too, with many unresolved discussions about her future.

Then there was the invitation to become chair of the board of trustees for a national charity working with adults with learning disabilities and headquartered locally. The stroke happened the night before the meeting when he was meant to be taking over. Perhaps providence has prevailed?

Dad makes a conscious decision. The Christian call is counter-cultural and he wants to be a witness. He makes a choice to forgive them all, and commits each one to God in prayer.

My parents attend a large vibrant town-centre church. They have worshipped there, with the family, for nearly two decades and are well-known and loved in the congregation.

When the vicar hears news of the stroke, he sends the young curate on a pastoral visit to the hospital. Sitting in a high-backed, camel-coloured, faux-leather armchair to the side of Dad's bed, the curate leans slightly forward, his hands cupping his chin, his elbows leaning on his knees, listening attentively.

"God has promised He will take hold of my right hand and help me, and that I'm not to fear," Dad explains, "and it's that, together with the prayers of many people, which has been sustaining me during the days when my right hand feels helpless." His speech is improving, the slur is barely noticeable now.

The curate gestures that he'd like to lay hands on Dad and pray with him for his healing but, before he can continue, Dad makes a suggestion

"I've been reading my Bible a lot in here," he says, gesturing to the hospital ward with his left hand, "and today I've been led to re-read the 'Prayer of Faith' verses in James 5, which talk about how, if anyone is sick, they should call the elders of the church to pray over them and anoint them with oil in the name of the Lord, and how the prayer offered in faith will make the sick person well."

He pauses a moment, and the curate nods to confirm that he knows the passage.

"I'm happy for you to pray with me now," Dad continues, "but I've been told I've got a tumour on my adrenal gland and I don't believe it's of God, so I'd really like you and the vicar, and maybe some other church leaders, to pray for me and anoint me with oil. Would this be possible?"

"I'm sorry to hear this," the curate responds kindly, care and compassion evident in his response. "Let me see what I can do."

Feeling buoyed by his conversation with the curate, Dad calls over one of the nurses who he knows to be a Christian because of conversations they've been having, when time allows. "Would it be possible to set aside a small room so that my church leaders can pray with me in private?" he asks her. "Sure," she responds. "Just let me know when you have a time and a date."

A couple of days later, the nurse pushes Dad in a wheelchair down a bright white corridor, illuminated only by artificial neon light strips in the ceiling. Wheeling him into a spacious naturally-lit side room containing a handful of chairs and a cupboard containing medical equipment, he finds the vicar, curate and another church leader standing and chatting, and she leaves them be, closing the door quietly behind her.

The three men quickly gather around the wheelchair and, after an exchange of pleasantries and a quick update on the prognosis, Dad leans forward to enable them to lay hands on his back, around the area where his adrenal glands are located.

Claiming spiritual authority in the room, the vicar places his right hand on Dad's back and, full of faith, he begins to pray aloud. "Father God, we thank you for Keith," he says. "We pray, in the name of Jesus, for his healing and health, and we ask you for full recovery from his stroke, and for you to take this tumour from his adrenal gland."

Immediately and instantaneously, before the vicar has finished praying, at the mention of the name of Jesus an intensely hot burning sensation ignites in his back. It's exactly where his adrenal gland is located, and he feels faith rising.

As Dad sits back in his wheelchair, the vicar picks up the vial of anointing oil and continues, "Keith, I anoint you now with the sign of the cross in the name of Jesus," he declares, ever so softly, making the sign of a cross on Dad's forehead with his thumb and forefinger, each covered with a thin film of oil.

Before he's even able to articulate what's happening, tears well up from nowhere and Dad begins to cry.

Laughter is a much needed tonic, especially the belly-aching, bend over double, side-splitting stitches, tears streaming down the cheeks, kind of laughter.

An American former PhD research student and an old neighbour are both supplying Dad with a steady stream of jokes; they come in the post and Mum brings them with her during her daily visits. Dad has always shared the same sense of humour as these two men, but the anecdotes seem funnier than usual at the moment.

"Your emotions have been affected by the stroke," a portly nurse tells him. "It's entirely to be expected that you'll now find funny things funnier and sad things sadder. You'll notice your laughter and tears will be much more extreme."

Dad is most acutely aware of this when faced with the occupational therapist, a positive-minded, brown-haired, middle-aged man, who is doggedly determined to get him walking again. It's an intensive hard graft. Every. Single. Day. But the nurse is correct concerning his emotions. Comedy and tragedy seem to intermingle. He's never sure whether the exercises are going to lead him to laugh or to cry.

It's a momentous day when he holds a pen again in his right hand, and puts the pen to paper. Claiming the promise of Isaiah 41:13, he writes a coherent sentence. It's slow and slightly spidery, but it's legible.

"Keep writing, Keith," the occupational therapist urges him. "Keep using your right hand as much as possible."

"The registrar was wrong," Dad declares, recalling his haunting pronouncement, "I *am* going to write again, because God has promised he will take hold of my right hand and help me, and I'm not to fear."

Dad is sitting in a small room at a specialist hospital in a neighbouring city. Mum is in the waiting room with good friends, a married couple who have driven them there.

He has just had an X-ray taken of his adrenal gland, and some other related tests, and they are now being analysed, along with his test results, by a grey-haired endocrinologist who's a specialist in Conn's syndrome. Looking up, he peers over his glasses, evidently baffled.

"I really don't understand," he says. "Something must have gone wrong with the tests." He's holding up some pieces of paper and pointing to the X-ray, lit up on the screen. "For some utterly inexplicable reason, your X-ray and test results are both completely clear."

Looking the endocrinologist straight in the eye, Dad seizes the opportunity, "Two days ago, my church leaders prayed for me and anointed me with oil, in the name of Jesus," he explains calmly, as if matters of faith are entirely normal for everyday conversation. "I felt a burning sensation in my lower back, and I believe God healed me there and then. The fact you can't find the tumour is evidence that he has indeed healed me."

The endocrinologist, an expert in all manner of hormone-related diseases, has never heard anything like this before. He sits wide-eyed as he listens to Dad's explanation, clearly confused.

"Well, in all the years I've practised medicine, and in all the cases I've seen of Conn's syndrome," he says, "I've never come across a tumour just disappearing." He pauses for a moment, and then continues, "This is quite remarkable."

There's no room for doubt: the tumour has vanished without trace.

Dad's family doctor has initiated an appointment at the local surgery.

"Well, take a look at this," he says to Dad, holding two X-rays up to the light pouring through the window. One is from the local hospital, clearly showing a tumour on his adrenal gland. The other is from the specialist hospital, clearly showing no tumour at all.

"As far as I can see, there's absolutely no evidence of a tumour on your adrenal gland anymore," he muses, clearly puzzled. "It seems to have completely disappeared."

Dad is looking up at the window from his wheelchair, so he can see exactly what the doctor is pointing out in the X-rays, and he knows, deep down, that God has healed him.

"It's because I asked my church leaders to pray for me," he tells the doctor. "I know I've told you before that I'm a Christian, but I genuinely believe God can, and does, heal people when we pray for them in Jesus' name."

The doctor expresses surprise. He has no faith of his own, but he's not cynical or sceptical. "You're not the first patient who's claimed healing through divine help," he says gently, with a smile, "and I'm sure you won't be the last."

Being pushed around in a wheelchair is an eye-opener to Dad. He has long been an ardent advocate for people with disabilities, particularly since my youngest sister was born with severe learning difficulties. But suddenly, sitting in the wheelchair, he's on the other side and it's as if he's become invisible. People avert their gaze and look the other way, not knowing what to say or do. They won't even catch the eye of whichever family member is pushing him. Emotionally, it's exhausting.

One Sunday afternoon in mid-summer, I am with him, pushing him along a footpath by the river. Mum is walking alongside us. People are enjoying picnics, playing games, sunbathing on the large expanse of grass to the side of the path. Others are walking along the same path as us. They glance in our direction, tentatively offering sympathy, followed swiftly by pity, catching my eye and then turning away. I find it unnerving. This isn't supposed to happen to you when you're in your twenties.

Eventually it gets too much. "Anyone would think I don't exist," Dad remarks with incredulity. "But I'm perfectly capable of seeing, of thinking, of engaging with them. I may not be able to walk, right here, right now, but I'm still me. Disabled or not, I'm still worthy of respect."

If anything, the callous cold-heartedness of these strangers spurs him on in his determination to get better. His physio and occupational therapist also encourage him to keep going.

The stroke has killed some parts of his brain, so he's learning to train alternative parts to do all the things he's been doing since childhood – things he has taken completely for granted; things he doesn't even remember learning when he was young; things that make all the difference to daily life.

"My body is so lopsided now," he tells me, "I'm prone to imbalance." I recognise what he's saying as his left side keeps trying to compensate for what his right side can no longer do.

"Well, at least your speech is no longer slurring, Dad," I encourage him. "You're improving all the time."

Every small sign of progress feels like a step in the right direction. The day when he no longer needs to be pushed around in a wheelchair. The day when he walks with the help of two sticks, then one stick, and eventually no sticks at all.

The hardest test comes about a year after the stroke, at the Transport Research Laboratory, when his driving skills are assessed. Mum doesn't drive, and never has, so she's been reliant on lifts from friends and family, or public buses. For several hours, Dad's visual, cognitive and physical abilities are rigorously tested. Even getting behind the wheel of a car again takes more courage than he's anticipating. But he passes with flying colours, his driving licence is reactivated and, most important of all, his independence is restored.

While Dad has been clear that he's forgiven the university, his decision about whether and, if so, when to return to work is a much harder call to make.

His secretary, an older lady, is kind, cautious and softly spoken. All through the long months that Dad has been in hospital, she has faithfully brought him crucial papers, articles, references and items for scrutiny and to sign off, leaving less urgent items for others. He may have had a stroke, but his brain is still alive and active, and he remains committed to his students and colleagues. He also relishes every opportunity to write, repeatedly claiming the promise God's given him to take hold of his right hand and help him, and not to fear.

For a full year and a half after the stroke, the university keeps him on their books. He gives a few ad hoc lectures, as a favour, in response to demand. But mostly this timeframe is about ensuring his academic research and publications are included in the university's external examination exercise, so that they score highly enough to secure further research grant funding.

In the end, the decision makes itself, and there's a mutual agreement that Dad will retire early on ill-health grounds. It's far from ideal as he loves his work and doesn't want to give it up, but he knows he's done his best and could not have done more.

It's a sunny Sunday morning in early autumn, six months on from the stroke, and Dad is standing in a stream of sunlight pouring through ancient arched windows to his left. The vast vaulted ceiling towers above him, parallel rows of solid stone pillars having held it in place for more than 800 years. During his four long months in hospital, the church he knows so well has been renovated and reordered. The old wooden pews have been removed and fresh, clean cream-coloured floor tiles have been installed, together with underfloor heating. So now, stretching out in front of him, lies row upon row of terracotta-coloured cushioned wooden chairs, filling the building from front to back.

He has slowly hobbled his way to the front, with the help of a stick, and now he's standing in front of a packed congregation. It's the middle of a morning service. Despite years of lecturing and public speaking, it's hard to find the words to convey the immensity of the testimony he's about to share, at the vicar's request. He knows God has acted in the months following the stroke, but it's difficult to find the exact words to convey the emotional rollercoaster that's undergirded all that's happened.

Placing his Bible in front of him on the lectern, and leaning on his stick, he opens it at a bookmarked page and reads from Isaiah 41:13 before testifying to those who are listening.

"The Lord is my God," he says. "He has taken hold of my right hand. He told me not to fear because he would help me, and he has taken my fear and he has helped me. I am right-handed and I was told that I'd never write again, but God has taken hold of my right hand and helped me to write.

"If even just one person leaves the service with a sense of awe and wonder at God's goodness; if even one discovers that God still speaks today; if even one understands that God works wonders and miracles when we least expect them; if even one recognises the power in the name of Jesus; if even one learns that God is always faithful to his promises, then it will have been worth it."

CHAPTER 3

Beautiful inside and out

A complicated birth (2010)

"For you created my inmost being;
you knit me together in my mother's womb.
I praise you because I am fearfully and wonderfully made."

Psalm 139:13-14

This story is about Rebecca, the younger daughter of my friend, Marianne, and her husband, Luca. It tells of her complicated birth and all that followed. It also features her older sister, Annalisa, and other family members. Marianne and I met in our twenties, and have been long-standing friends ever since.

"Please pray. The doctors don't think she's going to make it through the night. She probably hasn't got much longer left."

Standing in the dark, I'm aware of the faint glow of a light sensor being activated by a cat in my neighbour's back garden, coming through the curtains, and my heart sinks as I digest what I'm reading. It's a little after midnight and a gentle ping has roused me from my slumber. It's unusual for me to leave my phone switched on and near me when I'm sleeping, but I've made a promise to be available for emergency prayer cover. Now I've leapt out of bed and I'm clutching my phone in my left hand, my right hand scrolling in autopilot as the fluorescent screen beams its message into the darkness.

The fog of sleepiness has lifted abruptly. Fumbling for my glasses on the bedside table, I slide them on to my nose, just to be sure my eyesight isn't deceiving me. Sitting on the edge of the bed, I feel the folds of the duvet rise up to envelop me, and I instinctively raise my arms into the air, phone still in grip, arch my neck back, raise my face towards the ceiling and cry aloud into the darkness, "Why, God? Why?"

It's an act of defiant faith; a vain attempt to pray. It's all I can do.

I pause for a moment before stating the obvious. "She's so little, Lord," I declare, desperation rising in my voice. "Please give her a chance at life. Please don't let her die. Please, Lord, please."

In the stillness, the silence is deafening.

When I meet Marianne, it doesn't take long for us to become good friends.

We are part of an informal friendship group connected to two vibrant town-centre churches. All of us are in our twenties and thirties, living in a handful of shared houses across the town. Evenings and weekends see us carefree, hanging out, having fun.

My house has a particular magnetic pull. My American housemate is friendly, fun and extraverted, with the warmest of smiles, and she has an exceptional gift of welcome. Those who meet her are brought from the margins into the centre of the fold, and made to feel part of our family of friends almost instantaneously. People can't help being drawn to her. So, when she announces that she wants to host a women's weekend away, everyone is eager to commit to come.

It is springtime and we are heading to a beautiful location – an eclectic group of women, travelling together in convoy. Hedgerows have grown fresh green leaves. Hosts of golden daffodils are bobbing in the breeze. The trees are sprinkled with pink and white blossom. Women from all walks of life have gathered to get to know God and each other better. Officially it is a "retreat" but we spend more time talking than praying, and the food is so good that there isn't much fasting. In between some simple teaching sessions we go for a group walk, and that's when Marianne and I get chatting.

She is much quieter than me, initially coming across as shy and reticent, but her warmth and care quickly come through whenever she breaks into a smile, her face framed by a mop of curly brown hair. She's working as a palliative care nurse at the time, whereas I'm a Legal Aid solicitor. But we both share a love of arty-crafty hobbies, long walks in the outdoors, and faith in Jesus.

Over the years since – no matter where we are living, what we are doing, how life is treating us – we are always able to pick up where we last left off. It's one of those friendships that has overcome the tests of time and distance.

We are chatting on the phone when Marianne announces that she might have met the man of her dreams – and I can hardly contain my excitement. In all the years I've known her, we've been waiting, longing, praying for this day.

He has recently moved to the town where she lives because a change of job has forced him to relocate. He's a committed Christian and has started attending her church, which is how they have met. Her being half Dutch, half British, and him being Italian, they both regard themselves as Europeans and have plenty in common. He cooks her pizza and pasta; she introduces him to walks in gorgeous countryside; and it doesn't take long for a firm foundation of friendship to blossom into romance.

Both Luca and Marianne are well into their thirties. Neither of them wants to waste time or emotional energy if their relationship has no future, so they have several frank conversations near the outset, before they make any long-term commitment to each other. This includes one about children, during which they establish that both of them want to be parents, either naturally or through adoption.

By the time I meet Luca, he and Marianne have been dating for three months – and they are already engaged! We hang out together for a weekend, and what's clear to me is that he brings out the best in her. He's larger than life, in more ways than one; his thick dark hair frames his face, which lights up when he smiles; and he's kind, gentle and respectful. Marianne seems radiant, happy and confident in his presence.

They seem really right for each other, and Luca has my seal of approval.

Marianne and Luca marry in May, less than a year on from meeting, in a wonderful Christian wedding surrounded by family and friends. After a honeymoon in sunny Tuscany, they return to the UK and, although they initially consider waiting, they quickly change their minds and start trying for a family straightaway, not knowing how long it could take to get pregnant in light of their ages.

Within a year, they have two miscarriages.

The first time, Marianne gets short, sharp, painful contractions, which keep coming without warning. When she's hospitalised, the radiographer reveals that there's no longer a heartbeat on the ultrasound. At eleven weeks' gestation, she and Luca are about to start telling people. The disappointment cuts deeply. The pain is excruciating and nothing, not even morphine, will suffice.

The second time is slightly easier. The pregnancy is at eight weeks' gestation when Marianne has an extremely heavy period, which goes on for several days. She knows she's lost the baby and she finds it hard to fight the feelings of failure.

Just as they reach their first wedding anniversary, Marianne conceives for a third time. Despite their track record, she and Luca are cautiously optimistic; with each month that passes, they feel more assured that perhaps this baby will make it through. However, it's not an easy pregnancy. Marianne can't seem to shift the feeling that it's somehow her fault she's not been able to carry her babies to full term, personally blaming herself. When this is combined with an underlying fear of further miscarriages, she experiences unusually high anxiety levels.

When the baby's due date comes and goes, and a further two weeks pass by, Marianne is told she needs to be induced. Labour is long and drawn-out, lasting over eighteen hours. Marianne keeps passing in and out of consciousness and Luca, who stays throughout, keeps crying because he can't bear to see his wife in so much pain. When the baby's head gets stuck, the midwife calls for an emergency caesarean-section and

Marianne is too tired to argue. It's been over twenty-four hours since either of them have slept.

Annalisa enters the world with a yelp. Her parents operate in an autopilot haze of sleep deprivation, wondering where to find the manual that ought to be given out with all newborn babies! Their flat is filled with all the paraphernalia that comes with first-time parenting as they grapple with breast feeding, nappy changing and discerning between different types of cry – and the trauma of the birth is quickly smoothed over by happy hormones and the passage of time.

When Marianne conceives again, she is less stressed and more relaxed about the pregnancy. She and Luca have always wanted two children, if they can, and this time she knows that nothing is inherently stopping her: she can carry a baby to full term; it doesn't have to end in miscarriage.

The baby's due date comes and goes, and time keeps ticking. Ditto the induction date.

Then, just as Marianne is getting out of bed, fluid floods the mattress. Her waters have broken. Contractions are beginning. The baby is on the way.

Luca calls the hospital and they are advised to come in. "Second children can sometimes come notoriously quickly," he is told.

Everything feels reassuringly familiar. They park in the same hospital car park as last time, enter through the same double doors to the maternity wing, and are allocated the same delivery suite. Nevertheless, Marianne is feeling vulnerable, nervous and uncertain. Annalisa's birth was complicated and traumatic and haunting memories keep flooding her mind.

What's different is the make-up of the medical team. She's never met the midwife and there's an obstetrician there from the outset this time, just in case of complications. But it's unclear who's in charge; whether Marianne's birth plan preferences will be followed; if a caesarean section will be required.

"How can we be certain that the same things won't happen again?" she asks Luca.

"Let's pray for protection, and entrust you and the baby into God's hands," he says, squeezing her hand.

The obstetrician encourages her to give birth naturally, and Marianne pushes, but the intense pain is unbearable.

"Please can you give me an epidural?" she cries out in agony, directing her question towards the midwife, who defers the decision to the obstetrician.

"An epidural is fine for where we've reached in labour," he says, looking at the midwife and then at Marianne. "You might feel a little numb, but it will ease the pain best."

Marianne is in too much anguish to be able to articulate anything. It's Luca who verbalises consent.

As the anaesthetist inserts the needle, the pain almost instantaneously disappears, along with all sense of feeling below the waist. She's being asked to push, and she feels sure she's pushing, but she's lost all sensation. Her head is muzzy; she's finding it hard to think straight. Everything around her is operating in slow motion.

Suddenly there is a commotion. Coded conversation is taking place over her head and she feels utterly helpless. "What's the matter?" she asks. "Have I done something wrong? Is the baby going to be OK?" No one answers her. Everyone's eyes are on the machine that's monitoring the baby's heartbeat and Marianne suppresses a rising sense of panic.

"There's no cause for concern," the obstetrician says, his tone of voice trying, but failing, to be reassuring. Marianne and Luca look at each other, knowing a "but" is coming, and then the obstetrician continues, "But the baby's heartbeat is slowing down and we're not sure why."

The obstetrician pauses for a moment, searching for the right words. "The baby seems distressed, so we need to get her out as soon as possible," he explains, looking at Marianne. "That means we're going to have to give you a caesarean section".

They barely have time to digest this news before Marianne finds herself being wheeled to the operating theatre, where a small incision is made in readiness. The familiar feeling of déjà vu takes over. "You can do it," Luca tells her, holding her hand. "You've been here before." His presence is a safe and steady constant in the midst of all the turmoil.

Unaware she's even doing it, given the epidural has suspended all sense of feeling down below, she unwittingly keeps on pushing. Within moments, the baby's head emerges. There is a gasp. Nobody is expecting a natural birth. Not when Marianne is lying on the operating theatre, cut and ready for a caesarean section.

Rebecca announces her arrival with a couple of cries, followed by a deathly hush.

The obstetrician is holding her in his arms. "It's a beautiful baby girl!" he declares, handing her over to the midwife, and turning to sew closed the incision in Marianne's abdomen.

"Her name is Rebecca," Luca responds.

The silence is deafening.

"What's the matter? What's wrong with her? Why isn't she crying?" Marianne asks. Lying flat on her back, being sewn up, she is completely debilitated, unable to move. Pushing down her anxiety, she knows instinctively that something is wrong.

The midwife is looking down at the baby in her arms, studying her face and body for any glimpse of an explanation. It's only seconds, but it feels like hours.

The midwife and the obstetrician exchange glances. They press the panic button and people appear out of nowhere. Everybody is talking at once. Somebody they haven't met is performing CPR on Rebecca. Nobody explains what's going on. It's all happening in a haze.

"Why can't we hold her?" asks Luca, trying to assert some authority, distressed to see that Rebecca is writhing and arching her back.

Something is seriously wrong.

Realising that Marianne and Luca are not being briefed, the paediatric consultant interjects with a response. "I'm afraid your baby isn't well. She's having seizures and we're not sure why." She pauses a moment, scanning their faces with compassion, before continuing. "We're going to have to take her to the Special Care Baby Unit. We need to look her over and do some tests to find out what's happening."

Even as the consultant is speaking, Rebecca is being placed in an incubator and whisked out of the room, surrounded by medics manoeuvring the machines that are monitoring her vital organs. The sense of urgency is palpable.

The consultant looks at Luca and offers him a choice. "Would you like to come with us, or stay here with your wife?" He hesitates, torn in two.

Still lying on the operating table, exhausted and incapacitated, shock turns into tears and Marianne starts weeping inconsolably. Luca doesn't know how to comfort her. Their precious baby has been born and they haven't even held her yet.

It's all happening in slow motion.

By the time Luca locates a wheelchair for Marianne, and assistance to help her off the operating table and into it, Rebecca has been gone for half an hour.

"Why did the midwife not assert her authority?" Marianne asks Luca. "Why did she let the obstetrician decide on an epidural? How long until it will wear off? How long until the caesarean cut will heal up?"

Luca has no answers. It's hard not to feel angry, even in the shock.

Rebecca is lying in a clear plastic incubator. Filtered air is being pumped through it at a perfect temperature. She wears an oxygen mask, connected to a ventilator, helping her breathe. Hooked up to an intravenous drip, dangling a large saline bag of solution, her tiny body is covered in tubes and wires. Every so often, she arches her back and has a seizure.

Luca cries, Marianne cries, Rebecca cries. Through their tears, they sing songs over her that they have been singing to her in the womb. "Twinkle, twinkle, little star" is the song that soothes her the most.

"We believe there's acid in her blood and we're just running tests to see," the paediatric consultant explains to them. "We think there's been some irritation of the fluid around the brain, which is why she's having seizures."

"What's caused it?" Luca asks, trying to make sense of what's happening.

"We don't know," the consultant replies, kind and compassionate. "I know it's distressing to see her in this state, but she's breathing well. What we can't tell you is whether there's been any brain damage."

"I don't understand," Luca says, bewildered. "How could this have happened?"

"As I say, we don't know, and we may never know," the consultant responds gently, bending to sit in a chair at the same height as the wheelchair, so that she can communicate with Marianne at eye level. "We're just testing Rebecca," she says. "If she's deteriorating, then we'll have to transfer her to a larger hospital, about half an hour's drive away, where there's a specialist unit."

Marianne looks on, silently praying as the consultant systematically checks Rebecca's heart rate, muscle tone, reflexes and breathing rate again.

"Please can I hold her?" Marianne asks, tears welling up as she makes the request. "Something's clearly concerning you, but I've carried her for nine months, and now . . ." Her voice chokes with emotion and trails off mid-sentence.

"Let me see," says the consultant.

Rebecca is three hours old when Marianne finally gives her a cuddle, delicately negotiating the tubes and wires. She gingerly passes her to Luca, who carefully takes hold of her in his arms, tells her he loves her, and then pops her back in the incubator with precision.

A few hours later, Luca starts mobilising prayer support. "Please will you pray?" his message reads, before explaining what has happened. It's been sent to close friends and family, one of whom is me.

It feels surreal when they overhear a conversation intended to be out of earshot.

"All her organs are shutting down in order of priority," the paediatric consultant is telling the obstetrician, referring to Rebecca, "and I don't understand why." She pauses while he ponders for a moment.

"I don't understand either," muses the obstetrician, "but I know that the brain will be the last organ to shut down if there's been a shortage of oxygen."

"Was there enough oxygen during labour?" the consultant enquires.

"Totally," asserts the obstetrician emphatically. "We noticed the baby's heartbeat was slowing down towards the end of labour, but it wasn't any cause for concern."

"I just hope she doesn't die," muses the consultant, "because we can't do a brain scan until she's stopped having seizures and is stable."

Hearing the consultant talk about Rebecca dying sends Luca spiralling. He turns to prayer, and sends out another update. As soon as I receive it, I pray.

⟡

The Special Care Baby Unit smells sterile and pulsates with mechanical bleeping and buzzing. Each piece of equipment creates a rhythm, keeping time, occasionally announcing a warning, consistently meeting the needs of the precious babies being cushioned in each incubator. It creates a life-giving melody, merging with the hum of hushed whispers.

Rebecca is no exception. She is attached to a ventilator because she doesn't have enough oxygen in her blood, so she is struggling to breathe. She has a line going directly into her stomach, feeding her tiny amounts of formula milk, and a number of probes that are measuring her heart rate, pulse, blood pressure and other vital signs. Her utter vulnerability is overwhelming.

Yet, despite the best endeavours of both machines and medics, her condition is deteriorating and a decision is made. Within the next hour, she will be transferred to a specialist Neonatal Intensive Care Unit (NICU) in another hospital, further away from home.

After an interminable age, the Acute Neonatal Transfer Service (ANTS) ambulance arrives amidst a whirlwind of activity. Marianne and Luca watch while Rebecca is disconnected from everything that's been keeping her alive in her incubator, sedated with a small shot of morphine to stop the seizures, and prepared for the ANTS ambulance to whisk her away.

Medical histories are checked. Permissions are sought and granted. Everything is efficient. Nothing is forgotten; the t's are crossed, the i's dotted.

"She's a big baby, isn't she?" the ANTS nurse comments, as it becomes clear that Rebecca will only just fit into the ANTS ambulance incubator. "We're used to premature babies in our service, not full-termers." She makes sure all the equipment is working as it should and then, standing in the frame of the doors of the ambulance, she looks down at them reassuringly. "Her weight will give her a good fighting chance."

It's a struggle to articulate how anxious they are feeling. Luca bends down to hug Marianne, and they cling to each other before they part company. Marianne follows Rebecca in an ambulance, but Luca travels separately by car.

The new hospital feels enormous compared to the one that's been "home" for the last forty-eight hours – before, during and after the long labour. Their arrival is anticipated and Rebecca is wheeled out of the ambulance and straight into her allocated cot in the NICU, where her brain, lungs, liver and kidneys are all scanned.

The ambulance delivers Marianne to the door, where she's left in her wheelchair, waiting for a hospital porter to push her to the NICU. Alone with her thoughts, tears stream down her cheeks, unchecked. She feels exhausted, utterly helpless and incapacitated in this new unknown environment. Sleep deprivation is making her robotic. She lost a lot of blood during the delivery and her head feels light, her body is weak, and she's still completely numb below the waist.

She is shooting prayers aloud into the atmosphere, as arrows from a bow, in the hope that some of them might hit the bullseye. "Oh God, why has this happened?" she asks. "How could things have turned out like this? Please watch over Rebecca."

"Why are we crying now?" A smiling portly middle-aged man is walking towards her, whistling, and he introduces himself as a hospital porter. His upbeat voice and cheery disposition put Marianne immediately at ease. "Come on now, have a hankie," he says, passing her a wad of tissues. "Let's be getting you along to where you need to be now, shall we?" A wan smile breaks across Marianne's face.

Marianne and Luca arrive separately but almost simultaneously at the NICU, and are greeted warmly by a smiling nurse. "She's in the best place possible," she reassures them, taking them over to Rebecca's incubator.

When the World Health Organisation declares a swine flu pandemic, the National Health Service has no choice but to take emergency precautionary measures to avoid potential cross-contamination. Babies, children and the elderly are particularly vulnerable. It has arrived, unannounced, from Mexico, and nobody knows how long it will stay. For the foreseeable future, there will be restrictions on visitors to all intensive care units, especially neonatal ones.

Annalisa is desperate to meet her newborn sister. But the swine flu restrictions mean she can't. It's parents only in the NICU – and even then they are required to ensure antibacterial handwashing on entering and leaving.

She misses Marianne, but is too little to articulate it in words, so it comes out in other ways and Granny, who is on hand to provide childcare, is reporting that she isn't her usual self. Instinctively, she's picked up that something unusual and unexpected has happened.

Despite Luca's best efforts when he returns home at night, he can't seem to appease his little girl. She wants her mum and no one else will meet the mark. Last thing at night, she asks for her. First thing in the morning, she asks for her. Luca is caught in a no-win situation.

When Rebecca unexpectedly stops breathing, the medics swiftly intubate her, inserting a long thin tube down her throat and into her lungs, connected to an oxygen monitor, enabling her to breathe. A portable X-ray machine is wheeled into place to ensure it's been accurately aligned and her tiny newborn chest begins to bob up and down again, her breathing rhythmic but laboured. The monitor beeps incessantly, reminding everyone in earshot that she's being kept alive artificially.

Marianne and Luca are standing on each side of her hospital cot, watching over Rebecca with profound parental love, care and concern. Her whimpering cries are gagged by the tube that's currently keeping her alive, and this sight and sound cuts deep into the core of their being, but there is nothing they can do. They both feel utterly helpless.

Looking up, they see the paediatric consultant approaching them. She is wearing a crisp white coat, a stethoscope dangling around her neck. She is accompanied by a senior nurse who invites them to sit down. Her face is grave and serious as she pulls up two tan leather-cushioned chairs next to the noisy monitor.

The consultant's manner is brusque, her voice sombre, as she breaks the shattering news. "Rebecca's condition is extremely serious and we don't expect her to survive the night," she explains in a strong Nigerian accent. She pauses to allow her words to penetrate, unwittingly creating a dramatic effect. "If she stops breathing again, we don't think we should resuscitate her because her brain damage will be too great."

"Are you wanting our permission to turn off the machines that are keeping her alive?" Luca asks tentatively.

"We don't actually need your permission," the consultant replies, "but we'd obviously prefer it if you agree." Luca is listening carefully; Marianne is fighting back tears. "At the end of the day," she continues, "it will be Rebecca's doctors who decide."

Her words pierce deep and then the shock rises up, a fist punching the air, as the enormity sinks in. "Are you saying our daughter has deteriorated so rapidly that she could die?" asks Luca.

"Yes," says the consultant. "Her life is at risk."

Luca feels distraught. He and Marianne are being asked to make the most difficult decision either of them has ever had to face. "How on earth are we meant to respond?" he muses.

"Please," he pleads with the consultant, his voice choking through the tears, looking up at her and the senior nurse. "Please can you give us a few moments alone together?" He reaches towards Marianne, putting his hand on her knee in case it's not obvious who "us" means. "We need to talk in private about what you're asking of us."

Their wishes are respected, and the consultant and nurse leave the room. His words hang in the air as the door closes behind them, and the atmosphere is tense.

Somehow, through the fog of three nights' sleep deprivation, tears streaming down their faces, Luca and Marianne hold each other and pray as they try to process all that's been happening these past three days.

Whatever the ultimate outcome, they know beyond knowing that they are being carried by the prayers of others. Christians across the UK, Netherlands, Italy and beyond are petitioning God for Rebecca's life.

By the time the paediatric consultant returns to the room, Marianne and Luca have committed Rebecca to God, trusting him to see her through the night ahead. If Rebecca stops breathing again, she may suffer catastrophic brain damage. They know her medical team will do what they can to save her, but they also know she could deteriorate so much that they have no option but to take the difficult decision to turn off the machines that are keeping her alive. All they will be able to do is watch and pray.

"We're Christians," Luca tells the consultant confidently. "There are lots of people praying for Rebecca, and we believe God will heal her and bring her through the night."

Luca wants the world to know Rebecca's name. He wants to register her birth. Whether she lives or dies, he wants her existence to be officially recorded.

It was while she was still in the womb that he and Marianne decided on her name. It means "beautiful", and they feel sure she will be, both inside and out. It's also easy to pronounce in their native languages – English, Dutch and Italian.

As he drives to the registry office, Luca thanks God that he knows Rebecca's name, echoing the words of David, on her behalf, from Psalm 139:13-16 in the Bible:

"For you created my inmost being; you knit me together in my mother's womb. I praise you because I am fearfully and wonderfully made; your works are wonderful, I know that full well. My frame was not hidden from you when I was made in the secret place, when I was woven together in the depths of the earth. Your eyes saw my unformed body; all the days ordained for me were written in your book before one of them came to be."

The registrar is clearly distracted. She has been out for a lunch appointment which overran. Arriving late for her afternoon shift, she runs up the stairs and is out of breath and apologetic as she enters her office. The faint aroma of alcohol follows in her wake. She slides into the chair behind her desk to survey who's waiting for her and sees Luca sitting patiently in the waiting area.

His head is full. All through the night, he's been trawling through online medical journals, trying to analyse what the doctors have been telling him. He needs to quench his insatiable need to know, to understand, to problem solve. He wants to know why Rebecca is not responding; whether something hasn't been spotted; what it's going to take to get her better.

The registrar comes to the door of her office and beckons him in.

He's barely taken his seat when, "I'm sorry I'm late," she says sheepishly and slightly tipsy, rummaging through her handbag to find a nail file. "I've been out for lunch with my daughter, you know, and we went to that new little bistro which just opened up last week on the other side of town, only the parking was terrible and then I got stuck in traffic getting back here on time, so I'm sorry I'm late . . ." She is looking at her finger nails, not at Luca, her semi-articulated thoughts tumbling out and tailing off.

It takes all his willpower not to vent his frustration.

"It was a lovely little place, but it wasn't half busy, I guess because it's new and lots of people are seeing what it's like. Anyway, there were some amazing specials on the menu and we just had to try them." She pauses and half looks up, nail file in one hand, fingers splayed out on the other hand while she inspects the nails. Her mindless chatter is irritating Luca, but she is utterly oblivious. "It was a shame there weren't more staff in today as the service was slow, but you should try it some time," she tells him, putting down her nail file and wiggling both sets of fingers in the air with a flourish.

The last thing he wants is to try a new bistro. Banal things don't matter. Not when there's a battle between life and death going on over your daughter.

She reaches across her desk for a book of blank certificates, and picks up a pen, poised and ready to write. "Birth can be such a stressful time," she exclaims, "but as long as the baby is healthy, the rest really doesn't matter, does it?" She raises her head to give Luca eye contact, and there is a pregnant pause.

"My daughter is currently in the Neonatal Intensive Care Unit," he informs her, his words slicing the atmosphere. "She's in an extremely critical condition and she could die."

The registrar's face fills with remorse and she finally falls silent, shifting awkwardly in her chair.

Less than ten minutes later, Luca leaves the office, clutching the completed paperwork. He feels upset with the registrar. "At least if the worst happens, I won't have to register her birth and death at the same time," he calls out after he leaves.

As dawn breaks on a new day, hope rises on the horizon: Rebecca has made it through the night. She is stable, fighting – and alive.

Luca and Marianne have been keeping a watching vigil by her bedside, praying for her constantly – and allowing the prayers of Christian friends and family to sustain them, intermittently sending emergency updates, like the one that woke me not long after midnight.

It's the weekend and the neonatal paediatric consultant is meant to be off duty today. Instead, he's in the NICU and looking at Rebecca's notes. He introduces himself, and explains that he's been monitoring her vital organs. He shows them the portable ultrasound that he's been using. "The only change I've made is a slight adjustment to her ventilator," he explains, "as I'd really like us to wean her off it as soon as we can."

"See here," he says, pointing towards various charts on two monitor screens next to Rebecca's incubator. "She's got a strong constitution and she's clearly fighting." He pauses for a moment. "What we don't know is whether there's been any brain damage. It's simply too soon to tell."

"What are her chances of survival?" Luca asks, voicing the question that's been burning inside ever since her birth. "Will she make a full recovery from all this?"

The consultant turns his head away from the monitor and looks Luca in the eye. "Based on all my years of specialist experience," he responds, softly and reflectively, "I honestly think she's got about a fifty/fifty chance." He studies Luca's face, and then turns to look down at Marianne in her wheelchair, bringing her into the conversation. "Remember that I'm used to dealing with tiny premature babies," he muses, "not full-termers like Rebecca."

Marianne silently reaches for Luca's hand.

She knows she has to prepare – psychologically and emotionally – for God to take Rebecca. "What if the worst happens?" she asks Luca. "Are we ready for it?" She can feel fear gripping her heart.

There is pandemonium in the NICU.

Nurses are frantically running around, communicating in coded hushed whispers. Machines are frenetically bleeping and buzzing, broadcasting a message of urgency. "Listen to us!" they demand. Graphs on display screens are furiously spewing out spikey scenes – mountain peaks followed by valley troughs on endless repeat.

Rebecca's organs have shut down. All of them, one by one.

At this precise moment, her tummy is ballooning, round and taut. To an experienced eye it would appear that her kidneys are failing, and possibly her liver too. Why else would she be retaining fluids?

The neonatal paediatric consultant strides into the room. The atmosphere shifts and he unwittingly creates a sense of calm.

"Her heart and lungs are working overtime," he declares, peering at the monitors over his spectacles, while grabbing the clipboard crammed with papers which a nurse is thrusting into his hand. He pauses to read the latest entries. "Her potassium levels appear to be low," he pronounces, pausing. "Far too low," he adds.

He turns and consults with the nurse. "When did she last urinate?" he asks her.

"Nearly three hours ago," the nurse replies.

"Let's give her a dose of diuretics," the consultant suggests. The nurse agrees and duly obliges. However, an hour later, Rebecca is still not responding to treatment.

"Should we really be keeping her going?" a junior doctor asks. "Wouldn't it be kinder to turn off her ventilator and let her die?" There is no emotion in his voice. He is simply making a suggestion in light of the available facts.

"It's too soon to make that kind of decision," the consultant responds firmly. "We don't yet know whether Rebecca will recover."

There is a hushed silence.

"Quick! Look!" Luca's voice is upbeat. He beckons Marianne with an unexpected urgency, grabbing her attention as she wheels past the NICU security desk after a quick comfort break.

"Why? What?" she responds, but the answer becomes obvious as she peers down at Rebecca in her incubator. She gives an involuntary gasp, turns to Luca and smiles.

Their baby's newborn beauty is no longer marred by the long thin tube that's been carrying oxygen into her lungs.

Rebecca is breathing on her own.

The ventilator has been removed and oxygen is now being pumped into her incubator, where she lies asleep, her chest bobbing gently up and down as her lungs learn to operate without assistance.

A nurse comes over to check Rebecca's vital signs. "She's doing well," she remarks. "We're weaning her off the dopamine and morphine now, so hopefully she'll wake up soon." She pauses a moment before continuing reflectively, "One thing's for sure. You're not going to see her have any more involuntary convulsions."

The memories of Rebecca writhing in pain, her back arching in distress, her body contorting, is one that Marianne and Luca will be glad to expunge from their minds. It's something that their friends and family have been praying into, and today they can be sure that God has heard.

The vacuum-suction sound of the breast pump is whirring full pelt. It's a sound that's become familiar during the past week. But today is different.

Today, Rebecca is one week old. Today, she is going to be given Marianne's milk. Today, the intravenous line into her tummy button is going to carry it directly into her digestive system. It's not simply going to be pumped, labelled and frozen; it's actually going to be used.

Breastfeeding without a baby at the breast is painful. It's not just the physical pain caused by the mechanical contraption; it's the emotional pain of absence, the acute reminder that your baby is not where she should be, latching on.

Marianne is in turmoil. Tears trickle down her cheek, hormones kicking in, as the pump grinds on. Whir and click. Whir and click. Whir and click.

Once Marianne is mobile, she returns home with Luca. For the first night since the birth she is back in her own bed again, surrounded by comforting familiarity. She is still questioning what happened, still feeling fearful and tearful, still in immense pain – partly the incision made in preparation for the caesarean section that never came, partly the rips caused by the natural birthing process. Her hormones are wreaking havoc.

Leaving Rebecca at the hospital has been painful. She feels bereft.

"Will she be OK?" she whispers to Luca, lying back against the pillows. "Will the medical team be kind to her? Will

God watch over her?" She doesn't wait for answers before she succumbs to exhaustion and falls into a fitful sleep.

It's still dark when she wakes, remembers where she is, opens an eye and discovers a toddler standing at eye level by the side of her bed, staring at her with wonder in her eyes because her mum has returned home. Granny is standing in the doorway, watching.

Annalisa's squeals of joy are contagious, her cuddles a delight.

A prayer update has come round. I am making breakfast when my phone gently pings to announce its arrival. I grab it and start to scroll.

Rebecca is stable, the message is informing me, but she is failing to fully respond to treatment. Her breathing is laboured, so she is back on ventilation again and has had an electrocardiogram to assess the condition of her heart.

Her stomach is swollen, round and taut like a ping pong ball, which Luca is finding distressing. She's not urinating, but her medical team are at a loss as to why because her kidneys and liver are functioning fine. A catheter has been inserted into her bladder, and a long needle into her tummy to release the fluids and relieve the pressure on her lungs, but nothing seems to be working. The consultant in charge of her case has been calling other hospitals for specialist advice.

It feels like a setback.

But the amazing news is that one of their friends knows the neonatal paediatric consultant. They used to attend the same church as him. It means Rebecca is in the care of a Christian who "just so happens" to be the consultant in charge of this hospital's NICU. Such a small detail, yet so significant. It's a reminder that God is in control.

Please will we pray?

"Oh God," I cry aloud, still holding my phone where I'm standing, leaning back against my kitchen units, "please don't let Rebecca die. You've brought her so far in this last week and a bit. Please heal her tiny body. Please give the doctors wisdom to know what treatment will work. Please protect her from all stress and trauma. Please, God, I'm asking in Jesus' name."

Over the weekend, Marianne and then Luca are able to stroke and cuddle Rebecca. It's awkward, given all her wires and tubes, but they want her to feel their touch and know they are there. Rebecca opens her mouth to respond. She is trying to cry, but no sound comes out. They alleviate their upset by singing gently over her, creating some semblance of normality.

The neonatal paediatric consultant is working the Monday morning shift. Marianne and Luca are relieved to see him again, and he greets them with a warm smile.

"We've received and discussed the results of the electrocardiogram with the radiologist," he informs them, looking at them across Rebecca's incubator. "What we can see is that fluid seems to be building up in Rebecca's abdominal cavity, and this is compromising her heart and lungs." He pauses a moment to ensure they are following him. "We want to insert a large needle into her abdomen to drain the fluid," he continues, "but this will need to be done by specialists." He names a hospital in a huge city. "They will also be able to do a baby MRI scan," he adds, "because we still don't know the extent of her brain damage."

Marianne reaches out and holds Luca's hand. "How soon will this happen?" she asks the consultant, anxious about the potential impact of another transfer on Rebecca.

"As soon as a cot becomes available in the NICU there," he says, "and as soon as we have an accurate diagnosis."

Visits home are hard. Annalisa has caught a cold and a cough, which she is keen to share and her parents are keen to avoid. Every night she wakes up coughing and crying. She wants to see her baby sister and doesn't understand why she can't. She's also missing Granny, who's had to return home and is no longer on hand to help with childcare. Tempers are frayed; sleep deprivation is starting to kick in.

Luca's paternity leave is also coming to a close, but his company are compassionate and his colleagues understanding. They also have a steady stream of friends from church who are blessing them by bringing meals.

Together, they forge a new rhythm: Luca goes to the hospital in the morning while Marianne looks after Annalisa at home. At lunchtime they overlap at the hospital, before Marianne takes over in the afternoon while Luca goes to work. Both of them keep dosing up on vitamin C to fend off the germs, as the last thing they want is for Rebecca to catch a cold and a cough.

"Medically speaking, she shouldn't still be with us. It makes no clinical sense." A new consultant has been studying Rebecca's records, clearly puzzled by the difference between what he's reading and what he's observing.

"We're Christians," Luca interjects. "The hospital chaplain has been praying over her regularly, and we've got many friends and family, all over the world, who are praying for her too. Maybe their prayers are making a difference?"

"Her progress has been exponential in the past few days," the consultant continues.

It's a few days now since the huge city hospital was mooted as an option for their specialist expertise and their baby brain scanning services, but a referral has not yet happened. The fluid retention has suddenly stopped; she now has normal urine function. The ventilator has been turned off; she is breathing independently. Such a rapid turnaround is a source of mystery to her medical team.

The only unknown is the extent and severity of her brain damage.

"Now she's stable, we'd recommend a baby MRI scan because, at the moment, we can only guess what damage has been done," the consultant explains gently. "But it will need the specialist equipment at the huge city hospital; are you OK with that?"

"Yes," they both say resignedly, in unison.

On the Monday morning that she turns three weeks old, Rebecca has a baby MRI scan. The previous evening she was transported to the huge city hospital by blue-light ambulance. Luca has slept fitfully in a room set aside for parents adjacent to the NICU, and Marianne has followed by train after entrusting Annalisa to Granny's care once again.

Three doctors have been discussing the results, one of whom is a top paediatric neurologist. They are united in their opinion. "Rebecca has two areas of damage on her brain, both of which are quite small and localised, as far as we can tell," she explains, her tone kind and compassionate. "One relates to her balance and movement; the other, her focus attention span."

"What does that mean?" asks Marianne, feeling frightened by this prognosis.

"The first area of damage means she's probably going to struggle to coordinate her hands and fingers with her eyes. It may come with time, but she's likely to be slower than other children at the same age, and I think we should expect delays in some of her developmental stages – sitting unsupported, reaching for things, walking – that kind of thing. She might need physiotherapy, but we'll need to keep assessing her to see."

Marianne struggles to absorb what she's hearing, and Luca gives her hand a reassuring squeeze.

The neurologist continues. "The second area of damage means she may have difficulty with tasks that require concentration, and she may need occupational therapy."

"Is there anything we can do about it?" asks Luca.

"Not really," the consultant says. "In the long run, she should be able to do most things, but she will need to have regular check-ups with us over the next few years so that we can keep her under observation"

Marianne visibly relaxes; her sense of relief is palpable. "It's because so many people have been praying for her," Luca remarks, squeezing her hand again. "God has heard us."

It's a sunny Sunday morning in early spring and Luca and Marianne are standing on a stage in a room without natural light. The high ceiling reveals that this building used to be a warehouse, but it's now owned by a church who run all manner of ministries from it, including Sunday services. Rebecca is in Luca's arms and Annalisa is holding on to Marianne's left leg, trying to hide her face from all the people looking up at her, one of whom is me.

Sitting alongside me are Luca's family, who are visiting from Italy, and Marianne's parents. We are part of a packed congregation, several hundred strong. It's the middle of a Sunday morning church service and we've paused for Rebecca's dedication, a time of giving thanks to God for her life and committing her into his care.

Since leaving hospital at four weeks old, she's been developing as a happy, healthy, normal baby – bonding, crying, sleeping, feeding, gaining weight – and Annalisa is loving having a little sister. Anyone meeting her now would be none the wiser about her rocky start.

The senior pastor hands the microphone to Luca, who proficiently explains the rollercoaster ride of Rebecca's first four weeks of life. "We couldn't have done it without your prayers and support," he tells the congregation as he draws the story to a conclusion. "We've had such a profound sense of God's presence with us, carrying us, and it's been such a huge comfort. Thank you if you're one of those who have prayed for us or helped us practically. God used you in ways you may never know. We feel so blessed."

The congregation prays collectively for Rebecca and we welcome her into God's family, the church community, recognising just how much there is to celebrate.

Marianne and Luca keep a watchful eye over Rebecca's development, understandably concerned about the neurologists' prognosis of potential brain damage. But time and again, Rebecca exceeds expectations and confounds the experts. As a baby, she is determined to move, commando crawling as soon as she can. As a toddler, she sits for half an hour at a time, fully focused on completing wooden jigsaw puzzles. In a group setting, she's never a passive observer.

Rebecca's health records folder is huge, splitting at the seams because of all the paperwork generated during her first four weeks of life. Every six months it gets opened when Luca and Marianne faithfully take Rebecca back to the hospital for check-ups. She passes each one with flying colours and is formally discharged when she reaches age three. She is fine for her age and doing all she should be doing. There's no evidence of her having any of the anticipated brain-damage-related developmental problems.

Meeting Rebecca now, you will come face-to-face with a girl who is happy, sociable and expressive. She's a fearless explorer, always taking risks and trying new things. She loves to make people laugh and is cheeky, funny and often clowning around. More than anything else, she's full of life, a walking witness to the God who made her beautiful, inside and out.

CHAPTER 4

Power in the name of Jesus
A woman with stomach cancer (2006)

"Now faith is confidence in what we hope for and assurance about what we do not see."

Hebrews 11:1

This story is about my friend and former colleague, Karen. At the time, we were working together for a charity which supports vulnerable children around the world. It tells of how she was diagnosed with stomach cancer and what happened subsequently. It also features her husband, Martin, her parents and her sisters.

I am sitting in an independent café, tucked into the corner of a shabby shopping precinct that has seen better days. The pale-yellow laminated table top has clearly only been cursorily cleaned as my cup of tea keeps catching where it's still slightly sticky. Opposite me sits my friend and colleague, Karen, in her early thirties, her long dark hair framing her heart-shaped face, her fringe in need of a trim.

"Thanks for the coffee," she says, the inflection in her soft Welsh lilt ending the sentence on an up. Her hands are cupping the mug for warmth, the handle pointing towards me.

"My pleasure," I respond.

Karen has just returned from a holiday in South Africa with her husband, Martin, and I can tell she wants to share something important. It doesn't take long for it to come out.

"You know how I've been gaining weight and throwing up in recent months?" she says, softly spoken, looking down at her rather large stomach. It's more of a question than a statement. So I nod, aware that she's been experimenting with various different diets in an attempt to shed the unwanted pounds.

"And you know how I've taken pregnancy tests that have come back negative, and blood tests that have proved inconclusive?" she continues and, again, I nod. "Well, while I've been away, the symptoms have got worse and my family doctor is now referring me for an MRI scan." She pauses a moment, nervously biting her bottom lip. "She thinks it might be cancer."

I feel shock surging through my body, followed swiftly by a strong sense of denial. "That can't be right," I declare defiantly, "you can't have cancer."

Even the suggestion of such a terrible disease simply makes no sense. Karen is kind. She is warm and welcoming, generous and gracious, full of humour, full of life, full of faith. She makes everyone around her feel special. She makes everyone laugh.

"I'm telling you because I want you to pray," she reveals, letting me know the date and time for her appointment at the hospital. Without hesitation, I stretch out my hand to her across the sticky table top and pray aloud for her healing, in the name of Jesus. A surge of conviction rises up within me, confident God has heard me.

When Karen and I meet it's the spring of 2001, and we are both attending an international conference in the Netherlands. The venue comprises a cluster of Dutch-designed buildings, situated in a vast, flat rural landscape, with occasional waterways weaving through the freshly planted fields. The conference centre is crammed to capacity, every bed taken, with delegates from more than sixty nations, mostly in the Global South. All of them are Christians working with, or on behalf of, vulnerable children. All are here to share what they are learning in their different country contexts.

It's during the opening session of the second day when I find myself sitting next to Karen in a row of interlinked wooden chairs, beneath the cavernously high white ceiling of the conference centre's main auditorium. In the midst of all the delegates, most of whom are twice our age, Karen stands out from the crowd. She turns to me with a smile, open and warm, as I nervously ask whether I can sit next to her. She exudes an unusual air of confidence.

Striking up conversation, I discover that, although originally from South Wales, she's been living in South Africa for several years. She has painstakingly pioneered a network for people working with children at risk in Cape Town, and it soon becomes clear that she embraces danger and difficulty without question. Working out of a makeshift office in a shed at the end of a friend's garden, she helps abandoned children find night shelters with spare beds, and assists the projects who care for the children, helping them to track any who go missing.

She is clearly in her element at this conference, surrounded by kindred spirits who are collectively striving to make life better for vulnerable children in all the contexts and cultures they represent.

When our conversation continues into the coffee break, I know I've found a new friend, and the backdrop to her story emerges over the course of time.

Growing up alongside coal mines and steelworks in the industrial heartland of South Wales, Karen comes from a close-knit family. Although most of them make no pretence to profess the Christian faith, her grandma regularly talks to her about Jesus. "I pray for you and your sisters every day," she tells Karen, teaching her the tunes of familiar Welsh hymns.

Karen develops a strong sibling bond with her two younger sisters. Pushing them on the swings at the play park, she frequently prays and sings over them, much to her grandma's delight.

Warm, witty, kind and clever, she has an endearing manner which charms even the most hardened soul. She is always putting other people first, even when done with a wry smile and a practical joke. Her imagination is vivid and she spends hours writing reflections or whimsically dreaming about the future. At age eight she has a dream that, one day, she will work with children in Africa. "The dream was so vivid," she explains, "I could see that my job was to open tins of peaches and feed them to the children." It is a dream she holds onto for years.

Doggedly determined in her studies and exams, she's the first in her family to go to university, and she soon sets off to study undergraduate business studies in a nearby city, a short distance along the coast from her home town.

One sunny day during her final academic year, she climbs a hill, not far from the city. Taking a seat on the grass at the top, she stops to absorb a beautiful panoramic view. The golden brown and red rust colours of the trees are signalling the start of autumn, and the sun is shining on the rooftops of the buildings which scan out to the docks and, beyond them, the sea. Overwhelmed by the beauty of the scene in front of her, she starts to pray. "Oh God, if you're real," she negotiates, "please will you show me?" In an instant, a sense of peace engulfs her. "While I was praying, something came over me," she explains. "I felt embraced by a tremendous peace."

Heading back down the mountain, she feels sure she's had an encounter with God and, returning home, she finds a Bible which she begins to devour, reading it hungrily. She also starts to pray and can soon be found conversing with God on an almost constant basis.

The following Sunday she visits a local Baptist church, where she describes her encounter on the hill to the pastor and the lady sitting next to her. Neither of them is phased by it and they both agree it sounds like she met with God. At the end of the service, the lady invites her to lunch with some other students and Karen gladly accepts, relishing the opportunity to talk about matters of faith. It's not long before she's a permanent fixture, a familiar face, in the congregation.

Whereas her faith used to be an idling engine, God has now pressed the accelerator and revved it into life.

After Karen graduates she becomes a management consultant, working for a local borough council in South Wales. But she misses academia and returns to university, where she completes a Master's degree in philosophy. Wowed by her intellect, her supervisor endeavours to persuade her to study for a doctorate. "Let me pray about it," she tells him, much to his surprise.

Throughout the course of that long hot summer, the more she prays, and the more she consults with her church pastor and others whom she trusts, the more she senses a growing call from God to prepare for missionary service in Africa. She is unclear which country; she just knows she needs to get ready.

As the new academic year arrives, and autumn merges with the tail end of summer, Karen moves away from South Wales to train for mission at a popular Bible college. An imposing red-brick building, based on the edge of a large cosmopolitan city, she soon settles in, making many friends with people from all over the world; she emerges with a distinction a year later. It is then that she applies for a voluntary placement and is delighted to be matched with a local Christian organisation, which is serving the needs of people who are living in poverty in Cape Town.

Despite the best-laid plans and preparations, arriving in South Africa is a culture shock for Karen as she experiences, for the first time, the continent's beloved kamikaze traffic, pot-holed roads, street-stall vendors, lilac jacaranda trees, rust-red earth, smell of tropical rain, and the incongruity between rich and poor.

Sitting in an administrative, office-based role, she feels far removed from the frontline work of the organisation she's serving. However, she lives in a destitute neighbourhood where abuse and knife crime are rife, homeless children are coerced into joining gangs, and drugs are openly sold on street corners in broad daylight. Her heart breaks at what she witnesses and she soon starts to respond to the needs on her doorstep, building trust with those who are willing to let her into their lives.

Six months soon turns into a year and, before she knows it, Cape Town is becoming "home".

Returning to the UK for an international mission conference at the end of her placement, she meets a young enthusiastic red-haired Danish entrepreneur who is setting up a new networking organisation, linking together people and projects who are serving children at risk around the world. "Would you like to join us?" he asks Karen. "You could pioneer a citywide network in Cape Town."

The vision is inspiring. The opportunity is timely. His pitch is passionate and persuasive. The only challenge is a lack of funding. "All of us are self-funded at the moment, so you'd have to be a volunteer," the Dane explains, "but I'm doing what I can to raise enough to pay salaries at some point in the future."

Thankfully, Karen has built a strong relationship with a philanthropic Welsh businessman, who she knows through the Baptist church in her university city. That year, he sells his company and decides to use part of the proceeds to provide seed funding for start-up businesses in Cape Town. With the profits from this venture, he generously releases funds to financially support Karen and the work she is undertaking, including provision of office space and accommodation.

"We seek to coordinate local organisations working with children at risk, across the city of Cape Town," she explains to a journalist during an interview with a South Wales newspaper. "We equip existing organisations and help new ones get established, and we bring them all together in a supportive network."

South Africa forges and forms Karen's faith and future.

Late one starless night, her car breaks down while she's driving through a notoriously violent township. Knowing she will become an instant target if she stays in her car, she hides in a nearby bush, praying until dawn. Another time, she's due to meet Winnie Mandela when the van she has hired breaks down. So she stands on the side of the road, prays and lays hands on the bonnet, and the engine fires into life again. When her sister comes to stay, Karen takes her to church and she's so visibly moved by God's presence that she becomes a Christian. And when she's asked to spend time in Zimbabwe, helping a colleague replicate the network model in Harare, ever alert to spiritual matters, she has to keep avoiding the witchdoctors who are keen to be rid of her.

There is also the time she meets her husband, Martin.

She's never short of marriage proposals, usually from inappropriate men in unexpected places. But it soon becomes clear that one of them is not going to give up. Sitting on a train, quietly reading her Bible and occasionally looking up to gaze out of the window, Karen catches Martin's attention as he sits opposite her, facing against the direction of travel. Trying desperately to ignore his imposing rugby-player build, he strikes up conversation with her and, before she disembarks the train, he insists on taking her number, intent on pursuit. Romance soon blossoms and they marry in 2002.

One of the things that most attracts Martin to Karen is her kindness, and they are both hardwired to fearlessly defend those who are needy and vulnerable.

When they decide to relocate from South Africa to the UK, if they aren't housing one of Martin's South African security-guard friends, they are providing a roof for a waif, stray, orphan or outcast with nowhere else to go. They also sign up to start fostering; on one occasion taking in a troubled teenage girl, her angry father turning up at their house late one night, only to flee at the sight of Martin's enormous silhouette in the doorway.

Whenever Karen faces challenges, she responds with faith, grace and humour. She frequently seems to find herself in the most ridiculous situations, regularly causing friends and family to double up with side-splitting, belly-aching laughter. It's as much the expressionless, straight-faced way that she tells her tales, with the soft lilt of her Welsh accent, as in the stories themselves.

On more than one occasion, sitting round a large communal table in our dilapidated office, with a group of colleagues lingering after lunch, Karen entertains us with her comedy recollections.

"Once, while browsing in a porcelain shop, I reached up high for an ornament, knocking off balance an entire shelf of china," she says, "but I leapt to grab it, to prevent it from landing on the floor – only for the man behind me to bump against the exact same shelf, sending it into a seesaw, and causing all the contents to domino down to the ground with an almighty crash." We laugh in unison.

"On a long-haul flight, I accidentally hit the emergency alarm when I used the toilet, causing the air stewardess to come running," she tells us. "I reassured her it was a false alarm, only to turn the wash basin tap so hard that it snapped, creating an uncontainable water fountain. I was so panicked, I had to hit the emergency alarm again, and the same air stewardess came running."

"My family despair of me," she concedes. "On one occasion, I offered my services as a driving instructor, accompanying my sister while she practised – only to watch in horror as we ploughed through a barrier and over an occupied manhole cover." She pauses a moment. "I also took my mum and sister out on the river in a rowing boat, but the boat kept rotating in circles and almost capsizing – and then I realised there was a rope attaching it to the bank." Again, we laugh.

Karen's self-confidence means she regularly strikes up conversations with complete strangers, and she never shies away from sharing her Christian faith. If she believes God has spoken to her about a situation that someone might be facing, she has no qualms in happily walking up to them, introducing herself and telling them what God has said.

She's hard-wired to cope with adversity through faith, fun or both.

On a hot summer's day in 2004, Karen is at her parents' home in South Wales, catching up with the family. Standing in the centre of the living room, the French windows pouring sunshine in from the colourfully planted back garden behind her, her sisters are sitting on one of the sofas and her parents are on the other.

"I keep putting on weight and I keep throwing up," she explains, "and both seem to have got worse while we've been on holiday in South Africa." She pauses a moment before continuing, "None of the diets I try ever seem to work, and I know I'm definitely not pregnant."

Leaning forward to listen, the older of her two sisters, a registered nurse, gently speaks out a suggestion. "Karen, I'm not a specialist, but your symptoms suggest to me you might have cancer." She allows her words to sink in as Karen's mouth drops open, visibly shocked. "Why don't you ask your family doctor for a referral to the hospital for tests?"

Heeding her sister's advice, Karen visits her doctor who is hugely understanding.

"My hands are tied though," she explains, "so even if I refer you today for an MRI scan, the soonest you'll get an appointment will be in at least four months' time." She speaks with compassion. "It's just because all the hospital waiting lists are so long at the moment."

As Karen prays with Martin, she starts to wonder whether there might be another option. "Do you think I could be expedited if I pay to be a private patient?" she asks.

"It might be better than waiting for a referral through the public health service," he concedes, "although I don't know where we'd find the money."

Contacting her church pastor and other trusted friends, she describes the situation and asks for their advice. One by one, they respond – expressing concern, committing to pray, and offering to contribute financially towards the costs of a private patient referral. It quickly pays dividends.

Rather than waiting more than four months, it takes less than two weeks to get an appointment.

The consultant oncologist is a kind and caring middle-aged man in his early fifties. Balding slightly, he has an affable manner which quickly puts Karen at her ease. He has a harder job persuading her mum, who has accompanied her, to cast aside her anxieties. Welcoming them into his consulting room, they discover a desk to one side, some book-lined shelves and a translucent white screen on the other, and a window at the end, looking out over the hospital car park.

"Please take a seat," he invites them, gesturing towards the two leather-cushioned, metal-framed chairs in front of his desk. Clasping Karen's MRI scan results in his hands, he uses colourful magnets to pin them to the screen on the wall and peers over his spectacles perched on the end of his nose, to study them. "I've got to tell you," he says reflectively, "your scan is telling me that you've got a malignant tumour in your stomach. It looks to me like a retroperitoneal sarcoma."

There is a sharp intake of breath as her mum hears her worst fears confirmed, while Karen shuffles into a more upright position, her hands cupped protectively atop her burgeoning tummy. "What does that mean exactly?" she asks.

The consultant catches Karen's gaze and points to one of the images pinned to the screen. "See here," he explains, using his forefinger to indicate, "the tumour starts at the base of your spine and it looks as though it's been growing gradually over many years, but it's now become so big that it's pushed all your organs to one side to make room." He screws his eyes into a squint and peers in closer. "It actually looks as though the tumour has attached itself to your liver and this large vein." He hones in and points. "That vein is connected to your heart. Can you see? It takes blood from the lower part of your body and returns it to your heart."

Karen, usually so articulate, is struggling for words. Her shock is palpable. "What are my options?" she eventually asks. She can't help noticing that the scan pictures appear to show the tumour has hair growing on it. "It looks like some sort of alien being inside me," she jokes.

"We could try to shrink the tumour through chemotherapy," the consultant informs her, "but we can't remove it through surgery because it's attached to your liver."

She can feel the tears welling up, and is grateful when her mum reaches out to take hold of her hand. "But I want to have children," she sobs, "so I can't have chemotherapy."

As numbness sets in, there's only one option left. "I'm going to mobilise people to pray," she says, as much to herself as those in earshot. "I know God can heal me."

I feel uneasy when I discover Karen's email in my inbox, remembering our recent café conversation.

"Please will you pray?" I read. The tone is emphatic. "The doctors have given me a stomach cancer diagnosis," she explains. "I have a huge abdominal tumour which has wrapped itself around the vein to my heart, attached itself to my liver, and entangled itself with my other vital organs. I urgently need surgery, but I'm told it's impossible while the tumour's attached to my liver."

Karen's email exudes faith. Spurred on by the miracles she has witnessed while living in Cape Town – where she has seen street children healed of sicknesses, delivered from demons and, in one instance, raised from the dead – she and Martin are imploring friends and family to pray and fast for her healing.

"I don't believe this is of God," she declares with faith-filled insistence. "I don't believe he wants me to die, because there are still things he wants me to do. So I'm asking you to pray, in Jesus' name, and to fast too if you're able, for the mighty power of God to heal me."

There are a lot of us on that mailing list.

The temperature is soaring and people are stripping off layers of clothing, exposing pale British skin to the sun for the first time in months. Karen and Martin are hosting her parents in their rented house in the south of England. With her health deteriorating fast, and unable to muster enough energy to climb the stairs, she has started to sleep on the sofa. She knows that time is of the essence and, on this particular Sunday morning, she's determined to get to church, and invites her parents along too.

The congregation hire out a school hall to host their Sunday services. Made up of people of all ages and stages of life, the worship music is provided by a band; the singing is joyful and vibrant; the preaching is straightforward and Bible-based. When prayer is offered at the end, Karen gets up from her seat and walks to the front, slowly but unhesitatingly. Martin follows, while her parents watch.

A cluster of friends gather around her, laying hands on her stomach and praying for healing in the name of Jesus. As they do so, the power of God comes upon her and Martin has to reach out to steady her when she starts to shake uncontrollably.

That afternoon, back home and lying on the sofa, Karen becomes acutely aware that her cancer-ridden stomach is starting to shrink in front of her very eyes.

"Your whole body is glowing and trembling," her dad remarks, dumbfounded by what he's witnessing.

"It's because there are so many Christians calling out to Jesus for me," Karen states, her faith immovable.

Later that evening, she takes an international call from a friend in Russia. "God's given me a vision," the friend reveals. "He's shown me that the tumour will be lifted up and out of you like a parcel."

Karen shares this with Martin. "It's a prophetic promise," she says, "and I'm going to claim it."

A few days later Karen and her mum are, once again, sitting on the two leather-cushioned chairs in front of the consultant oncologist's desk, nervously waiting for the results of another MRI scan.

While she's casting her eye over the titles of the books on the shelves and her mum is gazing out of the window onto the hospital car park, the consultant walks into the room. "I have good news," he announces excitedly, holding aloft a wodge of papers as he shuts the door behind him. His eyes are twinkling as he peers over his spectacles at the two women.

Karen sits upright and pivots round to listen; so does her mum.

"I don't understand how the tumour has detached itself from your liver," he announces with a huge grin, "but that's exactly what's happened."

Karen turns to her mum, wide-eyed. "Was that what Sunday was all about then?" she asks, and her mum smiles and nods.

Even as she explains to the consultant what happened when she was prayed for, he stops her short. "The good news, Karen," he says, still grinning, "is that I can now operate."

Shell-shocked, she sits in disbelief while practicalities are discussed. "Let me look at the lists," he says, taking a seat at his desk, where he starts to scroll through a calendar set up on his computer monitor.

Before she knows it, she's been booked in for an operation in a fortnight's time. "You may not survive the surgery," the consultant confesses, "but it's better for me to try than not."

"It gives me plenty of time to get people praying," she says, "I feel sure this isn't of God."

In the days leading up to her operation to remove the tumour, people from places as far apart as Cardiff and Cape Town are on their knees, pleading with God for Karen's healing. Spurred on by her tenacity and faith, some pray tentatively, while others ooze confidence.

During those days, three separate people, located in three different countries, each contact Karen independently to say they feel God has given them insight. All of them have the same message, something they could not possibly have made up, even if they had tried: *her cancer has been caused by a curse from a witchdoctor during the time she was living in Zimbabwe.*

What they say resonates with Karen, and she knows immediately which incident God is highlighting. "I know what I need to do," she tells Martin. She recalls what happened, where she was, the altercation that occurred with the man in Zimbabwe. She remembers what words were spoken, the discomfort she felt in his presence, the sense of unease she had as she walked away. She forgives the witchdoctor, repents of any part she played, however inadvertently, and asks God to forgive her. As she does so, her spirit lifts, and so does her countenance.

"I am even more resolute in light of this revelation," she tells us in her next prayer email, "for I know that if the cancer has a *spiritual* cause, then it can (and arguably should) be confronted with a *spiritual* solution. The bottom line is this: I belong to God, and the Holy Spirit in me is greater than the spirit who lives in the world," quoting 1 John 4:4 from the Bible. "We need to command the cancer to go, because the power and authority we have in Jesus' name is greater than the power behind any demonic curse from a witchdoctor."

It's the kind of theology I have read about in books but never encountered in person, so I push myself to participate. "In the name of Jesus," I pray out loud, "I speak to the cancer in Karen's stomach and I command it to go to the foot of the cross of Christ, where I believe it's been defeated by Jesus' death and resurrection."

There is something strangely comforting in knowing I am one of many dotted around the world, praying similar prayers. I am not in this by myself, and I am in awe at all God's been doing for her. Confessing my doubt, I realise he's teaching me something simple, yet profound.

I'm learning that, when Christians call on the name of Jesus and claim the authority they have been given in the name of Jesus, God gives them immense power through the Holy Spirit and it is the same power that raised Jesus from the dead. Because Jesus was raised from the dead, everything sinful and demonic has already been defeated, including curses from witchdoctors, meaning we can call on the name of Jesus with complete confidence.

God has got me on a very steep and speedy learning curve.

"Please will you sign this form, giving your consent for surgery?" asks the consultant, now a familiar face, handing Karen a clipboard, paperwork attached, together with a ballpoint pen.

She and Martin are sitting on upright chairs in an airless consulting room at the large teaching hospital in their nearest city. It's a sweateringly hot day and the room has no natural daylight. Hesitantly, she takes hold of what's being held out to her, removes the pen lid, and starts to read the small print on the paperwork.

As she does so, the consultant continues. "As you know, your tumour is a retroperitoneal sarcoma, which is an extremely rare cancer. There are only eight of us in the UK who specialise in it, and four of us are here today to operate on you." His tone is calm and kind, but serious.

Karen nods to indicate she understands, and he continues, his voice becoming gentler. "We've already told you how serious this operation is, and I know you know. But looking at your X-rays, MRI scans and the other preliminary tests we've conducted, we're estimating the likelihood of you dying during surgery could be as high as seventy-five per cent." He pauses a moment to consult his notes. "However, your cancer's so unusual that it's hard for us to be sure."

Karen is utterly unfazed by this revelation. "I have people praying for me," she replies confidently, "and I believe Jesus has already healed me."

He is amazed at her assurance.

The surgical team comprises four consultant oncologists, each summoned from their respective specialist hospitals around the country. Although they have all agreed to operate, they are of one mind about her case. At best, they are expecting various secondary complications; at worst, they anticipate she may not make it out alive. Martin holds Karen's hand as she is anaesthetised, waiting with her until she loses consciousness, before watching her being wheeled off for surgery.

When the operation is over, pulling his surgical face mask up and over his head, and removing his see-through thin plastic gloves, the lead consultant oncologist pushes open the swing doors of the operating theatre, and strides purposefully towards the side room where Karen's relatives are nervously waiting. When his frame appears in the entrance, significantly sooner than they are expecting, Martin leaps up from his chair.

"How has it gone?" he asks.

Breaking into a broad grin, the consultant reveals his surprise, clearly delighted, as well as confused. "I really don't understand it," he reveals, "but when we sliced opened her stomach, we were astonished to discover that the tumour had shrivelled, died, unattached itself from the vein to her heart, and separated itself from her liver and all her vital organs, so we were easily able to cut it free." He pauses a moment before adding a detail. "It was huge, weighing in at more than fourteen pounds, so it took all four of us to lift it out."

Silence fills the room as shock mixes with a palpable sense of relief.

"Wow!" says Martin, gasping. "It would certainly explain why her stomach's been shrinking in recent weeks."

"Indeed," says the surgeon, "but it's also bewildering. None of us have ever known anything like it." He takes a breath. "For a tumour to be heavier than a baby and to come out that smoothly, it's just incredible. That's why it's taken us only six hours, rather than the twelve we'd anticipated." He smiles.

"So she's going to be OK then?" Martin asks.

"She's now in recovery," the surgeon explains. "When she comes round, we will be seeking her permission to report her case in the leading national medical journal, because a retroperitoneal sarcoma like this one is so rare." He stops for a moment to scan the room, struggling to find the right words.

Eventually he simply says, "It makes absolutely no sense, and I don't say this lightly, but I'm wondering whether I've just witnessed a medical miracle."

Lying on her back in a white metal-framed hospital bed, wearing only a pale diamond-patterned open-backed hospital gown, Karen is becoming aware of acute intense pain throughout her upper body as the anaesthetic starts to wear off. She is in a room on her own, for which she feels grateful. It has a huge window which looks out over a local housing development.

Seeing her open her eyes, Martin takes hold of her hand. "How are you feeling?" he asks. "You've been sleeping peacefully."

"I'm still here, thanks to God," she smiles wanly, "but I need some painkillers."

Tentatively, she raises her hand to the neckline of her loose-fitting gown. Lifting it a few centimetres, she bends her chin down to her chest to take a sneaky peek. Where her stomach has been bulging in recent months, although far from flat, it now looks to be a much more normal size. Atop it lies a huge red-raw wound, bound tightly together by a neat line of stitching.

When the consultant swings by the end of her bed, wearing a crisp white coat, clipboard in hand, and his spectacles dangling on a cord slung around his neck, he bursts into a broad smile at the sight of Karen. Giving her a summary of the surgery, he then says simply, "None of us have ever seen anything like it. We're all wondering whether we've witnessed a medical miracle."

"I believe Jesus has healed me," Karen states simply, before proceeding to tell him that God loves him and wants a relationship with him.

He looks at her amazed. "I'm not a man of faith myself," he says, "but what's happened to you is so utterly unexplainable that I've got to concede a higher being may well have been involved."

Later that day, she's wheeled into a windowless room for a PET scan, where she's invited to swallow a dye containing radioactive tracers, and a junior doctor runs an imaging test over her abdomen area. The consultant oncologist surveys the scan on a screen, which clearly reveals the huge hole that the tumour has vacated.

"You're going to be on a long road to recovery now," he advises Karen, "and although I know you don't want chemotherapy, I have a professional obligation to remind you that it's the only other option available if we're going to guarantee getting completely rid of the cancer."

"I'd rather rely on prayer and trust in Jesus," Karen calmly tells him.

In the week that follows, while she remains in hospital, Karen becomes so convinced of the role that her Christian faith has played during this gruelling time that she shares her powerful testimony far and wide. The lead consultant oncologist and a junior doctor in the surgical team are both deeply impacted by what they hear, wondering whether to weave this into the report they are writing about Karen's case for the leading national medical journal. Her sister, too, finds her faith deepening in light of what she's witnessed.

"Jesus has saved my life," Karen repeats enthusiastically to all who are willing to listen.

During her recuperation, Karen is sure of what she needs to do next, and she sets her mind to do it.

While living in Cape Town, God gave her a vision which has not diminished since she returned with Martin to live in the UK. It's a vision for an incredibly powerful programme that will protect vulnerable children throughout the world, through the upholding of international standards.

Karen is fiercely protective of standards. She knows from first-hand experience in South Africa and Zimbabwe, that the vast majority of Christian childcare practitioners have no formal training in organisational development. Most of their projects and programmes are run using very basic standards in areas such as governance, financial accountability, fundraising, child protection and staff care.

Having already conducted various pilot schemes in Cape Town and Harare, and having encouraged colleagues to do likewise in other countries, she has ample evidence that there will be an enormous demand for the type of assessment, training and delivery that the programme will provide.

Her focus and tenacity are admirable. Nothing seems to deter her, not even the huge discomfort she experiences as she recovers from such invasive surgery. Whether working from home in relative peace, or in the office surrounded by me and other colleagues probing into her wellbeing, she is driven by her vision. Determined to keep going, she displays a steely determination as she tirelessly devotes her time to developing the new programme.

Using her amazing academic aptitude, she delves into the quagmire of international quality frameworks, producing a collection of criteria appropriate to the global Christian community, who are providing invaluable care to vulnerable children. At the same time, she negotiates funding deals with multiple donors to pay for the programme to be rolled out in numerous countries.

Her dedication to the vision sees the birth of the Quality Improvement Scheme (QIS) less than two years on from her operation. In the following months, it starts to be rolled out for use, reaching thousands of Christian childcare projects and programmes within the first year, and benefiting innumerable vulnerable children around the world.

Apart from some occasional back pain originating from muscles which were displaced during her operation, she seems to be well. She cultivates an attitude of gratitude, determined to make the most of life, counting her blessings in the ordinary and mundane, and becoming an advocate for appreciating the people around her.

When she attends hospital for a check-up, an initial scan suggests there might be some minor problems, but there's no obvious cause for concern and the consultant oncologist does not propose any immediate action. However, it's not long later when Karen is admitted to hospital with breathing problems. Two years on from her operation and the cancer has returned. A tumour, just as vigorous as the last one, has invaded her lung.

She's had a growing inner conviction that God might be giving her only two more years of life, but nothing tangible to root it in. When she explains it to me and others, she likens it to Hezekiah, a biblical king who became ill and was at the point of death. "He pleaded with God to remember him for having walked faithfully and with wholehearted devotion," she tells me one crisp cold morning, as we stand in the office kitchen, both holding mugs of steaming tea, "and God then revealed that he'd heard Hezekiah's prayers and that he'd add fifteen years to his life." She pauses a moment before continuing. "I feel this might be me; that God might have healed me for a set time and purpose." I struggle to absorb what she's saying and she reaches out to me with a hug.

Even if this is true, Karen is determined to fight for life. She can regularly be heard ranting and raving at God, reminding him of why he should heal her in Jesus' name. But when he gives her a vision of a caterpillar turning into a beautiful butterfly, she reluctantly wonders whether it might be a metaphor for her earthly body being exchanged for a heavenly one.

Deep down, she longs for another medical miracle, but her relapse happens quickly.

"If God is calling me home, then I'm ready," she tells Martin. "I'm angry about it, and it's testing my faith to the limits, so don't get me wrong. But I also feel I've fulfilled my earthly purpose now that QIS has been born, and I'm at peace that he's in control."

"If Jesus calls you home, Karen," Martin asks her, his South African inflection more pronounced than usual, "would you like me to ask him to bring you back?" She has now been moved into a local hospice where she's receiving palliative care, and they both know the end is likely to be imminent.

Both of them have witnessed a person being raised from the dead during the time they lived in Cape Town, so Karen is utterly unfazed by such a simple question. Smiling weakly up at her husband as he sits by her bedside, she hesitates a moment. "I'd like him to show me around first, so I can see whether I like it," she tells him.

The following day, as she surrenders her fight for life and breathes her last, Martin marches purposefully around her bed praying, out loud, African-style. They are in a ground-floor room, and the curtains have been drawn against a cold, dark, winter's afternoon. "Oh Lord, I'm crying out to you now, please bring Karen back to life, in Jesus' name," he implores, the volume in his voice getting louder with every word he utters and every step he takes. "Please work a miracle and raise her from the dead, I'm pleading with you now, Lord, in Jesus' name."

"Are you alright in there?" asks one of the hospice nurses, pushing the door open slightly with one hand and gingerly poking her head into the room. Seeing that he's shouting in prayer, rather than shouting for her, she quickly backs out again, silently shutting the door behind her.

A few moments later, mid-prayer, Martin stops in his tracks when he hears a still, small voice, which he recognises immediately to be God. "I've shown her around now, Martin," he senses God saying, "and you can let her go, because she likes it here."

Martin's demeanour instantly changes, and a sense of peace overwhelms him. Raising his arms in praise, still marching around the bed, he loudly starts singing songs of Christian worship, interspersed with prayers of surrender. "I praise you Jesus for who you are, and for all that you did for us through your death and resurrection," he cries out loud. "I thank you, Lord, for Karen's life, and for all that you achieved through her while she was here on earth. I thank you, Jesus, for showing her around her new heavenly home. I praise you that she likes it there."

Once again, the hospice nurse tentatively pushes open the door and peers into the room to assess the situation. Satisfied that he's simply singing Christian worship songs over his wife, albeit rather loudly, she leaves him in peace.

Later that day, I'm boiling the kettle in my kitchen, poised to make a cup of tea before I head to the evening service at my church, when I take the call from Martin – and I know immediately that she's gone.

"I felt God enabling me to surrender and let her go," he tells me. "Instead of mourning, he's helping me rejoice, because Karen is now with him in her heavenly home."

I put my phone down on the kitchen counter and I pray, tears trickling down my cheeks, asking God to comfort her family.

The long wooden pews of a small Baptist church in South Wales are crammed to capacity with Karen's friends and family. The auditorium and the overhanging horseshoe-shaped balcony are full, and there is standing room only at the back. Some are wearing bright colours, but most are dressed solemnly. All are grasping a cardboard booklet order of service, showing a head and shoulders photo of Karen on the front cover, her beautiful beaming smile radiating out.

I'm standing in the midst of a large group of colleagues who have travelled together to be there. Our hushed whispers are silenced when the organ starts to play, and we turn to watch her simple brown wooden coffin being brought up the aisle and placed in front of the altar. It feels surreal.

One of the Bible readings comes from Hebrews chapter 11. It starts with, "Now faith is confidence in what we hope for and assurance about what we do not see," and ends with, "All these people were still living by faith when they died. They did not receive the things promised; they only saw them and welcomed them from a distance, admitting that they were foreigners and strangers on earth." It feels strangely apt.

It's been chosen wisely and well, and there are ripples of agreement when the eulogies remind us that Karen was a woman of fierce faith who died still believing what God had promised her.

Sitting in my pew, reflecting, I realise how much Karen's faith has impacted me. She's shifted my perspective on life and death. She's also helped me fully understand what it means to pray for healing, knowing there's power in the name of Jesus.

CHAPTER 5

All it takes is one split second

A married couple in a head-on car accident in the UK (2006)

"[He] will not die but live,
and will proclaim what the Lord has done.
The Lord has chastened [him] severely,
but he has not given [him] over to death."

Psalm 118:17-18

This story is about a horrific car accident involving my younger brother, Adrian, and sister-in-law, Ruth. At the time, they had been married three years. The story also features other family members, including me.

(For the observant amongst you, yes, this is the same Adrian who features in the opening chapter of this book and, yes, he has indeed been involved in two serious car accidents.)

"As soon as you get this message, please phone home," my dad's tear-filled voice is urging me. "Adrian and Ruth have been involved in a terrible accident."

Fumbling with my handset, panic and nausea threaten to engulf me. Hands shaking, heart racing, feet unsteady, I slump onto the grass. *Please pick up*, I plead silently as I dial all the familiar family numbers, each one clicking through to voicemail. Clutching tightly onto my phone, time stands still, and I find myself praying.

All around me are strangers enjoying the early evening sunshine which bathes the rural French campsite where I'm on holiday – chatting, cooking and sharing food together. I watch them in slow motion, rooted to the spot, shivering.

When the call eventually comes through, Dad's voice is cracked with emotion. "There's been a terrible car crash," he tells me, tears free flowing. "Adrian is in intensive care with a serious head injury, unconscious and fighting for his life. Ruth is in the same hospital with multiple broken bones. Their injuries are really serious and, in Adrian's case, life-threatening."

There's a moment's hesitation before he continues, "Please can you get home as soon as possible?" he urges me. "The doctors don't think he'll make it through the night."

My brain short circuits as I process the news. Adrian is my only brother; Ruth is his wife.

All it takes is one split second for life to turn upside down.

This holiday in France has been a long time coming, with its sleepy street cafés, historic sights, and bike rides through beautiful vineyards and olive groves.

Recent months have been difficult and I'm exhausted. I've lost a friend to cancer. My job, with an international charity working with vulnerable children, has recently felt relentless – and I've not long returned from a particularly challenging African work trip, which has unearthed some issues which will take time and tact to untangle. At the same time, I've just completed my second academic year of part-time studying for a Master's degree, and all that's left to complete is my dissertation. Now, finally resting and recuperating, my phone is switched off and I'm only turning it on once a day.

That day's check-in brings an abrupt end to my holiday.

Standing, looking out at the river running along the rim of the campsite, uppermost in my mind is the question *Why?* I am wrestling in prayer when I sense God softly speaking, bringing words to mind from Psalm 118:17-18 in the Bible: "[He] will not die but live, and will proclaim what the LORD has done. The LORD has chastened [him] severely, but he has not given [him] over to death."

It feels like a prophetic promise, and I hold onto it tightly, sharing it later with family and friends.

It's a warm and sunny Thursday at the end of August 2006.

Adrian and Ruth have just spent an hour or so at our parents', on route home from visiting friends, sitting in the garden, drinking tea, catching up, and sharing hopes and dreams about the future. One in particular stands out: Adrian and Ruth are considering a year abroad before buying a house and starting a family.

They met and dated when Adrian was working in a day-care centre for adults with learning disabilities, and Ruth volunteered there during her pre-university gap year. At well over six-feet tall, Adrian is an emotionally intelligent, caring, gentle giant, while Ruth is beautiful, resourceful, strong and steady. Married now for three years, life stretches out ahead of them, a blank canvas waiting to be painted.

Before they set off for home, Dad prays for them in the hallway, a habit formed when we were small. His faith has deep roots, dating back to his Christian conversion as a student. On this particular occasion, he prays for angels to watch over Adrian and Ruth as they drive home – and clear guidance for the future.

They soon reach the section of road that snakes through a small village, spanned by olde-worlde red-brick cottages. Many are covered in beautiful climbing roses and scented honeysuckle; some have decorative shutters adorning the windows; one offers home-grown vegetables alongside an honesty box perched on a ramshackle table, worn with the weather. The speed camera cautions drivers to slow down.

Less than a mile beyond the village, without any warning, the driver of a red Audi coming in the opposite direction loses control on a bend, on the brow of a hill, hitting Adrian and Ruth's car head-on, on the wrong side of the road.

The combined speed is estimated to be at least 100mph.

The two cars meet in a collision of tangled metal, glass, plastic, tarmac and human flesh, as the force of the impact concertinas Adrian's beloved old blue Golf, and squeezes the enormous engine of the Audi up and out, from where it is tossed into a field on the far side of the road.

Another driver, following shortly behind the Golf, slams on his brakes, pulls to the side of the road and calls the emergency services. Traumatised by what he's witnessed, the police take a statement, his life suddenly entwining with two strangers.

The police are anticipating fatalities, believing both drivers to be "goners".

Traffic backlogs as the road is closed for six hours while the fire brigade try to disentangle the cars, and paramedics assess and treat the injuries at the scene. A decision is made to take them to the nearby hospital, known for its medical expertise in neurology. Ruth is transferred by air ambulance, while Adrian is rushed by road, blue lights flashing and sirens blaring.

In excruciating pain, and aware of the whirring sound of the helicopter blades, Ruth is extricated from the passenger seat of the car. She's broken her right leg in several places and both her feet are mangled. Although initially lucid, she passes out on the stretcher.

Adrian's car is too old to have airbags. His chest has taken the full brunt of the steering wheel on impact, and his head has collided with the windscreen. He has sustained a serious head injury, broken several ribs and punctured a lung. He has also fractured numerous bones in his neck, hips, elbow, wrist and hand.

His breathing is erratic, his pulse weak. He is only just hanging onto life.

When Dad answers the landline shortly after 10pm that Thursday evening, an unfamiliar woman introduces herself as a senior nurse at a well-known hospital in the city where Adrian and Ruth are living. His heart sinks as she asks him to verify his name and his relationship as Adrian's father.

"Are you sitting down?" she asks, clearly adept at delivering bad news.

"Yes," he replies from the swivel chair at the desk of his book-lined study.

"I'm afraid I have to let you know, as next of kin, that your son's been involved in an extremely serious car accident." Her voice is kind and compassionate. "It hasn't been fatal," she says, "but his injuries are life-threatening."

His heart is pounding as she gives him directions to the Intensive Care Unit. "I urge you to make your way as quickly as you can, but please drive safely," she says.

Yelling upstairs, with a sense of urgency, to my mum who is getting ready for bed, he quickly fills her in and she pulls her clothes back on. Ever practical in a crisis, raising four children has taught Mum to multi-task. Adrian is her only son – and they are close. Flinging things into an overnight bag, mind racing, she verbally processes the practicalities, and urgent calls and arrangements are made.

Praying in the car as they drive, they suddenly see a long line of cars snaking towards a police roadblock on the edge of the village, just ahead of the scene of the accident. Each car is being turned around and sent on a detour. Winding down the window when it's their turn, Dad's voice chokes up. "The accident, up ahead there, involved my son," he explains. "We've been told by the hospital to get there as quickly as we can. What's the best route to take?" Bending down to eye level, the policeman has an empathetic attitude and gives them clear directions. "Drive safely," he says.

It's nearly midnight when my parents eventually reach the hospital.

My journey home from France takes place in slow motion. Sleep eludes me, my appetite vanishes, and I can't stop crying. It feels like a hazy nightmare. I pray continuously through the early hours.

Listening to worship music, I remember a song from Adrian's and Ruth's wedding: "Blessed Be Your Name" by Matt Redman. At the time it felt like an unusual choice, but now I can see its relevance – a defiant declaration of God's goodness in all the seasons of life.

Based loosely on Job 1:21, the lyrics speak of how God's name should be praised whatever the circumstances. Back then, we sang with them as they embarked on marriage and all was as it should be. Now we are singing with them in the midst of the anguish of a horrific head-on car crash.

As soon as I reach home, I dump my camping kit and head straight to the Intensive Care Unit (ICU), where I find my parents and the older of my two sisters. We hug and hold each other. Tears are pouring down our cheeks. Words are meaningless. Five months pregnant with her first child, my sister is distressed and the baby is kicking in the womb.

Venturing into the ICU, I am confronted with a plethora of wires and tubes attaching Adrian's body to multiple machines. Each of them beeps at a different pitch, while fluorescent graphs and charts monitor all his vital statistics. The room is unbearably hot. Adrian is naked apart from a white cotton cloth that covers his unconscious body. His breathing is laboured and uneven. His punctured lung causes each side of his chest to breathe out of sync with the other. His face is a mess. His body is bruised, battered and broken.

I am ill-prepared for the vast number of stitches, cuts, lacerations, bruises and swelling. I am equally ill-prepared when, without warning, he shouts out repetitive phrases, his voice deep and gravelly: "Oh boy", "Help me, Jo", "Hold my hand, Mum", and "Amen". He is clearly confused and concussed, oblivious of his surroundings and circumstances.

Compounded by an utter lack of sleep and having not eaten since lunchtime the day before, when I was still in France, I keel over and faint.

It's Sunday evening, seventy-two hours on from the accident, and I'm sitting on a pale wooden chair in the large city-centre church which I've been attending for the last five years. One of the church leaders announces from the front that there's been a terrible car accident involving my brother and sister-in-law. "Life is fragile," she declares. "Let's stand together now and pray for this couple." I'm not sure how she's heard the news, and I feel utterly overwhelmed.

The volume is immense as chairs scrape and people rise to their feet, simultaneously offering up their prayers. It's a phenomenal sound; I can hear tears, cries, shouts and heavenly languages reverberating around this recently refurbished old building with its incredible acoustics. This is a church that has never met Adrian or Ruth. Yet they are prepared to stand alongside me, and them, as members of the same Christian family. It's utterly humbling.

After the service, the church leader introduces me to a nurse who has come to the front to make herself known. "I was on duty in Accident and Emergency at the hospital on Thursday night," she informs me, speaking against the background hubbub of multiple conversations within the packed church building, "and there were a disproportionately large number of Christians on that particular shift, and all of us were praying when Adrian, Ruth and the other driver were admitted." I am amazed. "We all thought Adrian was a goner," she says. "None of us expected him to survive the night." She pauses a moment before continuing. "My colleagues can't stop talking about him. It's an absolute miracle he's still alive. It makes no medical sense." Our conversation flows easily, the words tumbling out, as I explain how Adrian and Ruth are from Christian families. "I'm not surprised," she says. "One of my colleagues keeps commenting on Ruth's peace, and I'm convinced it's supernatural."

God's reassurance continues when three friends, separately, seek me out. Each of them tells me how God has shown them there are angels in Adrian's ICU room. Some are standing guard, battling in the spiritual realm, and warding off the enemy. Others are ministering to him, defending the healing that's happening.

Faith rises within me. "Please, Lord," I pray, "open my eyes and ears to see and hear these angels."

Both cars are taken to a local police compound and, when my parents visit to retrieve the belongings that have been salvaged, they are appalled.

"Looking at what is now a crushed and mangled mess of metal," Dad reports, "I don't know how Adrian's come out of it alive." He pauses a moment and then continues, "But much of the driver's area in the Golf seems to be intact, so they clearly don't have an outstanding safety record for nothing."

"It turns out the policeman on duty on the night of the accident is a Christian," Mum interjects. "Isn't that amazing?"

"Absolutely," I agree, thinking of all the Christians on duty at the hospital that night as well.

"The police don't understand how the Audi's enormous engine ended up in a field on the far side of the road," Dad continues. "All they will say is that none of them would have survived if it had stayed put." It's a sobering thought.

"I prayed for angels to watch over them when they left our house that day," he recalls. "I'm convinced God sent some to protect them as the accident happened." Even as he speaks, a vivid picture is emerging. "Angels could easily have squeezed the engine up and out, and tossed it out of the way."

My parents are traumatised, having to pass the scene of the accident every time they travel between their home and the hospital. Debris is strewn along the edge of the road, each piece a heart-wrenching relic from the cars involved. "Some of that debris is from my son's car," Dad tells me he wants to yell. Assuming the other driver regains consciousness, the police will issue criminal proceedings against him. The skid marks imply he was speeding; there are also suggestions that excess alcohol was a factor involved. Not knowing what happened is the hardest, so the police issue a press release, appealing for witnesses. "News in Brief: Two Hurt in Road Smash," it declares, before describing the accident with clinical accuracy. "Reading it is so surreal when it's talking about members of our family," I remark to my parents, showing them the column in the local newspaper.

All around, life continues as normal. For me, it's on *pause*, and the days are passing with no real sense of when *play* will be resumed.

Work have been gracious in granting me compassionate leave. "It's the week of the office move," our HR manager reminds me. "Everyone will be involved, so one of us will pack your desk for you." I had forgotten; my pre-holiday life feels an eternity ago.

Sleep is a struggle, but I'm being given supernatural stamina to pray in the early hours, pleading with the Lord for Adrian's life. Friends and acquaintances across the nation and beyond, report of being woken in the night and prompted to pray. On several occasions, I wake with a strong sense that I'm picking up the prayer "baton" from one of them and I run with it awhile, before handing it on.

At my parents' church, a group from the congregation have committed to pray before, during, and after every Sunday morning service. Dad phones the ICU for an update, which he relays to the vicar, who then leads collective prayers, frequently getting everyone up on their feet as they do so. With 24/7 prayer going on, I'm comforted to know God never slumbers or sleeps.

Adrian has acquired some temporary tattoos. An orthopaedic surgeon has deftly drawn arrows in black marker pen, pointing to each of his broken bones. "We won't be able to operate unless and until he regains consciousness," he explains. "The breathing tube needs to be out of his mouth, and his temperature needs to stop sky-rocketing."

Adrian's chest heaves lopsidedly, a sober reminder of his punctured lung. His limbs are covered in goose bumps, involuntarily shivering despite the sweat pouring from his forehead. His eyes periodically flicker open, his gaze failing to focus.

The doctors are at a loss. "We've done every conceivable test, but we can't work out the source of infection," one of them reveals.

Through floods of tears, I cry out to God again. "In Jesus' name, please stop this fever," I write in my prayer journal. "Please reveal if the infection has a spiritual root, not a medical one. Please minister to his spirit, even though his body is unconscious."

When I'm not at the hospital, my lodger is providing prayerful and practical support, fielding phone calls, cooking meals, encouraging me when my faith starts to flag. Together, we adopt a worship song by Brenton Brown, "Everlasting God", playing it on continuous loop.

Crafted from a place of great pain, with words from Isaiah 40, the lyrics permeate my home, infusing the atmosphere. "Oh Lord, our family are waiting on you; we need your strength," I pray repeatedly, the music blasting at full volume. "You alone are our hope. You alone can deliver Adrian from death. Please defend Adrian and Ruth. Please comfort them. Please lift them up on wings like eagles."

Praying with my lodger, she has a strong sense that God's glory will be revealed through what happens to Adrian and Ruth. She also has three words – peace, promise and provision – and asks God to give them peace beyond understanding, fulfil his promises to them, and provide for their needs.

To my utter surprise, I have a picture of them holding a baby boy, and wonder if it could be a prophetic promise. Trusting that it could be, I pray in faith for blessings on their children, grandchildren, and subsequent generations.

Ruth's high-pitched, blood-curdling screams of agony come echoing down the hospital corridor when her dressings are changed.

With multiple breaks in her right leg, it's now in plaster. All the bones in her feet have been shattered, but only the big toes have been splinted; the others are too small for surgery. The blood keeps congealing over the bandages wrapping her feet, ripping away flesh when removed. The nurses are kind, but their comforting words do little to sooth her anguish.

Her emotions have been anaesthetised, paralysed by the trauma. "I'm so pathetic," she keeps saying, but nothing could be further from the truth. She's made of strong stuff, stoical, pragmatic and practical. Even as she forces down food and painkillers, only to vomit them up again, she's already planning for what will happen when they leave hospital.

Leveraging herself into a wheelchair with support from two nurses, she's determined to get to the ICU. "I want to see my husband," she says. Her broken leg, straight and rigid, sits at right angles to her body, making manoeuvring awkward. When she inadvertently catches it, the sharp burst of pain is too much and she faints.

When we discover that the other driver may not have valid car insurance, it puts the potential for compensation into jeopardy. It's hard not to feel angry with this man – for driving above the speed limit for the road, under the influence of alcohol and, now it seems, illegally. How could he have been so selfish?

Even though he's lying unconscious in a different ICU bed, in an equally life-threatening state, I'm facing inner turmoil. "It was almost easier when he was anonymous," I say to Dad. "Finding out the facts about him is making it difficult."

"You've got to forgive him," he responds.

I decide to seek counsel from an old friend who's a personal injury solicitor, and she reassures me.

"A fund exists for accidents caused by uninsured drivers, to cover the costs of compensation claims," she explains to me, and I slowly exhale, relieved. "It means Adrian and Ruth will have an avenue to pursue compensation for their injuries and other losses, if it turns out the other driver is uninsured," she advises.

Adrian is thrashing his arms and legs, and pulling at the breathing tube in his mouth. Such disorientation is distressing to witness.

"We're going to sedate him to keep him unconscious," an ICU consultant explains. "It will help his body heal." His eyes are kind.

"At least we know he's not paralysed," I remark, and he nods agreement.

"But it will be a while until we know the full extent of his head injury," he advises.

I find myself crying out to God again in prayer. "Oh Jesus, please normalise his temperature and make the fever flee," I write in my prayer journal. "Please heal his lung so he can breathe without assistance. Please heal the broken bones in his neck, ribs, hips, elbow, arm, thumb and wrist. Please protect his neck from the risk of paralysis. Please heal his head injury so he has no brain damage. Please release him from trauma and shock, and restore his life."

On the day that Adrian is moved into a side room in the ICU, he's fighting interlinked infections in his blood, chest, lungs, sinuses, kidneys and liver. His yellow complexion indicates jaundice.

"He's very, very sick," the ICU consultant informs us, "and although we're doing all that we can, he may not make it." He doesn't mince his words.

"There are many people praying," Dad responds with conviction. He has faith for Adrian to fight this.

The consultant smiles and continues, "We're isolating him to reduce the risk of cross-contamination and to identify the source of the infections." He pauses a moment. "The blood infection is a particular mystery," he adds.

A blood transfusion follows. So does kidney dialysis to flush the fluids through his system.

"Oh Lord," I pray, "our very life is in our blood. Without it, we die. But Jesus' blood, shed on the cross, brings life. This feels like a spiritual battle." And in response, I sense the Holy Spirit's whisper: "He will not die but live, and will proclaim what the Lord has done."

Before I went to France, my car passed its annual safety and roadworthiness test, but I was advised that the tyres were nearing their legal limit. Today, I'm heading to the garage for new ones.

"Why haven't you brought it in before now?" the garage owner asks me. He's a man in his fifties, down-to-earth and genial, his portly belly disguised by his oil-stained baggy blue boiler-suit.

I begin to explain what's happened when he interrupts me with a string of expletives. "Excuse my language," he says, "but I know about that accident." He pauses a moment and then, "The guy who was driving the Audi, he's a mate of me and the missus."

He awkwardly wipes his hands on an oil-stained cloth, avoiding eye contact as I stand, stunned, rooted to the spot.

"My missus got a call from his ex, late that evening. She wanted us to go with her to the hospital, so we dragged ourselves out of bed," he explains. "What we found was horrific." He bites his bottom lip. "None of us understand where he was going or why he was driving down that road."

The other driver is fifty and going through a divorce. He's the landlord of a local pub. He also has a name.

I realise I can no longer view him anonymously.

"My family are committed Christians," I share. "We're praying for your friend." He looks surprised. "You might want to let him know," I add.

"That's humbling," he mutters. "I'll let the missus know."

Nothing prepares us for the emotional rollercoaster ride that follows the three separate occasions when we're told, "Adrian is very, very sick. He may not make it through the night tonight."

The first time it happens, a South African friend is helping me with the garden. "Adrian has taken deteriorated again," Dad informs me. "The ICU have told us to prepare for the worst." Indignation rises within me and we pray aloud over the phone, commanding the enemy to stop trying to steal my brother's life.

Calling my friend in from the garden, we fall to our knees and a tangible sense of God's presence fills my living room as we pray and worship for the next few hours. While we do so, she has two pictures in her mind's eye. One is of Adrian, like Jonah, in the belly of the whale. Her sense is that, although he's currently in the darkest depths, God knows he's there, and God will cause him to be discharged. The other is of angels, double human height, standing shoulder-to-shoulder around Adrian's bed. Some are on guard fighting for him; others are ministering to him and working with the medical staff. We finish by breaking bread and wine, praying for the protection of Jesus' blood.

The following morning, my faith is riding high when the phone rings. "He's made it through the night," Dad updates me, clearly relieved. But we both know we're not there yet.

The second time it happens, my lodger has cooked dinner and we've just sat down to eat. "The ICU have rung," Dad tells me, "and Adrian is very, very sick again." He pauses a moment, fighting back tears, before continuing. "His kidneys aren't working, his lungs are struggling, and his blood remains infected. I've been told that he may not make it through the night."

Returning to the table, my appetite gone, I sit and pray with my lodger. She's immediately reminded of the story of Jonah. Grabbing her Bible, she finds the story and reads of seaweed being wrapped around Jonah's head, yet God restoring his life from the grave, suggesting this could be a metaphor of Adrian's situation.

Suddenly, in the depths of my being, I know that God is going to get the glory for what happens. Breakthrough is going to come, and they will be given a beautiful testimony, but an almighty spiritual battle still needs to be won before we get there. "He will not die but live, and will proclaim what the Lord has done," I declare aloud at the table.

I feel surer of this than ever when Dad calls the following morning. "He's made it through the night," he reassures me.

The third time it happens, my parents are staying overnight and I take a late-night call on the landline while they listen from the sofa. "Adrian is very, very sick," the ICU nurse informs me. "He may not make it through the night." She goes on to explain, "We've managed to identify which type of bacteria is causing the infection in his blood, but the usual antibiotics aren't working." She pauses a moment and then continues, "We're also still unable to identify the source of the infection. All the specialist consultants are baffled."

"What if the source is spiritual?" I ask Dad. "If so, the medics may never be able to identify it."

"Let's pray and ask God," he suggests.

"Oh God, we forgive the other driver," I pray, "We bind and silence everything demonic coming against Adrian, in Jesus' name. We command the bacteria, infections and viruses to go, in Jesus' name. We speak healing into all his vital organs. May your kingdom come, on earth as it is in heaven."

As we finish praying, my lodger appears in the doorway, clasping her phone. "I've just taken a call from my mum who's been praying for Adrian," she tells us. "She feels he's like Jonah, in the belly of the whale, but God will give him hidden treasures there, and he will be discharged." Then she turns and heads upstairs.

By the following morning, Adrian is being described as "stably unwell". In medical terms, this is progress.

During the course of the next few days, I find myself pondering.

Three times we received the same medical pronouncement: "Adrian is very, very sick; he may not make it through the night."

Three times, in response, God prompted a Christian to remind us of the Bible story of Jonah, with its prophetic promise of pending discharge out of the darkness.

It only slowly starts making sense when I complete the paperwork to register Adrian and Ruth with the fund for compensation claims caused by uninsured drivers, and reach a question I can't fully answer: "*Where did the accident take place? Please provide as much precision in identifying the location as possible.*" A quick call to the police to obtain this information from the official records, and I discover the accident took place opposite a signed entrance for "Nineveh Farm".

In the biblical account, God asks Jonah to go to the city of Nineveh with a challenging message. Jonah refuses and runs away, ending up on a ship in a storm at sea, from where he's thrown overboard and swallowed by a whale. Three days later, he is spewed out onto dry ground.

Jonah and Nineveh are inextricably linked.

"What do you think God might be trying say?" I ask Dad. "If the accident was at Nineveh, and if Adrian is being likened to Jonah in the belly of a whale, does it mean he'll soon make it out?"

"Perhaps their testimony of what God's going to do for them might be a challenging message for some," Dad suggests, "but we'll need to watch, wait and see."

When I head to the hospital after work, I discover two of Adrian's and Ruth's church elders anointing him with oil. "We've just done the same for Ruth," one of them says, his eyes twinkling.

It's hard to concentrate on anything other than praying and I've become very un-British, doing away with dignity and decorum. Each small sign of progress feels a significant answer to prayer. Adrian's kidneys start to produce urine again. His blood pressure normalises. His breathing evens out. Best of all, the infection vanishes from his blood.

"We don't know where it started, and we don't know where it's disappeared," the ICU consultant concedes. "To be honest, we're all a bit baffled."

"There are so many Christians praying for his healing, in the name of Jesus," I say with a smile, "that I'm not surprised." He looks bemused, and I add, "His church leaders have also anointed him with oil."

"I'm not a person of faith myself," he reveals, "but others have said before that prayer makes a difference."

"We need to move him out of the side room to reduce his temperature," a young, blonde-haired, ICU sister informs us. "It will be cooler in the main ICU ward. Besides, he no longer needs it, now the infection in his blood has gone."

I'm unnerved when I discover that the reason the bed has become available is because the other driver has regained consciousness and no longer needs intensive care.

Part of me feels angry about the injustice. "Why, God?" I write in my prayer journal. "Why have you allowed him to come round so soon, while Adrian's still sedated? When will it be his turn too?"

Another part of me feels compassionate. "Oh God," I write, "I'm aware this man has had a bleed on the brain. Please heal him and restore him to his friends and family."

About two and a half weeks after the accident, I hear the angels singing.

It's a Sunday evening and I decide to go to church, sneaking in late, hiding at the back and leaving before the end of the service, not in the mood to make small talk with well-meaning people.

It's almost dark by the time I get to the hospital, and I find Adrian still in the side room on his own, his temperature soaring. The sister on duty is the same young, blonde one who's been mooting when to move him back into the main ICU ward, and I greet her warmly when I see it's her.

Cycling up to the hospital, I've been asking God how best to use this time, and I've sensed I need to march around the metal-framed hospital bed, African style. It's a bit of an obstacle course, with his body attached to various machines via wires and tubes, but I persevere. I pray aloud. I read portions of Scripture aloud. I sing worship songs aloud. I command everything not of Jesus to leave. I commission the angels of Jesus to protect him and minister to him.

It's then that I hear them.

"Can you hear that singing?" I ask the sister on duty, standing still, mid-circuit.

"What singing?" she asks me from her chair in the corner of the room, beyond the foot of Adrian's bed.

"It sounds like praise and worship music," I reply, "like a heavenly choir, multiple voices in harmony."

She looks at me quizzically, wondering what on earth I'm talking about. I pause, and then continue, more pragmatic now. "Is the radio on? Or a CD playing?" I enquire.

"No," she says, pointing me to the shelf beyond Adrian's bedhead. There, amidst various medicine bottles, magazines, CDs and other paraphernalia, is a portable radio CD player. Without saying a word, we glance at it, and then each other, both acknowledging it isn't turned on.

"Maybe it's angels?" It's more of a question than a statement of fact. "Lots of people praying have sensed there are angels here," but I stop mid-sentence as I realise what I'm suggesting.

Sitting forward in her chair, she looks at me again, this time with care and compassion. "That wouldn't be the first time I've heard that said," she tells me. "Prayers do seem to help people in ICU, so maybe you're right, maybe it could be angels." She pauses momentarily. "But I haven't seen any, and I can't hear any either."

We both stop talking.

I'm still rooted to the spot, midway along the side of Adrian's bed. I close my eyes and my spine starts to tingle. All around me, whichever way I turn, I can hear beautiful choral music. Multiple voices are singing in heavenly harmony, saturating the atmosphere with hope and joy. The angels are rejoicing over my brother, motionless in bed. His body may be sedated, but they are ministering to his spirit.

Overwhelmed, I fall to the floor, on my knees, weeping.

The day Ruth is discharged from hospital feels momentous – a small step towards normality.

Rather than returning to their rented home – a beautiful small converted barn with high-beamed ceilings, multiple hidden steps and higgledy-piggledy floors, tucked away down an unmade lane – she moves into a ground-floor apartment adjoining the house of a couple from their church. Her parents have already moved all their possessions between properties, so she's surrounded by familiar possessions. She's also got help on hand next door if needed.

Her leg in plaster, her swollen feet still bandaged, she's mastering the art of manoeuvring her wheelchair with ease. "It's a relief to be out," she concedes as she welcomes me into her new home, "and it shouldn't be long before I can transition to crutches."

My parents and I are sitting on opposite sides of Adrian's hospital bed. His eyelids are flickering, but his gaze fails to focus. The kind-eyed consultant is updating us on progress.

"Now the puncture in his lung is healing, we're starting to wean his breathing off the ventilator," he explains, "so we're reducing his sedation." He pauses a moment before continuing, his tone serious. "We need to assess whether any swelling on the brain is causing his blood infection."

As the consultant walks away, Dad decides to lighten the mood. "You'll be pleased to know your favourite football club were promoted to the Premiership at the weekend," he informs his son with a smile – at which Adrian immediately wiggles his eyebrows!

"Did you see that?" I ask incredulously. My parents nod in unison, and Mum reaches out for Dad's hand. "I never knew football could elicit that kind of reaction," I jest, and then I realise Dad is blinking back tears.

For the first time since the accident, we have witnessed a flicker of interaction.

In the biblical story of Jonah, it takes three days until there's a turning point in the story. For Adrian, it takes three weeks.

It's then that ventilation is removed and he starts breathing by himself. Each inhalation and exhalation sounds laboured and erratic, but his chest no longer heaves quite so unevenly. Head back against his hospital pillow, eyes open, an oxygen mask covering his face, his neck brace rigidly in place, he looks baffled and forlorn.

Overnight, the blood infection disappears and his temperature, blood pressure and pulse all return to normal.

"We've nicknamed him Miracle Man," a young ICU nurse reveals affectionately. "There were several occasions when we honestly thought he was a goner." She gazes down at her patient, who she and her colleagues have tenderly nursed through the past three weeks. "Now look at him," she says smiling. "He really is a Miracle Man."

"His voice box has been temporarily damaged, so he's going to have laryngitis unlike anything he'll ever experience in his life," the kind-eyed ICU consultant jokingly reveals, "so you may need to help him understand, if he starts to notice and complain about the pain."

The following morning, Adrian is moved out of ICU and onto the Trauma Ward, which Ruth only recently vacated.

"We're going to miss you, Miracle Man," the young ICU nurse calls out cheerfully, as he's wheeled away.

"Now he's breathing independently and the blood infection has abated, we've been given a window of opportunity to operate," an orthopaedic surgeon explains to my parents, shortly before Adrian is taken to theatre. "On the scale of life and death, fixing broken bones has been low priority up until now."

Surgery is long and complicated, and Adrian only returns to the ward in the early hours of the morning.

The broken bones have been meshing in a chaotic manner during the past three weeks, every which way they wanted. Some of them have had to be re-broken to get them to align as they should, especially in the elbow where the joint needs to pivot and rotate as well as bend.

"You'll need to be careful when you go through airport scanners," I tease him, "now your elbow is so full of metal screws and plates."

When I return to work, it's to a new location. The charity I work for is no longer renting a dilapidated office, spread out along a dingy first-floor corridor. Instead, we're now the proud owners of a purpose-built unit in a recently opened complex on the opposite side of town.

I discover my belongings on a desk assigned to me. My colleagues are in buoyant mood. The smell of new carpet combines with fresh paint to permeate our nostrils. The atmosphere is full of excitement.

I'm quickly assigned with organising our tenth anniversary celebration – a special thanksgiving event – to be attended by current and former staff, volunteers, trustees and supporters, some of whom will also contribute and participate.

It's a relief to be distracted from all that's going on at the hospital.

A charming elderly man is in the bed opposite Adrian's. "He's entertaining us by singing word-perfect renditions of 'Amazing Grace' and 'Oh God, Our Help in Ages Past'," he informs us, "but it's mostly in the middle of the night, interspersed with cries of 'Jesus, help me,' and utter gibberish."

If it wasn't so serious, it would be comical.

My parents and I are sitting around the bed when the kind-eyed ICU consultant pops in for a progress update.

"The trouble with head injuries is that they are all unique," he explains. "Adrian's head injury is serious, but we don't yet know how it will affect him. All we can say with certainty is that he'll have some extremely vivid hallucinations while the sedation drugs wear off."

Adrian articulates thoughts without precision, randomly throwing them out there. Only long-term smokers have voices more hoarse and gravelly. His favourite topic for pontification is fishing. "Can't you see the fish swimming around the trawler?" he asks nobody in particular, "Can't you hear the lady fish talking together? Don't you think the men fish feel left out?"

When I head towards the loo, "Watch out for the octopuses and peacocks," he cautions me, before adding as an afterthought, "and the sharks and whales."

"It's because the beds in ICU create the sensation of lying on water," one of the nurses explains.

"Am I in hospital?" he asks Ruth, as she manoeuvres her wheelchair, her plastered leg sticking out straight, parallel to the bed.

"Am I safe here?" he asks me. "My head feels very vague."

He thinks the charming elderly man in the opposite bed is our uncle. He thinks he's in different locations; a new one every day. He thinks he's out at sea, in a boat, fishing for food. He thinks he's in church when I read the Bible or pray with him, responding loudly with an emphatic, "Amen!"

"He's definitely keeping us amused," a nurse chuckles. She's holding a bowl of pureed food in one hand and a spoon in the other. He tries to take hold of both, but his hands won't coordinate and he misses his mouth. "We need to get these calories into you," she chides, as she reclaims the spoon and feeds him like a child. "Thank you," he responds politely.

I'm feeling frightened.

What happens if this is it? Will his language remain nonsensical? Will he never be able to feed himself? What has this head injury done to him? I find myself praying for his full restoration and recovery. And then, a gentle whisper, "He will not die but live, and will proclaim what the Lord has done." I hold onto it tight.

The leaves on the trees are turning from green to golden, the nights are drawing in, and there's a nip in the air when Adrian contracts MRSA, the bacterial infection so common amongst hospital in-patients.

It's the early hours of the morning when he noisily clambers out of his hospital bed, waking the other patients in the ward. Disorientated by being upright, he wobbles and loses balance, his weakened legs collapsing beneath him. Clattering to a heap on the floor, the sling from his arm hangs loose, and blood spurts from a cut, freshly hewn in the thin skin under his eye. Grabbing his neck brace, he tries to yank it off, utterly frustrated by its iron grip.

Before the night-duty nurses can come to the rescue, he has two epileptic seizures in quick succession.

"His CT scan has revealed a bleed on the brain," the consultant neurologist, who's been updating us, explains. A middle-aged man, his tone serious; he's clearly used to sharing difficult news. "It will be a while before the repercussions become clear, but he'll probably be confused when he wakes up." He pauses a moment, looking down at Adrian, sleeping peacefully on his back, his head propped up by hospital pillows, oblivious to the commotion he's caused.

And then, an addendum, "We've also found MRSA in his chest drain, so we're dosing him up with antibiotics and putting him in isolation in his own room." My heart sinks. "How has this happened?" I ask him. "He was doing so well." He concedes it's a setback, but he seems confident it can be overcome.

There's only one thing to do: when the consultant leaves the room, we pray.

It's the last day of September, exactly one month on from the accident, when Adrian wakes up.

The call comes through just as I'm joining my colleagues in setting up the venue for today's work celebration event. My spirit soars, my heart rejoices, my step is light, and my smile is wide. I welcome staff, volunteers, trustees and supporters, including my parents, and watch as the occasion that I've been organising falls into place. Ten years seems significant for a charity that started out in an old-fashioned red phone box.

"Adrian waking up is the best present we could have received," Dad tells me, through tears, at the end of the event. "God has answered our prayers."

"He will not die but live, and will proclaim what the Lord has done," I respond with a smile.

Walking together into Adrian's hospital room, tears free-flowing, we embrace.

Calm, clear-headed and completely himself, he converses with us as though nothing has happened. Polite with the nurses, thoughtful with his visitors, concerned for Ruth's wellbeing when he sees her in a wheelchair, he is as considerate and caring as ever.

The atmosphere is heady with delight as he plies us with questions, and we celebrate the return of the man we all love. We read him some of his many get-well messages, and he's moved to tears. We recount his incredible hallucinations, and laughter reverberates around the room. We share the many Bible verses, prophetic promises and prayers that have sustained us, and he's deeply moved.

"You're affectionately known as Miracle Man around here," the nurse smilingly reveals, clearly delighted to be on duty today.

It's as if the plug has been pulled on the past month. All the tense uncertainty, the unspoken fears, the endless waiting, the unceasing prayer cover, the audacious trust in Jesus. All of it's been released.

Excruciating pain greets Ruth when her toe pins are removed.

"You'll need further surgery to correct the alignment of the bones in your leg where they aren't healing properly," one of the surgeons tells her.

She's a strong woman, so she takes this news in her stride. "Your persistence will pay off," Adrian reassures her, acutely aware that the broken femur means one of her legs is now about an inch shorter than the other.

"At least I can wear normal shoes and socks again," she replies, happily replacing the wheelchair with crutches, and a dogged determination to learn how to walk with them.

"Perhaps God is teaching you to rely on him," I suggest to her. "God has sovereignly allowed your life to change forever, and I wonder whether he wants your vulnerability and patience, in exchange for learning to lean on him for his strength and leading." She seems willing to consider it.

We are caught off-guard when we learn, by chance, that the other driver is being discharged from hospital.

He has a permanent head injury, requiring supported living accommodation for the foreseeable future, possibly forever, meaning he may never drive again.

In light of this, the police seem undecided about whether to prosecute him, but it's a fine line between justice and mercy.

A groundswell within me wants justice. Why should he not be brought before a court for what he has done? His stupidity and selfishness on the night of the accident has turned Adrian's and Ruth's lives completely upside down. Surely he should be held to account for that?

But the more compassionate part of me sees the need for mercy. If he's never going to drive again, what will a court case achieve? His head injury is permanent, so is that not punishment enough? Surely we should just forgive and forget?

Over the following weeks, Adrian struggles to come to terms with how close he's been to dying. He keeps weeping when he realises what might have happened.

With words like "unbelievable", "fantastic", "amazing", "incredible" and "miraculous", the doctors are running out of superlatives to describe the speed and scale of Adrian's recovery. "There's a reason we've called him Miracle Man," one of them jokes.

His head injury is assessed for specialist rehabilitation. All his broken and cracked bones gradually mend. Following fervent prayer, the MRSA tests eventually come back clear. His interest in the outside world increases and he takes accompanied trips out of the hospital, building these up over time.

I am sitting by his bed when he has a vivid hallucination. "I can see the American military climbing through the window to get me," he tells me earnestly. "Can you stop them?"

I look at him, amused. "An air ambulance has just landed on the helipad," I inform him gently. "We're a few floors up in the hospital, and it's just a few hundred metres in that direction." I nod towards the window and he looks alarmed, clearly confused. "Perhaps your brain has scrambled what's happening," I suggest, but he isn't convinced.

We're all adjusting to the new reality, and sometimes there are setbacks.

His social inhibition isn't what it should be; he frequently says what he thinks. His memory has lost its edge; he needs prompts to remember things. He gets bogged down in detail when describing things, preferring literal to abstract concepts. His batteries never seem to fully recharge, so he gets unbelievably tired.

"These symptoms are typical for the kind of head injury Adrian's sustained," the consultant neurologist reassures us. "Compared to others, he's doing remarkably well."

I am on a much-needed weekend away, when my parents call.

"We heard this evening that Adrian's been discharged from hospital," Mum tells me. I can tell she's smiling; the joy is palpable in her voice. "The doctors are still calling him Miracle Man," she says. "They never thought he'd be well enough to leave so soon."

Dad interjects from the other extension, "One of the members of our church prayer group, a consultant, has told us that, clinically and medically, Adrian shouldn't be alive." His voice chokes as he continues, "He says it's a miracle he's still with us."

"It *is* a miracle," I reply. "But God told us, 'He will not die but live, and will proclaim what the Lord has done,' and we've held onto that, haven't we?"

"Oh Lord," I write in my prayer journal that night, "thank you for bringing Adrian this far on the road to recovery. Thank you for hearing the prayers of so many; for working miracles; for confounding the doctors. Please help him adjust to life outside hospital; to the rehabilitation that's needed. Please continue to heal and restore him. I ask in Jesus' name. Amen."

On a Sunday evening in March the following year, Adrian and Ruth are invited to share their story on the local radio station. "Please pray that what we say will impact those listening," they ask in an email, sent in advance.

As I listen live, from home, they give full credit to the power of prayer in Jesus' name. "I was called Miracle Man for a reason," Adrian says.

The radio interview sparks interest, and churches and other venues invite them to speak.

It feels like the prophetic promise God gave us is now being realised: "He will not die but live, and will proclaim what the Lord has done." What a joy to witness it being fulfilled!

There's a sense of relief when the other driver is deemed to have valid car insurance after all. "Claiming compensation will be much more straightforward now," the solicitor advises.

Previously delayed medical treatments are suddenly expedited, with the insurance company picking up the tab. Adrian has surgery to remove unhelpful bone growth and scar tissue in his elbow, disentangle the nerve and remove some of the metalwork. Ruth has bespoke insoles made to even out the length of her legs. And both of them benefit from intensive specialist physiotherapy.

Decisions about returning to work are tricky. Will it be possible, given their injuries? How many hours will be reasonable? Will their employers understand their constraints and limitations?

Ruth returns to teaching, a year after the accident. Standing all day is demanding, and the pain in her feet is immense. Pupils, parents and colleagues are mostly oblivious, and some days are overwhelming, but a part-time pattern eventually emerges.

With Adrian, it's much more complex. Nearly two years on from the accident, it's considered appropriate for him to try to return to social work, despite the anticipated impact of his head injury. Assessments by neuro-psychologists and occupational health workers give him the go-ahead, with the aim of gradually increasing his hours in the coming months.

Much has changed in his two years' absence, including a team restructure, an office relocation, and a totally different client caseload. He feels like a new starter and, despite his best endeavours, it soon becomes clear that he no longer has the stamina, drive and mental agility to be effective. The head injury keeps leaving him exhausted, even when he's only working part-time hours.

There's no sense of shame, only regret, when he's forced to retire early on ill-health grounds. It's a difficult day for all involved. He's only in his thirties.

Hindsight is a wonderful thing.

All it took was one split second for life to turn upside down.

In the weeks and months that followed, we had to hold onto the prophetic promise that, "He will not die but live, and will proclaim what the Lord has done," even when circumstances were dictating otherwise.

Now, years later, it's about living with the reality of the long-term repercussions of what happened. For Adrian, it's the loss of memory and energy caused by his head injury. For Ruth, it's the constant pain in her legs. Their daily challenge is to hold this in tension with gratitude for the gift of life itself.

Financial compensation can never make up for what has been lost in terms of health, fitness, mobility, lifestyle and earning potential. But God has been faithful to his promise of peace, provision and protection.

"If we keep proclaiming what the Lord has done for us," Adrian reflects, "then that is enough."

CHAPTER 6

Hard pressed but not crushed

Twins born prematurely (2008)

*"We are hard pressed on every side, but not crushed;
perplexed, but not in despair."*

2 Corinthians 4:8

This story is about my friend and former colleague, Jackie. It tells of her journey into motherhood, and what happened when her twins were born prematurely. It also features her husband, Alex.

"Jo!" It's only a whisper but the intonation is willing me to wake, and I roll over in bed. "Jo! Are you awake?"

I open one eye. It's gone midnight and my housemate is standing at my bedroom door, her pyjama-clad frame in silhouette against the light on the landing. She peers into the darkness, trying to gauge if I'm stirring from my slumber. It's clearly urgent.

"Jo, I've received a text," she tells me, clutching her phone firmly in her right hand, concern evident in her voice. "Jackie's gone into labour."

Suddenly, I'm sitting bolt upright. "What? Why? How's that possible?" I exclaim, fully waking up, even as I try to articulate the words.

Jackie is pregnant, expecting twins. But this is June, and the twins aren't due until September.

Something has clearly gone wrong.

I turn on the bedside light, grab my glasses, leap out of bed, and peer over my housemate's shoulder to read the text on the phone she's holding out in front of me. The text has come from a mutual friend, one of Jackie's go-to people for emergency prayer cover. It urges us to pray, so we stand in the doorway of my bedroom and do just that, my heart and mind racing.

It is early in spring 2001 when I first meet Jackie at an international conference in the Netherlands. The venue is crammed to capacity, overflowing with people from more than sixty nations, all of them Christians working with, or on behalf of, vulnerable children. The atmosphere is alive with optimism about all that can be achieved. It is six months before 9/11 will irrevocably change the global landscape.

Based around a large cluster of typical Dutch buildings, complete with thatched roofs, the conference centre is in a rural location. Surrounded by flat fields, freshly planted with new crops, the waterways provide breaks in the landscape, some naturally meandering, others stretching out straight, clearly created artificially.

When Jackie suggests I join her for a walk around one of the fields adjoining the conference centre, I leap at the chance. Her smile is warm and welcoming amidst the sea of unknown faces.

The week before the conference, I have written my resignation letter, but I have yet to hand it in. The conference is my testing ground. Should I, or should I not, give up my job as a family and children's solicitor for a large law firm in the south-east of England, and take up the challenge of a newly created, self-funded advocacy role with the children's charity organising this conference? So many things have led me to this junction in the road of my life's journey, and I can sense God's hand guiding me.

Nonetheless, it's a far-from-easy decision. I am new to the sector and the conference is a complete culture shock. I am sharing a room with a diffident dark-haired Russian lady, who speaks halting and broken English – and a Singaporean lady who wears a continuous smile, sees the positive in everything, and for whom nothing is too much trouble. I have no idea what they make of me. My focus is to find out as much as possible about the organisation with whom I might end up working, testing whether I would fit with my potential co-workers and seeking God's will for the future.

The walk I take with Jackie meanders along a wide flat path that circumnavigates the fields to our left, elegant ash trees to our right, and it's not just the walking that's easy. Our conversation is deep, personal and free-flowing, and seeds of trust and vulnerability are sown from the outset.

Jackie is full of wise counsel, having also transitioned into the sector only a couple of years earlier. Being a similar age, she recognises the challenges of choosing to walk away from so much, and she understands the dissenting voices of those who struggle to understand. She listens carefully as I articulate previously private hopes, aspirations and reservations. She creates a safe space for me to be open. She puts me at ease about the life-changing decision with which I am wrestling.

We soon become firm friends.

Despite the best-laid plans, Jackie doesn't marry until she's in her mid-thirties. She's known Alex as a friend for a little over a year, but they have both been dating different people, and their social lives operate in largely separate circles, in part because Jackie is a Christian and Alex is not.

In the summer of 2004, Jackie and I take a holiday in Canada, a few hours' drive from Niagara Falls. Friends of mine, an older couple from a church I used to attend in my twenties, have generously given us the use of their lakeside holiday home for free. It houses four people, so we invite two other friends to join us and fly out together,

Arriving at the lake at dusk, none of us have clocked that we'll need to pilot a boat to get to our destination, which we can see in the distance across the water. Taking a deep breath, we pile in our luggage and freshly bought food supplies, leaving just enough room for ourselves, and the engine splutters into life, skimming over the lake as darkness starts to descend. Clambering out on the far shore I relish the night sky, studded with stars, and feel immensely grateful for the peace and stillness of such a remote location and good friends with whom to enjoy it.

A fortnight later, we're chatting away, cleaning our holiday home, ready to leave it as we found it, when Jackie suddenly stops mid-sentence. She is leaning on the broom she's using to sweep the floor, and gazing out the window.

"Can you see that 'A' in the sky?" she asks me, pointing to a cloud formation high above the lake. I follow her gaze and nod my agreement. "I wonder whether it's a sign," she ponders, leaning on the broom, and I look at her, bemused. "About Alex," she explains, pausing a moment. "Do you think God's giving me a choice?"

We have been talking about her friendship with Alex, on and off, throughout the holiday and the dilemma of whether it could ever become anything more. They have much in common, apart from faith, and this is what's been consistently holding her back. Aware of this, I struggle to respond. "I guess it could be God," I surmise, hesitantly, wondering whether it's normal for him to write letters in the clouds! "But what makes you think it might be?"

"Cleaning this lake house today," she replies. "It's given me a real sense that Alex's thatched cottage is the one I want to be cleaning. It's Alex I should be dating."

It seems an unusual way to make a decision. But her mind is made up and, within six months, she and Alex are going out.

Jackie is open about her Christian faith from the outset of her friendship with Alex, and he is equally clear about his atheism. He simply doesn't believe that there is a God or gods or any sort of deity. When Jackie persuades him to attend an Alpha course, it simply helps him understand what she believes and why, but it doesn't persuade him to change his mind. If anything, it increases the divide between them.

When they become more than friends and start dating, Jackie enters into the relationship, eyes and ears wide open.

She's always felt she should marry a Christian. Yet here she is, falling in love with someone who is completely antagonistic to Christ. She knows it will be difficult, but they have a rockier start than she'd been anticipating. Worse is that Alex doesn't intend to marry or have children. Such fundamentals for Jackie are simply not there for Alex.

Compared to many, their relationship is harmonious and they share a lot of common interests. Alex accepts Jackie's faith in Jesus, and Jackie releases Alex to God. They are both brutally honest with each other. However, ten months in and they split up.

The five months that follow are a time for heartache, soul searching and vulnerability.

"We don't want to walk away from something that could work," she tells me one weekday lunchtime when we've escaped the office for a walk around the block. "So we're grappling with all the potential pitfalls that could come up because of our lack of shared faith."

"What sort of things?" I ask.

"Big things," she says, before proceeding to give me some examples. "What happens if we have a crisis and I want to pray, but he doesn't even believe God exists? What happens if we have children and I want to take them to church, but he likes spending Sunday mornings in the garage working on a car or motorbike? What happens if I want to tithe some of our income, but he doesn't want to give any money away?"

When Jackie and Alex get back together, they have contended with so many combinations of questions and answers that will work for them, that their relationship is stronger than ever.

Observing as a friend, I admire their willingness to tackle these kinds of core issues ahead of time, certain they are laying firm foundations for what lies ahead.

Jackie and Alex are married on a cold crisp winter's day in the no-man's-land season between Christmas and New Year 2006. Family and friends crowd into the Anglican church building in their local village, just around the corner from the thatched cottage which will become their home, and the celebrations continue at one of the local hotels. Both venues are alive with candles and tea lights, defiant in the darkness that comes with some of the shortest days of the year. There is a sense of celebration.

They have been married about a year when they decide it's a good time to start trying for a family. By this point, Jackie is in her late thirties and Alex in his forties, so there's no time to lose. Within a month, they are pregnant.

The day of the twelve-week scan, Alex has a huge hangover and would rather be hidden away in a darkened room for the day. Rather reluctantly, he accompanies Jackie to the hospital, and the sonographer, who later turns out to be the lead consultant, invites them into a bright and airy room, full of natural daylight. Alex groans and puts his hand over his eyes.

Inviting Jackie to lie on the bed, the sonographer prepares her appropriately and holds a foetal monitor on her exposed abdomen. As she does so, Alex's car keys clatter onto the floor and he drops onto his hands and knees to retrieve them from under the bed.

"Did you see that?" the sonographer asks, excitedly, pointing out two clear foetuses in utero on the screen. "You're expecting twins!"

There is a bump as Alex hits his head under the bed. "Ouch!" he yells, part pain, part shock.

"Wow!" exclaims Jackie, craning her neck to see the screen clearly.

"There is nothing wrong with your babies," the sonographer says, moving the foetal monitor ever so slightly. "Listen to those heartbeats. They are as strong as anything." The boom, boom, boom of two distinct heartbeats is audible in the room as Alex emerges from under the bed, holding the car keys aloft. "Twins," Jackie says reflectively, her head spinning, trying to process the news. "Who would have thought it?" She's aware that, for someone of her build, for twelve weeks' gestation she looks more pregnant than most. But twins would explain it.

"Twins are my specialism," the sonographer explains, wiping Jackie's abdomen and printing off a picture of the twins in utero. "So you'll be seeing a lot more of me in the coming months."

It is early spring 2008 and I have been invited to join Jackie and Alex for dinner. I have barely crossed the threshold, ducking my head under the beam of the low ceiling in their thatched cottage, removing my shoes, hanging up my coat, before their news comes tumbling out.

Jackie gives me a hug and then, "I'm pregnant," she announces, with a broad grin. "We're expecting twins."

"Wow!" I respond. "Congratulations!" I pause for a moment. I've been expecting a pregnancy announcement, but not one of twins. "Do you have twins in the family?" I ask.

"None that we know about," Alex interjects, greeting me with a hug, "but we're trying to find out."

"We're so excited," Jackie continues, unable to contain herself, showing me the print of the twelve-week scan. "The scan revealed they are non-identical, a boy and a girl." I know, without any elaboration, that this is perfect; a fulfilment of her lifelong dream for a son and a daughter. "We've already decided their names," she tells me, her joy contagious. "The boy will be Christopher James and the girl Ella Rae."

It is so like Jackie to have pre-planned the names for her babies, long before they were even conceived, because she is one of those women who's been born to be a mother. Her ability to care, nurture and support other people and especially children, always putting their needs before her own, is something that comes naturally and easily.

All through her childhood and teens, her main ambition in life has been to find a husband, get married, and have children. As a young girl she would dress up as a bride, dreaming of one day having a son and a daughter and all of them living "happily ever after", to quote the well-known fairy tales.

Fascinated with motherhood, she would watch and observe how different families work, how different women raise their children, how different children develop. When her mum's best friend, who lived around the corner, gave birth to twins, Jackie was in seventh heaven! Still at primary school at the time, she more or less moved in, helping out in whatever ways she could.

When it's come to life choices in her school and college studies and, later on, in her career, Jackie's love of children has consistently influenced her decision-making and several of her roles have involved working with, or on behalf of, children. But her deep-down desire is to have children of her own.

It has never occurred to her that life could turn out any other way.

Jackie is doubled up in pain. Excruciating cramps keep ripping through her abdomen. It is a Saturday morning and she and husband Alex have just completed the course for first-time parents run by the National Childbirth Trust. Returning home to their beautiful thatched cottage at the edge of their village, panic is starting to set in. The twins are only twenty-four weeks' gestation.

"What if things go wrong?" she asks Alex, her mind whirring. "How will they survive?"

At church the following day, Jackie sets up a room in the hall, ready to lead the toddlers' group, but the spasms keep coming. Clutching hold of the back of a white plastic chair, she leans forward, letting it carry her weight, as she stands and contemplates what to do. A short while later, she's being admitted into hospital and given a steroid injection.

"It will help accelerate the development of the twins' lungs if they appear sooner than we're expecting," a consultant informs her, his demeanour matter-of-fact. "It's routine procedure," he reassures her when he sees her concern. "You're bleeding intermittently, so it's important we prepare for all eventualities."

The ad hoc bleeding continues for forty-eight hours. "This isn't what I was expecting," Jackie confides in Alex from her hospital bed. "What if the bleeding doesn't stop? I'm scared we might lose them."

"You need to rest," he reassures her, gently squeezing her hand.

Back at home, when the bleeding starts again, Jackie fights a rising sense of panic. Calling the consultant, he doesn't hesitate in admitting her back into hospital for the second time in two weeks, and she is too emotionally exhausted to question his decision. The twins are one day shy of twenty-seven weeks' gestation, and the pregnancy is taking its toll. "It's a precaution," he explains pragmatically, "so we can monitor you effectively."

She is shown past the nurses' station, the bins filled to overflowing with gauze and antiseptic wipes, the stacks of blankets on trolleys, and the curtained beds behind which women are waiting to give birth. Hers is in the corner, tucked away with a modicum of privacy, and she faces into a long day – and an even longer night. Nausea keeps sleep at bay and so does the noise of newborn babies making their presence felt, and the hushed and harried reassurances of mothers and nurses trying to placate them.

It is four in the morning. All across the hospital patients are dosing and dreaming, their immune systems repairing, revamping and regenerating, willing weak bodies to live. The ward is quieter now – no beeping, no footsteps. Somewhere in the distance, a television screen is flickering without sound. Reaching for her phone, she calls Alex. "The cramps keep coming thick and fast; the sickness is relentless," she tells him. "I'm feeling really frightened. Please will you come as soon as you can?"

Alex arrives to find two doctors deep in discussion, standing outside the curtain that encases Jackie's bed. Clipboards in hand, the conversation is heated, their voices carrying easily through the thin layer of pale, faded plastic.

"We should deliver these twins right here and now," says the one who's just examined her. "The mother is bleeding. Her blood pressure is sky high. The babies are in distress. We need to do an emergency C-section."

"I don't think it's quite so urgent," says the other. "I agree she needs a C-section, but surely it can wait until morning, when the consultant will be in?"

The consultant is a specialist in obstetrics and foetal medicine. Highly regarded in his field, he specialises in high-risk cases. A few hours later, Jackie feels a deep sense of peace when she sees him in charge of the sea of people, all swathed in sky-blue gowns, packed into the operating theatre. His very presence commands gravitas, and his team clearly respect him.

"Thank you, God, for such impeccable timing," she whispers under her breath.

Monitors are beeping. The fluorescent lights in the ceiling are piercingly bright, but the glare is soon blocked by unknown faces, hidden behind surgical facemasks, muffling instructions in coded language. Their hands pass instruments, their eyes glance at screens.

The epidural kicks in and she loses sensation. Alex is holding her hand.

In the operating theatre, the consultant lifts a tiny human bundle out of Jackie's body, covered in blood and mucus. "It's a boy," he pronounces, cutting the umbilical cord and handing him over for weighing. And then, moments later, he repeats the routine, this time declaring, "It's a girl." Christopher weighs not much more than a 1kg bag of sugar; Ella a little less.

"They are good weights for twins of their gestation," he reassures Jackie, who can only see their utter vulnerability. "Their heartbeats are strong, so we'll get them straight upstairs to the Special Care Baby Unit," he explains. Alex nods quietly.

Two nurses are bundling both babies into blankets, their eyes sealed. The monitors pulse steadily as the twins are placed into two incubators, each one a mass of tubes, wires, lamps, heaters and all the paraphernalia which comes with keeping two such tiny people alive.

Noticing Alex gazing down at his son and daughter, the younger nurse offers to capture the moment on camera. "It might be a while before you see them again," she tells Jackie, showing her the photos. Christopher seems peaceful; Ella less so, letting out a high-pitched cry.

"Stable," pronounces the consultant as he checks their heartbeats.

"Miracles, more like," says Jackie, emotionally exhausted, physically spent. She yearns to hold the babies she's been carrying for the last six months, and her eyes fill up as she watches their incubators being wheeled out of the room, together with the machines to which they are connected.

"This isn't how it's meant to be," Jackie tells Alex back in the ward, weeping softly in frustration and pain. "This isn't my motherhood dream."

Her sorrow doesn't last long. "Let's be showing you how to use that breast pump then, shall we?" A jovial, matronly, middle-aged nurse draws back the curtains with a flourish. She hands over a box of tissues, warmth in her smile, and launches into the logistics of demonstrating how to latch the pump.

An email prayer chain has been created by one of Jackie's church friends, and the opening email encourages us to approach God with confidence. The first few days are a rollercoaster and emails come through thick and fast.

Both babies are being assisted with additional oxygen. Please can we pray for their breathing?

They each have a tiny feeding tube installed through their nose, taped into position on their cheek, enabling breast milk to drip through, automated by a machine, one to two millilitres every hour. Additional nourishment comes through a central line inserted into their tummies, and the combination provides all the nutrients their tiny bodies need. Unfortunately, it keeps blocking. Please can we pray for their feeding?

They also have miniature flexible cannula tubes inserted into their veins, through which intravenous medication is administered at tightly regulated intervals, in a far from straightforward procedure. With Christopher it takes three attempts in three days, and an X-ray reveals it's slipped from his tummy, near his heart, to his thigh. Please can we pray for this too?

"We're going to have to insert his intravenous medication line into his head to stop it slipping," the specialist nurse advises, but the look on Jackie's face stops her mid-sentence. "It's a straightforward procedure," she reassures her, "but, if it fails, he'll need surgery."

Ella has high blood sugar levels, and Jackie high blood pressure. Please can we pray for both to come down?

"Ella is going to need an insulin infusion," the nurse informs Jackie, "and you're probably going to need a blood transfusion." It's not a prospect that Jackie relishes. Worse, her hands and feet are swollen, and her liver is malfunctioning. Yet she doesn't feel worried or concerned. Instead, she feels an indescribable peace, knowing she's being carried by the prayers of friends and family who are boldly bringing her situation before God.

Jackie is sitting in her hospital bed, reading a book.

"What's that you're reading?" asks one of the nurses, who's spied the back cover with interest.

"It's a Christian book," Jackie says, feeling slightly vulnerable, "about women in the Bible. Strong women. Women who had to stand their ground." She pauses a moment, wondering whether she might be overstepping the mark. "Why do you ask?" she enquires.

"I'm a Christian too," the nurse explains. "I had a feeling you might be."

It turns out the nurse goes to a well-known church in the city, and they have Christian contacts in common. "How amazing," Jackie says, "whenever I'm open about my faith, God always brings other believers, like you, alongside me."

"That's true," says the nurse. "We're never alone."

A week and a day after the twins are born, Jackie is discharged from hospital. Her liver has healed, her blood pressure has stabilised, the swelling in her hands and feet has disappeared, and her iron levels are such that a blood transfusion is no longer being mooted as an idea.

Not only that, but Christopher's intravenous medication line has stayed in place in his head without the need for surgery, and Ella's ability to tolerate more milk has increased. Both are starting to gain weight.

"Praise God!" she writes in an update to the email prayer group. "Please give him thanks for all the prayers he's answered this week. He's truly faithful."

In anticipation of Alex returning to work at the end of his paternity leave the following week, and owing to her immobility following the C-section, Jackie moves into her parents' house, where they can look after her while she recovers from the surgery. Their home is laid out on one level, which is much easier to navigate than the higgledy-piggledy floors of the thatched cottage.

"It's Ella," Jackie's text reads. "She's extremely sick at the moment. Her bowel is dying, so she's had to have half of it removed in emergency surgery, only she had a cardiac arrest in the middle of the operation. She's holding on, but she may not make it. It's all happened so quickly. Please pray."

I lean back against the kitchen counter where I'm making a cup of tea, and I cry aloud to God, pleading in prayer for this new little life, wrestling with this news.

It makes no sense, because Ella has been doing so well.

A couple of days ago, she was even being moved out of the High Dependency Unit to the Special Care Baby Unit, because she no longer needed such intensive support. Her photo had been emailed out, showing her wearing a tiny pink gingham dress, contrasting with a mop of dark hair on her head. Her hand seemed to be gripping firmly around Jackie's little finger, her knuckles white from squeezing so hard.

Later that day, an update comes out to the email prayer chain: Ella is currently fighting for her life.

She's contracted the devastating disease, necrotising enterocolitis (NEC), which is common in premature babies. It means the wall of her intestine has been invaded by bacteria, causing infection and inflammation. It won't take long for her whole bowel to be destroyed. Her medical team have done all they can – but the consultant doesn't expect Ella to live. She is heavily sedated and the drugs are preventing her from moving. Her vital signs are being carefully monitored every four hours.

Jackie is struggling, emotionally and spiritually. "I don't know why God is letting this happen, or how I'll be able to let Ella go," she says in an email to the prayer chain. "It's a miracle that she and Christopher are even here! If he's brought Ella so far already, please pray he lets her live, but also that his will be done. Please pray he gives me the endurance I need, for I sense this is going to be a marathon, not a sprint."

Christopher has an infection which is causing his heart rate to drop, putting him at huge risk. The nurses have to wake him up by tickling his toes. Each time they do so, the monitor screen shows a spike and then a steadying, so it must be good for his heart. He looks so vulnerable, a shock of dark hair on his head, his body wriggling in discomfort, microscopic doses of antibiotics periodically pumping through a long unsightly line penetrating a vein in his neck.

Jackie and Alex take it in turns to feed a couple of millilitres of her expressed breast milk to Christopher, using a syringe, through the tube up his nose, and he begins to develop a sucking reflex. When they stretch a hand into the incubator, he puts his hands up to his head, grabs hold of a finger and stretches his legs out straight. He is making incredible progress, against all the odds.

When Jackie and Alex are at home, or at her parents' house, life continues with the usual litany of laundry and chores and buying and preparing food. Even more so when Alex returns to work.

It feels as though they are leading a double life. One life is at the hospital, where they are holding out for baby cuddles, mastering the art of nappy changing and learning to ride the rollercoaster that comes with loved ones in intensive care. The other life is at home, where most of the neighbours are none the wiser and everything carries on as normal.

The overlap comes with Jackie's church home group. Not only do they coordinate and manage the email prayer chain, but they also organise for meals to be made, delivered to the door, and placed in the freezer when the fridge is full to overflowing. Two older ladies even climb through a window when they can't find the key to gain access, simply to clean the house. Their thoughtfulness, kindness and generosity are exemplary.

Even Alex is moved by the lengths that people are prepared to go to help them; their determination to stick around for the long haul; and their willingness to journey so closely alongside them, despite him not going to church.

Ella survives the surgery to remove half her bowel, is weaned off the drugs that are keeping her sedated, and is beginning to wriggle her fingers and toes again. She is being prepared to have a long line inserted for her intravenous medication, a procedure to match her brother's, meaning no more needles in her hands and feet.

But then things go downhill.

It's about seven in the morning and Jackie is getting dressed when the consultant calls. "Please can you come in, as soon as you can," he urges her. "Ella hasn't had a good night."

"Is she deteriorating?" Jackie asks, feeling fragile. She's just been trying to express breast milk, sitting in bed, but it seems to be drying up.

"Yes, I'm afraid she is," the consultant responds, as gently and kindly as he knows how. "Her breathing is laboured, even with the ventilator, so we are concerned her lungs are not developing properly." He pauses a moment. "Her abdomen is still distended, so we have run further tests which suggest the rest of her bowel is dying."

Jackie chokes back tears, trying to take in this information. She knew things were bad, but not this bad. "Is she distressed?" she asks, her heart breaking at the prospect of her little girl in pain. "Are you able to tell?"

"She is as comfortable as we can make her," the consultant reassures Jackie.

On the now familiar road route to the hospital, Alex is driving while Jackie is praying: "Please, God, we don't want Ella to suffer. I know she is in your hands, but it is hard to see how you are going to get the glory from this. Please, God, we would so love a miracle. May your will be done."

Throughout that day, Ella clings to life along a fine thin thread.

The night before, Jackie invited her church minister to the hospital to baptise Ella as a precautionary measure. The nurse on duty found a cross and covered it in gerbera flowers, and a simple service followed, entrusting Ella into God's tender and loving care. Her grandparents were also present.

Standing in the same spot now, the consultant is clear. "It's impossible to predict the quality of her life, but her long-term prognosis is poor," he tells them. "She will have to undergo multiple operations before the age of two to try and replace her bowel, and she may always have to be fed via a tube rather than through her mouth."

About four in the afternoon, the consultant announces that there's nothing more that can be done. He lifts Ella out of her incubator and hands her to Alex for a cuddle. He passes her over to Jackie who holds her carefully, acutely aware of her daughter's fragility and sickliness.

It is there, in her mother's arms, that Ella dies.

It is a Friday in early July. Her life has lasted not quite three weeks.

Through the haze of exhaustion that keeps threatening to overwhelm her, Jackie keeps playing a song on repeat, by Christian singer songwriter Lou Fellingham. Called "Hard Pressed", from her album *Treasure*, the song articulates Jackie's thoughts and feelings better than she can express them herself, giving her strength to keep navigating the highs and lows, blessings and battles, hopes and fears. It reminds her that God is constantly with her and she is never alone.

Lou sings powerfully into the headphones of Jackie's iPod.

The lyrics are loosely based on some verses from the Bible, written by St Paul in 2 Corinthians 4:7-9:

"This all-surpassing power is from God and not from us. We are hard pressed on every side, but not crushed;

perplexed, but not in despair; persecuted, but not abandoned; struck down, but not destroyed."

Time and again, she is witnessing God's all-surpassing power at work, answering prayers, surrounding them with support, and carrying them through this trial. Her faith is unshakeable. She is believing God for miracles. He is giving her hope to hold out for them, even when circumstances dictate otherwise.

The postman starts bringing bereavement condolence cards, which mingle on the mantelpiece with the new twin baby cards, a startling reminder of the thin line between life and loss.

There is a verse in the Bible, in the story of Job, which speaks of God giving and God taking away. It reassures Jackie that God understands, even when she doesn't; when the tears are in free fall; when grief comes unbidden in the night, reminding her of what might have been.

A senior staff nurse on the High Dependency Unit recommends Jackie join a support group for parents of premature babies, and she finds solace in connecting with others who have been on similar journeys.

Relatives rally around to provide support. Jackie's parents step in to visit Christopher when Alex has to work. Neighbours and friends appear to play their part. And Jackie's church family continues to provide a constant steady stream of practical provision and prayer cover.

But there is also an inner emptiness, a sense of loss, as if a piece of Jackie has died with Ella.

The antiquated hospital lift judders slowly up three floors. One, two, three. And Jackie gets chatting to another parent, heading in the same direction.

"We had a simple christening service with my church minister," she explains. "There was a cross, covered in gerberas, which are my favourite flowers, and ..."

She is stopped mid-sentence by a nurse in the corner, who has overheard them. "That was me," she says, hesitating before proceeding, "I chose those flowers."

Jackie is astounded. "How did you know they were my favourites?" she asks.

"I didn't," the nurse responds, smiling. "They just caught my eye when I went to choose some for the service."

"Thank you so much," Jackie says effusively, feeling deeply touched. "You have no idea how much they blessed me."

She steps out of the lift, seeing it as another little sign of God's goodness, always attending to the details in ways that nobody knows.

When Christopher is moved out of the High Dependency Unit to the Special Care Baby Unit, it is seen as a sign of progress. He is feeding well, putting on weight, and desperately trying to pull out the oxygen tube that is sustaining him, meaning the monitor keeps going into overdrive with bleeping. But the medical team are keenly aware that he could succumb to the same devastating disease that's taken Ella. So all contact is limited for fear of cross-contamination with infections.

The turnaround comes when Christopher turns one month old. His sucking reflex is developing, so the consultant wants to encourage him to feed from the breast or a bottle.

His long line remains in place, ready for any medication that might be required, but there is discussion about removing it. "The problem with the operation is the risk of infection," the consultant tells them. "There's a risk if we leave the line in, and a risk if we take it out." He pauses for a moment. "Either way, we will need to find another vein, so we can still give him intravenous antibiotics."

It's been nineteen months since I last entered the ancient church building in the heart of the village that Jackie and Alex call home, and the contrasts are considerable.

Back then, it was packed to the rafters, with standing room only for the latecomers; today, there are just a small select handful of people in the pews. Back then, we were rejoicing and celebrating as we witnessed Jackie and Alex's marriage; today we are mourning and grieving as we gather for Ella's funeral. Back then, it was so cold it could have snowed and outside was almost pitch black; today, the summer sunshine is dazzling us, and bright natural daylight is streaming through the stained-glass windows.

The simple white wooden casket, so small and delicate, is already on the altar at the front. It lies at the foot of the cross of Christ, covered in white and pink gerberas, a stark reminder of the brevity of Ella's life – all nineteen days of it.

I find a seat in the midst of the familiar faces of Jackie's and Alex's close friends and family, feeling honoured to be there. All of us are wearing bright and cheerful colours and the mood is one of thanksgiving, the atmosphere surprisingly upbeat.

The vicar who married them is officiating today's service. "I regret not praying more for Ella, while I could have done," he says, surprisingly us all with his honesty. "I believe God could have saved her, but we will never know why he didn't."

It is a simple and unassuming ceremony. We say some prayers and pause in the silence to reflect. Alex is in floods of tears, sitting in the front pew, his gaze fixed on the tiny white casket up ahead of him. Several of the neighbours are also getting emotional.

While we are reflecting, in my mind's eye I see a clump of stinging nettles and I pause to reflect on the picture. We try to avoid going near them, fearful they could sting us. But they actually contain healing properties. So it is with death. Part of us wants to avoid going near it, talking about it, fearing it will "sting" us. Yet it can actually bring healing. For Ella, she is no longer suffering or in pain. Surely that is healing in itself?

I am reminded of the verse in the Bible at the end of 1 Corinthians 15, where it says:

Where, O death, is your victory? Where, O death, is your sting? . . . But thanks be to God! He gives us the victory through our Lord Jesus Christ.

In the silence at the end of the service, we all pour out of the doors into glorious afternoon sunshine and, heading behind the back of the building, we gather to watch the oh-so-small coffin being lowered into an oh-so-small hole in the ground of the graveyard. Her baby body, born less than a month ago, is now being buried. "From dust you came, and to dust you shall return." It feels surreal.

As we gather together for cakes and coffee at the wake, the emotional toll on Alex and Jackie becomes clear.

"He took his best friend into the hospital to see Christopher this morning," Jackie tells me, "and he cried when the medical team presented him with a huge bunch of flowers." She pauses a moment. "It was even worse when he delivered them to the funeral directors. He got so upset, much more than he was anticipating."

"What about you?" I ask. "How are you doing?"

"I've cried a lot," she tells me. "But tears are releasing and healing, aren't they? They make me feel so much better."

"How's your faith?" I enquire. "Are you angry with God for taking her?"

"Not at all," she replies. "I don't believe God wanted her to die, but I don't feel angry with him for taking her, as I know she's not in pain now, and I was finding it so hard seeing her suffering and in so much distress." She pauses a moment, reflecting. "Besides, we've still got Christopher, and Ella will live on through him."

The operation to remove Christopher's long line goes better than anyone could have hoped. However, as anticipated, he gets an infection. It is tricky to cannulate Christopher's veins to receive the intravenous antibiotics, but they eventually find one in his leg. It helps that he's doubled his birth weight as it means his immune system is strengthening. There is a sense of relief when three consecutive blood tests reveal the infection has gone.

Unfortunately, it is only short lived.

"We would like him to have another six weeks on antibiotics," the consultant informs them, "just to make sure that all the infections are gone for good." He pauses a moment, takes a deep breath and continues. "But it means we're going to have to insert another long line as there's no way we can continue to use cannulas to administer antibiotics for that length of time."

Jackie's face expresses her disappointment, while Alex finds it hard to hide his frustration, wondering why they failed to think of this before the operation, rather than after.

"It's a routine operation," the consultant reassures them, but Jackie's mind is racing ahead, wondering how her son will cope with the twenty-minute journey in his incubator to the other side of the hospital. Again. So soon after the last time. She is thinking of the long corridors, double doors and lifts; the bumps and bends, twists and turns. And then the anaesthetic.

"He's still so little, so vulnerable," she says. "Will he be OK?" The consultant nods. "We'll do our best," he says.

Within the space of a week, Christopher has two sets of surgery.

The first operation inserts long line number two, but it becomes blocked. Nobody understands how it happens or who or what is to blame. Instead, he has a second operation which removes long line number two and inserts, instead, long line number three.

His cries of distress are heartrending. His reliance on oxygen is still apparent. He makes clear how much he despises the nil-by-mouth protocol in the hours ahead of having his anaesthetics.

Jackie is feeling utterly exhausted. One moment the nurses are suggesting that Christopher could soon be moved out of the incubator, into a cot, and are encouraging her to get his clothes ready. The next moment the consultant is the bearer of bad tidings. One moment he is settled and content, looking up at her, eyes wide open and attentive. The next she is settling his screams with her voice and touch. The highs and lows are an emotional rollercoaster ride – and she is only just holding on.

Breakthrough comes when Christopher turns ten weeks old and Jackie gives him his first bottle feed. It is as near to normality as she's known in the whole time since he was born.

"You really need to start preparing for Christopher being discharged from hospital," the consultant advises Alex and Jackie in early September, to their utter surprise. "We can't know for definite when it will be, but he's heading in the right direction, so I expect it will be soon."

The end is in sight and the sense of relief is palpable.

During the long weeks that follow the birth of the twins, Jackie's faith takes on a new dimension. She draws on her relationship with God, digging deep and trusting him in ways like never before.

"I often describe my faith in God being like a stone," she tells me, "hidden deep inside the core of my body, something solid and immovable, not necessarily visible but I know it's always there."

"Go on," I encourage her. "It's a helpful analogy."

"It still feels like that," she says reflectively, "but it's more like a diamond now than a stone, as if God has sharpened, crafted, polished and cut it." She pauses a moment. "I have felt his presence with me every step of the way through these long weeks. He's answered so many prayers and I've felt completely overwhelmed. But my faith is stronger for it. It's a unique and precious diamond of priceless worth."

I nod my agreement, as I can see this in her.

"What he's done for me is irreversible," she explains, "and I wouldn't change it for the world."

The day Christopher comes home is momentous.

Ten days before his original due date, and already three months old, the consultant simply says, "It's OK for you to go now," signing the release papers and clipping them into

Christopher's enormous file of medical notes, having just finished running a final set of tests. He looks up from where he's sitting, peering over his spectacles to make sure they have understood him. "You can take Christopher home today," he says with a smile.

They had expected a time of transition and adjustment on the "going home" ward, a halfway house between the Special Care Baby Unit and home. Designed for babies born prematurely, it enables parents to gradually take over responsibility for their care, but Christopher bypasses this step in the process. Everybody's been planning, but nobody's fully prepared.

When it finally happens, it's a sunny Saturday morning in early September.

As they strap him into his shiny new car seat, Jackie's hands start to shake. Tears roll off the end of her nose on to Christopher's tummy and he looks at her with big brown eyes. "I'm sorry for getting upset, but it's a big day today, Christopher," she tells him through her sobs. "We're taking you home from hospital."

"And we're leaving Ella behind," Alex interjects ruefully, his eyes welling up. "I hadn't expected it to feel so final." He climbs into the driver's seat in silence.

Friends and family form a welcome party. The house is decorated with banners, balloons and bunting, and there is a sense of hope in the atmosphere. Someone pops a bottle of bubbly and they raise a toast, while Christopher sleeps in his car seat, utterly oblivious.

A new normal soon sets in, with dirty nappies and changes of clothes; feeds, burps and projectile vomiting; sleep deprivation, and a steady stream of visitors keen for a cuddle. It's the pattern of parenting the world over, and Jackie and Alex embrace it wholeheartedly.

"I see no reason why you can't go ahead and try for another child," the consultant says to Jackie and Alex. "There's a statistical likelihood that you might conceive twins again, but there's no medical reason not to try."

His words are salve to her soul.

Jackie has always wanted a boy and a girl. It is a dull aching longing that starts to intensify during the adjustment period after Ella's untimely passing. So when a pregnancy test proves positive, and the twenty-week scan reveals she is expecting a girl, all her pent-up yearning bubbles to the surface and she can't stop crying.

Getting past twenty-seven weeks' gestation is stressful and pressurised. It is only when their baby girl is born at full term that Jackie realises how tense she's been and there's a palpable sense of relief.

They name her Anabelle. It is a name that means "favour" or "graceful" (Anna) and "beautiful" (Belle), a reminder that God has shown them favour and grace in giving them a beautiful daughter.

Jackie and Alex are acutely aware of every developmental milestone that Christopher has to hurdle and it draws them closer together as a couple. They and their marriage have been hard pressed – but far from crushed.

"What will be the impact of such a tough start in life?" Jackie asks Alex. "Will he be aware of the loss of his twin sister?"

"We'll just have to see how he fares physically, mentally, emotionally," Alex reassures her.

With each passing year, it becomes clear that Christopher is not afflicted by any of the complaints that are associated with premature babies. His immune system is strong. His lungs are fully functioning and he breathes easily. He has no sight, hearing or intellectual loss. Speech comes naturally and he quickly grasps new language. He has good hand-eye coordination, and loves throwing and catching balls. Concentration is never a problem and he has no difficulty focusing. The only noticeable difference is that he's just a little bit shorter and smaller than his peers.

Each time Christopher has a medical check-up, Jackie is reminded of how many people prayed for him and how many of their prayers God answered. His dense and detailed medical notes are the only clue to the different trajectory that "might have been".

Meeting Christopher now, you will come face-to-face with a maturing boy who is wise beyond his years. He is highly relational, with exceptional empathy and emotional intelligence, knowing exactly how to read people. He is kind, caring and compassionate. He is talented and teachable, popular amongst his peers. He is inquisitive, always asking questions, eager to understand how things work and why. He gives everyone and everything his full attention and total commitment.

He is, quite literally, a miracle.

A friend has a premature baby. Another has a baby die in the womb. Still another a stillbirth. Each baby lost leaves another precious person grieving and needing support.

"I'm able to mourn with those who are mourning; to walk alongside them; to tell them, with integrity, that I've been there too," Jackie tells me. "Baby loss sends us on such an unexpected and unknown journey, and not many people have travelled it."

She starts singing Lou Fellingham's lyrics: "*Miracles, you will do, as I come and put my hope in you.*"

"I pray this for all those who are going through something similar," she explains to me. "I have to trust God to give them hope, but it feels so freeing, knowing I can help; that I've got something to offer; that Ella's death wasn't in vain." She turns to gaze out the kitchen window and then continues. "At the end of the day," she says contemplatively, "I'll always be the mother of three children."

She pauses a moment, reflecting on all that she's gone through. "If me being vulnerable in telling my story helps even one other person, then that is enough."

CHAPTER 7

Building on God's grace
A church threatened with closure (2014)

"But now, for a brief moment,
the Lord our God has been gracious in leaving us a remnant
and giving us a firm place in his sanctuary."

Ezra 9:8

This story is about St Thomas' church. It features two couples, Al and Lucy, and Phil and Marian, whose combined history has intertwined with the church. I initially met Al and Lucy through one of Lucy's cousins, a friend since my teens. Lucy and I subsequently became friends through a shared love of writing.

"We have to make the most effective use of our buildings and the money it costs to keep them open," the Anglican Church Commissioners' notice reads. "We have been reviewing the mission and ministry of St Thomas', and can no longer keep the building open as a place of worship. We therefore regret to inform you that the church will soon be closed. You are kindly requested to make alternative arrangements for your Sunday services." Information is provided, detailing other local churches in their area of the city.

The congregation are stunned. They know their parish church of St Thomas' is struggling, but not enough to be closed.

Based on the outskirts of a northern English city, the church is located in a mixed area. Students from the local university live alongside young professionals in the Victorian terraces and the high-rise flats, some of which contain economically deprived households. Families make the most of the handful of playgrounds and send their children to the two schools, one of which is in special measures. Care homes accommodate some of the elderly residents, while others remain in large family houses in the more affluent area of the neighbourhood. The probation office is adjacent to the church building. Homelessness is commonplace.

Sunday services are currently attracting an average congregation of about twenty people, most of them elderly, some of them infirm. Numbers have been shrinking in recent years and the faithful few have been left with an uncertain future. At the moment, they rely on the kindness of the leaders of other local churches to meet their pastoral care needs and lead their communal worship – usually sung Eucharist with a robed choir. "It's like wading through treacle," one of the leaders remarks.

The church building was erected in the mid-1800s during the height of the Victorian era. It is laid out with wooden pews, an altar at the front and stained-glass windows on all sides. But the Church Commissioners, whose role is to manage the Church of England's assets, have got it on their radar. Historic buildings, like this one, are often sold and reassigned for other purposes. They are liaising with the city's bishop and other Anglican leaders in the diocese to discern what might be best, when they decide to give notice of closure.

The congregation might be few in number, but this is their church. What can we do? they wonder. How can we keep the building open? Surely St Thomas' has a viable future?

Organising themselves into a campaigning cohort, they reach out to a local vicar, who has been supporting them regularly in recent years.

"We don't want it to become a carpet warehouse," a man in his seventies declares philosophically. "Can we simply refuse to go?"

"Let's equip lay people," the vicar suggests. "It doesn't have to be run by trained professionals."

He takes his idea to the city's bishop, while the faithful remnant are praying. There is a sense of relief when the bishop agrees to give it one more go and refuses to sign the closure papers.

The first time I meet Lucy and Al, I'm staying in Northern Ireland with one of Lucy's cousins, an old friend from my teens.

My friend was raised overseas in a missionary family and, when her parents returned to the UK, they settled in my home town. We may not see each other often, but our friendship has a history; wherever in the world she, her husband and three daughters are based, I visit.

Lucy, Al and their children are on holiday, staying in a house a short walk from my friend and her family, so we meet up with them several times during the course of the week. Over dinner one evening, an incredible story begins to emerge, and it continues to tumble out when we take a beach walk a couple of days later.

Lucy and Al are warm, welcoming and generous-hearted; their children are a delight. Both in their thirties, Al wears glasses and has tousled dark hair, while Lucy is dark blonde. Their approach to life is easy-going and full of fun. Although we were attending the same church while they were students, our paths never crossed, but it has given us plenty of people in common and conversation flows freely.

It was during their student years when Lucy and Al met, thanks to various groups designed to bring together those with a shared Christian faith. After leaving university, they moved to northern England, where Al felt called to become ordained in the Church of England. As the daughter of a vicar, Lucy understands the joys and challenges this role will bring, and she supports his calling. Three years away at theological college follow for Al, before a move back north for four further years of practical on-the-job training as a trainee vicar, a "curate".

"We've always lived in the St Thomas' vicarage," Al explains. "It was left empty after their last vicar moved on, so the diocese decided to let a large city-centre church use it to house their curates, and I'm the third in a row to live there."

"We feel really happy there," Lucy tells me. "Our children are settled and we love being part of the community."

After the Northern Ireland holiday, Lucy and I stay in touch and, over the course of time, mostly because of our shared love of writing, we become friends. So I'm delighted when an opportunity later arises to visit.

Driving towards the city centre, I find the St Thomas' vicarage on a corner plot, where a main road and side street meet. It's a large detached, modern, brick-built house, with a sizeable wrap-around garden. Parking outside the front door, it feels strangely familiar. *This is where it all happened,* I think.

Later that evening, once the children are in bed, Lucy, Al and I sit in armchairs, cradling mugs of tea. The dual aspect living room is light and airy; the late spring sunshine is fading.

"Please take me back to the beginning," I say.

Heading towards the end of 2012, Al's curacy is drawing to a close and he is exploring options. There is a possibility with a church in the south of England. They have created a new role with special responsibility for ministry amongst university students, which could be a good fit for Al.

Lucy is saddened by the prospect of leaving the place in which they have settled as a family, but she is trusting that this job is the right one for Al, and starts to research schools and other opportunities.

As they pray about it, they decide that Al should pursue the post, so he has a long phone call with the vicar there and then heads over for an interview. By Christmas 2012 he has accepted the role and the news that they will be moving, in the summer of 2013, is announced in both churches.

It feels like a done deal.

But then, five months later, in the middle of May 2013, Al attends a special service at the cathedral, a vast and beautiful building. It is a celebration to commemorate Pentecost – when God gave the Holy Spirit to the disciples and other followers of Jesus in Jerusalem, the day the Christian faith began and the global church was born. Thankful that, for once, he has no clerical role to play, he sits at the back as a participant.

Halfway through the service a very strong sense of unease comes over him. While everyone around him seems to be engaging enthusiastically with what is being led from the front, Al sits, head in hands, praying silently. Seemingly out of nowhere, his mind starts to flood with serious doubts about moving south.

That night, unable to get the doubts out of his head, Al broaches the subject with Lucy. "I'm not sure we should be moving south," he announces, catching Lucy unawares. "I can't explain it, and I don't know whether it's God warning of difficulties to come or the Holy Spirit telling me not to go, but I just have an overwhelming sense that it isn't right."

Lucy sits up and listens, incredulity written all over her face. "I think it's probably just cold feet," she suggests. "Let's sleep on it, because things will look different in the morning."

A couple of days later, sitting in the study of his current church leader and boss, light pouring through the large windows, Al pours out his heart.

"It's so out of character for you, Al, that you really mustn't dismiss it," his boss says supportively. "Maybe you're just getting cold feet? But then again, what if there's something in it?"

Al feels grateful for this wisdom, and they pray together, asking God to make it clear.

There are no lightning bolts in the sky; no audible voices; no dramatic signs. There is simply a deep gnawing sense of unease.

It's less than six weeks until the family are meant to be moving.

It's a Tuesday, nine days on from the Pentecost celebration service at the cathedral, and Al and Lucy are sitting in the book-lined study of the vicarage at the church they are supposed to soon be moving to, and the atmosphere is tense.

They have driven all afternoon to get there for the five o'clock meeting, leaving friends at home on childcare duty. Nobody knows quite what to expect.

"So you're telling me that you no longer want to become our associate vicar?" The vicar is gazing out of the window onto the vicarage garden, biting his bottom lip as he tries to summarise what he's just heard.

Al has been laying bare some of his doubts about taking up the post, acutely aware of the ramifications of pulling out, and the vicar has done his best to persuade him to stick with his commitment. The last thing Al wants is to leave this church in the lurch – and the vicar facing the twin challenges of explaining to his congregation that he will no longer be coming, while also trying to recruit a suitable replacement.

"If God is in this," Al suggests tentatively, "then I'm sure he'll find somebody else, somebody better than me, to take the post."

With heavy hearts, Al and Lucy walk down the road to the church where a group of around a hundred students have gathered in the auditorium to hear Al teach. His topic is the peace of God in the midst of uncertainty, something he can currently speak about with authenticity. The hum of conversation as they break into small groups implies it's been well-received, but Al and Lucy don't hang around to find out.

Back in the car, they exhale. "Well, that was interesting," says Lucy, wondering whether they really are doing the right thing. "Yes," says Al. "Not the easiest of evenings." But as they talk it through together, God seems to bring clarity and unity to both of them.

"I feel sure we've made the right decision," reflects Al.

In the days following the pivotal meeting, Al becomes acutely aware of the knock-on repercussions: on the people in that church who have invested so much in their coming;

on Lucy and the children who are now living with significant uncertainty; on his current church who are getting ready for his replacement to arrive.

"Am I turning down a perfectly good job, which fits my talents and interests, on nothing more than a hunch?" he asks Lucy. "Or was it really God speaking and, if so, how can I be sure?"

Lucy is considering the practicalities of where they will live. The diocese want the St Thomas' vicarage vacated, not for Al's replacement who has been given a house elsewhere, but for a university chaplain, a Kenyan man, who has kindly agreed to provide ad hoc support to St Thomas'.

"I'm really sorry," Al informs the church, pressing send on his carefully crafted email, "but we won't be coming." God alone knows what will come next, how it will be funded, where it will be based.

"I feel really relieved," he confides in Lucy.

A few days after he has turned down the job, Al is sitting in his boss's study, surrounded by a sea of books and papers, updating him about his decision.

"I've got a suggestion," his boss announces excitedly. "With the worship director leaving to get ordained, his salary will be unused until we replace him, and that could take a while, so I'm wondering whether to pay you with the spare salary funds for the next few months, just to give you time to discern your next steps." He pauses a moment before continuing. "It would only be possible until the end of the year, but how about it?"

"That would be amazing," Al says, smiling.

"Your replacement will still take over your current curate responsibilities," his boss clarifies, "so you'll need to step back from those as planned, but I'm sure there will be things you can cover for us, and we can watch to see what opportunities emerge."

Al gets up to leave and, as he opens the door, his boss continues. "The other thing I need to tell you is that I had a dream, before all this happened, in which you didn't leave."

It takes Al by surprise.

"You've every right to be amazed," his boss grins, a twinkle in his eye. "I only remembered yesterday, when I was looking back through my journal."

The bishop is notified and, the following Sunday, midway through a collection for his leaving gift, Al makes a surprise announcement.

Standing on a podium at the front, looking out at a packed church, Al takes hold of a microphone. "Today I'm meant to be saying goodbye," he tells them. "However, for those of you who haven't yet heard, there's been a change of plan." A murmur ripples across the congregation and Al continues, "I'm going to be sticking around for a little while longer."

A queue of people line up to speak to him at the end of the service. "I'm so pleased you've decided to stay," one of them remarks. "I knew you shouldn't be leaving," says another. "We had a hunch that it wasn't right for you to take that job," still another one discloses. "I think you should stay and serve in this city," another pronounces. "You're key to the vision for the north," says still another.

"It's funny that people didn't say this earlier!" Al says to Lucy when he gets home. "But hearing all these encouragements brings home that we've built some really special relationships here. More and more I think that being in this city, and staying in the north of England, is a significant part of what God wants for us."

The bishop takes a call from the university chaplain, the Kenyan man who is due to be moving into the St Thomas' vicarage.

"My wife and I have been praying about it," he tells the bishop, "and we really don't feel it is right for us to move from where we are."

"You might as well stay in the St Thomas' vicarage for now," the bishop informs Al. "At least until the end of the year, while the city-centre church is paying you."

Al and Lucy are delighted.

Pausing the story at this point, Lucy and Al encourage me to speak with an older couple, whose story runs in tandem. They have arranged for me to meet them the following day.

Phil and Marian are in their sixties, silver-haired, kind, gentle and softly spoken. Their welcome is warm and, plying me with freshly brewed coffee, they invite me into their sunny garden, where we sit surrounded by the fragrance of flowers and blossom.

"Take me back to the start of your part in the story," I invite them.

Following a long career in secondary education, Phil decides to train for ordination and, as his curacy is coming to an end, he is wondering what next. One option is a paid post in a rural area, some distance from the city.

"How about St Thomas'?" Phil suggests to the bishop. "After all, thanks to the vicar who's mentoring me, I've been preaching there occasionally, so the congregation already know me a little."

"You know it's a non-stipendiary post there, don't you?" the bishop replies, contemplating the idea. "So we wouldn't be able to pay you."

Phil is fully aware. "I'd be OK with that," he responds. Because he has come to the Anglican ministry late in life, he has been accepted for ordination training on the basis that he may not get a paid post at the end of his curacy.

"One idea that's been mooted is for me to give St Thomas' a special mandate, to reflect the fact it only recently survived near closure," the Bishop explains. He seems to be articulating his thoughts out loud.

Phil is aware; it's the vicar who's mentoring him who's made the suggestion. So he nods his head in agreement.

"If I can sort out a special mandate," the bishop continues, "I could license you to lead that church."

Phil feels optimistic as he leaves the meeting. But he needs to know for sure, and discusses it with Marian. "Am I being called to serve St Thomas' congregation and community? Is it a setting that will also work for you, with your caring and compassionate heart for those on the margins?"

They have a house, so accommodation would not be an issue, and their adult children are all living independently with families of their own.

"Let's pray about it," Marian suggests, and both of them feel an increasing sense of peace.

And so, in the spring of 2009, the bishop licenses Phil as the unpaid priest-in-charge of St Thomas'.

"We simply built on the foundations of those who had gone before us so faithfully," Phil explains. "St Thomas' didn't have many mature Christians in the congregation at that time, and people were hurting and wounded, so all we could do was bring healing and love."

"They felt forgotten by the diocese," Marian interjects. "We had to be so gentle with them, but we knew God had given them to us to pastor, so we just had to trust his leading."

"Evangelism was hard work," Phil tells me, "but we started to see people in the community coming to faith and then to church. And they weren't all old. We even had some students." Marian cuts him off excitedly. "And families," she adds. "We felt so encouraged when we had to provide something for the children, as their families began attending our all-age services once a month. It felt like the beginning of breakthrough into the next generation."

"My desire was to help the congregation find their vision again," Phil muses. "God had so clearly rescued the church from closure. We just wanted to continue what he had started."

"We were praying," adds Marian. "We longed for St Thomas' congregation to comprise of more than twenty mostly elderly people, and God reassured us it was achievable. Speaking through the Parable of the Mustard Seed, one of Jesus' stories in the Bible, we sensed him say that St Thomas' would become a place of refuge, a place that people would call 'home', and that our role would be to help people find Jesus and dig deep roots in their faith in him."

"Gently and gradually, we introduced changes," Phil says.

While keeping their long, proud choral history with the robed choir and sung Eucharist, a "sing along with Phil" slot introduces some more informal worship songs to Sunday services. And when a substantial bequest is received, Phil buys and installs a projector and screen to use alongside the hymn books.

"I could have spent it all on repairs to the stonework," Phil muses, "but it seemed better to invest in the people than the building."

"It's OK, Vicar," a man in his seventies remarks. "We know we've got to change to keep up with the times, so you don't need to worry about us."

Spontaneous praying is an unfamiliar concept, so Marian uses simple liturgy to facilitate prayer. "Let's prayerfully imagine walking around the local area with Jesus," she suggests. "What do you encounter?"

Scouts and schools, social housing and homelessness, all are covered in prayer. On one weekday evening, they ask God to bring a family. The following Sunday, a family walks through the doors just as the service is starting. Another time, they ask for students and young adults. The next week, a woman in her twenties walks in, already a committed Christian. "God has told me he wants me to serve this church," she says, later becoming St Thomas' first parish assistant and developing a thriving student group. Expectancy rises as answers to prayer increase.

Infant baptisms are regularly requested and Phil invites the parents to watch a short explanatory film so they understand what is involved, and several families start coming regularly to church as a result. Marian starts a multi-cultural toddler group in the church hall. Phil offers a six-week course for adults wanting to be baptised or confirmed. "I had goose bumps every time I attended," one middle-aged businessman tells him afterwards, "especially when we learnt about Jesus' healing miracles."

Significant numbers show up for special services – Mothering Sunday, Easter, Harvest, Remembrance Day, Advent, Christmas – as well as weddings and funerals.

"The demographic was gradually getting younger, and growing numbers of non-churched people were finding faith in Jesus," Marian says.

"But then we had the issue of the parish share," says Phil.

In the Church of England, every congregation pays a "parish share" into a central trust fund, designed to cover clergy stipends, pensions, diocesan building maintenance and other associated costs. It's an ancient system, a levy on the adults who regularly attend Sunday services, enabling resource-rich churches to subsidise poorer neighbouring churches in the same locality.

For years, St Thomas' has struggled to pay their parish share. For years, they have faithfully found the funds. For years, they have had no paid vicar, vicarage or other obvious financial reward in return. Yet nobody complains.

It concerns Phil that, if the congregation continues to grow, so will the parish share.

"How will they financially cope?" he asks Marian. "Very few are wealthy."

The bishop is spearheading a new initiative, enabling churches to make a generous freewill offering rather than paying a strict parish share. Phil explains it to his leadership team one Saturday morning in the spring of 2013, and the news is greeted with good humour.

Many sitting around the table have expressed concern about the injustice of the parish share system, some publicly, many more in private, and Phil is aware of the tensions in the room. But he need not have worried.

"We have raised the money in the past, so surely we can raise it again in the future?" one elderly man points out. "Doesn't God ask us to be generous with what we have?"

Phil is reduced to tears by their large-heartedness. Instead of their contribution shrinking in size, that year, their freewill offering is for the same amount as their parish share in the previous year. "Let's pay it and see what happens," they tell him.

Year on year, their giving increases, and their generosity astounds him.

As Phil's retirement fast approaches, succession planning is uppermost in his mind.

"There is sadly no funding to pay for your replacement," the bishop informs him. "I fully support you and all that you're doing for St Thomas', but the only option available is to continue your post as non-stipendiary."

Phil is deeply disappointed. With the congregation now in the region of fifty regulars and growing, he had been hoping for a bit of room for manoeuvre. "What about the conversions, baptisms, weddings, funerals and all the special services?" Phil asks gently. "Don't they count for anything?"

"Absolutely, they count," the bishop responds with a kind smile, "but I'm afraid my hands are tied, and I've got more people in the diocese than I can pay, so I'm having to be creative to balance the books."

Within a week, the bishop has sent a potential candidate to visit. She is in her late fifties, a non-stipendiary vicar in a rural parish, but it's clear from the outset that she's not the right fit.

"Let's be more specific in our prayers," Marian advises Phil, full of faith. "God knows who he wants to send to replace you when you retire."

Using the prayers and readings from a well-known monastic community, she turns one of their reflections into a prayer, asking God to send the worker of his choice, and to keep others away so that they do not have to rely on advertising or other means. "Oh God, please, more than anything else," she prays, "bring the right person, for your purposes, in this place."

Not long later, on a sunny Saturday evening in the spring of 2013, Phil is lying in the bath, and his thoughts and prayers have, once again, turned to the future.

This time next year he will have retired and his two parish assistants will have both moved on, one for ordination training and the other for further study. He knows the congregation need continuity, but he can't see where it's going to come from, not when there's no money for St Thomas' to pay for a vicar, so he starts to pray.

As Phil is praying, a simple statement comes to mind: "The army of the Lord will come to help."

Puzzled, he shares what he's heard with Marian. "Could it be God speaking?" he asks her. "Does it mean spiritual warfare is on its way? Or simply that God has people lined up?"

"Why don't we keep praying and see?" says Marian.

Phil agrees, feeling a deep sense of peace and assurance that God is in control, and also a faint spark of hope.

"Unbeknown to either of us, God was dovetailing events in a neighbouring area of the city," Marian says, "and this is where Lucy and Al will need to pick up the story again."

Later that evening, Al, Lucy and I are sitting in their living room, once again clasping mugs of tea, as I update them with what Phil and Marian have told me.

"What happened next?" I ask.

That same sunny Saturday evening, Al is cleaning the bathroom. He has just scrubbed the shower, has now turned his hand to the loo, and is praying: "Lord, you've kept us here, in this city, in this house, but I can't see clearly what's next. Please can you show me?"

And then the seed of an idea comes into my mind: "You're living in the vicarage for St Thomas'. Why don't you offer help to the church and community that St Thomas' is serving?" So he swirls bleach under the rim of the toilet seat, and begins to ponder it.

Over the following few days, as Al prays about the potential possibility with Lucy, the idea seems to take root and germinate.

"What an excellent suggestion," his boss exclaims. "I'd be very happy to release you to help. Perhaps you could do mornings there and afternoons here? See what Phil says."

Al's email is short and simple, introducing himself, explaining the situation, and concluding with an offer: "Now that I know I will be staying put – and paid – for the next few months, I'm wondering whether I can be of assistance to you, the church or the parish. I can only offer mornings and only until Christmas but, if that will help, please let me know."

When it lands in his inbox, Phil is utterly amazed at such provision. "This is a wonderful answer to prayer, incredible timing, and a hugely generous offer," he types in his response, "but it's really important that you understand the needs of St Thomas' before you commit to get involved. How about we meet for a chat?"

A couple of days later, as Phil walks Al around the community served by the church, he witnesses something of Al's compassionate heart; he remembers Marian's prayer for people to come who are God's choice; and he accepts Al's offer without hesitation.

Al's involvement with St Thomas' gradually grows and he starts leading and preaching at their Sunday services, while Lucy and the children continue to attend the large city-centre church to avoid what would be a huge upheaval if they were to move church for just a few months. Al's heart for the congregation and community also grows, and starts proving popular, but it seems very unlikely he could ever be their vicar, because how would he be paid? The bishop has told Phil, clearly and categorically, that there is no money for a stipend.

"I think Al will be in post by Christmas," Marian tells Phil confidently one night in July. "I know there's no money, but I feel sure it's in the Lord's hands."

Phil is a lot less sure. "How can we expect Al's boss to pay him a salary beyond Christmas?" he asks her.

"I don't know how it will happen," Marian says reflectively, "I just know we need to keep praying."

It is early on a Tuesday morning in August and Al is running late. He was meant to be at a 7am prayer meeting at the city-centre church five minutes ago. As he wheels his bike out of the garage, he notices a bin bag on the front doorstep. He must have missed it last night when he put the bins out on the pavement just round the corner. He doesn't have time to deal with it now; it will just have to wait until next week's bin collection.

When Lucy opens the front door later that morning, friends are coming over and she is heading out for some supplies. There, in front of her, is a bin bag on the doorstep. Wondering why Al didn't put it out for collection, she thinks nothing more of it and crosses the road to the corner shop.

On her return, she realises the rubbish has been collected and this bin bag is not going to be part of it. She cannot recall anyone saying they would be dropping off hand-me-down clothes or books for the children. She looks closely and gives the bag a prod. It is too hard to be clothes, too soft to be books. She tries to rip it open, but it's been double bagged, so she gives it a yank. When she sees what's inside, her heart rate races and her hands start to shake. There before her lies a stack of neatly bundled bread bags, all of them packed with wads of clean, crisp, clearly new twenty-pound notes.

She has never felt so scared.

Standing in the doorway, Lucy glances up and down the road. The usual eclectic queue waits at the bus stop. A young man with headphones and baggy trousers saunters past. A mum pushes a black buggy on the pavement opposite. Everybody is going about their normal routine. Nobody is concerned with the vicarage. But somebody has put this particular bin bag outside their front door.

Heading into the house, she drags the bin bag inside, calls the police, and then Al.

Al is addressing a pile of admin, when Lucy calls. "Did you see the bin bag on the front doorstep when you left the house this morning?" she asks, clearly agitated.

"Yes," he replies, "but I was in a rush, so I didn't have time to put it round the corner."

"Al," she says, her voice trembling, "it's full of cash. I've called the police. They're on their way." She pauses for air and adds a detail. "It's all neatly bundled into bread bags."

An hour passes, during which she wonders whether she and the children are safe in the house while the bin bag is in their home.

Could it be drugs money? Lucy asks herself. *Or laundered money? Or money gained through illicit ill-gotten gains? What about the local estate with its known criminal gangs? Are we now a potential crime scene?*

She breathes a sigh of relief when two uniformed police officers ring the doorbell and introduce themselves as detective inspectors.

"This is quite something," one of them informs Lucy, explaining their lost-and-found procedures. "I've never known anything like this before."

"What will happen to it?" Lucy asks them, after giving them a statement. "Is it 'finders keepers'?"

"Not necessarily," the detective inspector says. "We will need to do a thorough investigation to try and establish where it has come from, and to rule out any criminal connection. Only then can we decide what should happen to it."

The following day, the police issue a press release asking anyone with information to contact them.

Lucy is in reflective mood. "Al," she ponders aloud, "do you think the money belongs to St Thomas'? Most local people know this is the St Thomas' vicarage, don't they?"

"I've been thinking the same," Al reassures her. "I keep wondering whether it's meant for St Thomas'."

"Well, I don't think we can claim it as ours," Lucy states introspectively, "as this house doesn't belong to us."

There is momentary silence and then Al vocalises what both of them are thinking. "Do you think the money could pay my stipend, so I can become St Thomas' vicar?"

Lucy nods her agreement. "Wouldn't that be an incredible answer to prayer?"

On a dull grey day in October, Al is catching up with the Kenyan university chaplain over coffee.

"Have you heard about the bin bag?" he asks, conscious that most people connected to St Thomas' are aware of the story, but by no means all. When the chaplain shakes his head, Al watches his jaw drop to the ground in disbelief as he starts to fill him in.

"This is amazing!" the chaplain pronounces, leaping out of his seat in excitement and astonishment. "Before I moved to work at the university here, I lived in Scotland," he exclaims, leaping up and starting to pace as his words come tumbling out. "While I was there, I had a dream, but the only person I told about it was my wife."

"Go on," encourages Al.

"In my dream, I was living in a vicarage in this city, and an old lady left a bin bag outside," the Kenyan explains, grinning broadly. "She told me it was 'for the ministry' and then turned around and walked away. When I opened the bin bag, it contained more than £100,000 in cash."

"Wow!" exclaims Al, as it suddenly dawns on him, "This was meant to be your house!"

He pauses a moment, wondering whether the bin bag could really contain that sort of sum. "Do you think your dream was prophetic, given by God, ahead of time?" he asks the chaplain.

"Yes," he declares emphatically. "I feel sure it's God's provision 'for the ministry' of St Thomas'."

"Maybe we'll never know if it was an old lady who left it," Al ruminates softly. "Maybe it was an angel?"

"Perhaps it doesn't really matter?" says the chaplain.

In November, Lucy takes a phone call from the police, who are keen to come over. It's been three months since their last visit and she's feeling nervous as she plumps cushions and puts the kettle on. At least this time there's no potential crime scene sitting on the doorstep.

"We have followed our lost-and-found procedures," the detective inspector informs them, "but we're still not clear how to account for the money." Lucy is unsurprised by this news.

"We recently uncovered a local drugs ring, and we have good reason to believe that this money is connected," continues the detective inspector, "but we can't put forth our evidence without putting certain parties at risk."

"Are we at risk?" asks Lucy.

"No," the inspector assures her, "it just means that, when the leader of the drugs' ring comes out of prison, if the money is his, he might ask what's happened to it." He looks Lucy in the eye, perched on the edge of the sofa, his hands clasping the mug of coffee she gave him on arrival.

"Am I allowed to know how much was in the bin bag?" Lucy asks. She and Al have been playing guessing games about the amount.

"Sure," says the inspector, handing over a formal letter. "There were sixteen bread bags in total, all of them containing bundles of twenty-pound notes, and the total came to just over £101,000."

Lucy's incredulity is palpable. There, on the paper in their hands, is written confirmation of the amount, a sum they had never dared to comprehend, despite the chaplain's dream.

When Al phones the diocesan office, he can hear the astonishment in the voice of the young woman who takes the call. "So, you're saying that this cash appeared out of nowhere; that you're not sure of the amount; that the police are trying to trace the owner; and that, if they can't, you'd like it allocated to St Thomas'. Is that correct?"

"Yes," says Al.

"We'll have to get advice from our lawyer, you know," the woman at the other end of the phone line is in crisp and efficient mode, "and also the bishop."

The diocesan lawyer is clear. In order to eliminate the risk of reprisal and retrieval, a court order is needed. "It will legally award the money to the church," he advises, "which eliminates the risk of any comeback against you in the event of a dispute in the future."

It is two weeks before Christmas when the case comes to court.

"Do we have written evidence from the witnesses that they have no intention of claiming this money in a personal capacity?" the magistrate asks the diocesan lawyer, pausing a moment before continuing. "Subject to that formality," she informs him, "we would be happy to make a court order allocating the money to St Thomas'."

The lawyer is hasty in asking Al and Lucy for suitable signed statements. He is hoping to get the case wrapped up quickly, but there are very few available court dates left between now and Christmas.

A week later, Lucy is strapping the children into the car after a swimming lesson when she switches on her phone and is amazed to find an email from the lawyer, stating that the court order has been granted.

That same day, Al is waiting outside the bishop's office in an imposing old building when, with impeccable timing, he receives Lucy's text updating him on the latest from the lawyer. "We've got the court order," he reads. "The money has been given to St Thomas'."

"What are your thoughts about the future?" the bishop asks him, and Al shares openly of his growing heart for the congregation and community of St Thomas', the lack of funding for a stipend, and the miraculous provision in the bin bag. "It sounds like the Lord to me," the bishop declares, clearly excited. "I'm sure the Holy Spirit can work in this way."

"Irrespective of what happens to me," Al says, "St Thomas' needs some long-term commitment – from you, from the diocese, from whoever is appointed to succeed Phil." The bishop nods sagely.

They do some simple calculations. "Three years is not enough," the bishop acknowledges. "Let me find the funds to extend it to five years and let me get my team to draw up a licence agreement, so that you can become St Thomas' vicar." He contemplates what lies ahead. "Don't worry, Al," he reassures him with a gentle smile, "we will make it work."

Despite the best endeavours of those involved, the news breaks on Christmas Eve.

"It's a Christmas miracle!" declares one local newspaper. "It's a Christmas windfall!" pronounces another. It seems everyone wants good news at Christmas. "The sum involved is four-and-a-half times what St Thomas' normally pays for its annual parish share," the broadcasters declare. "The police have found no criminal link to the bin bag of cash left outside a vicarage," another one declares, "so a court has decided that the sum should be given to the church to make sure the funds are used to benefit the local community."

Phil finds himself fielding inquisitive journalists and reporters, directing them to the diocesan press officer. On Christmas Day, he is invited for interview on the BBC *World Service*, and a local ITV news channel, but he politely declines both of them.

"You were right," Phil reminds Marian, "when you said Al would be in post by Christmas." She responds with a kind and knowing smile.

The city-centre church is excited and encouraged by Al's news, and they wish him well as he says goodbye. "I knew you'd stay in this city," one old man remarks. "It's good that St Thomas' isn't being turned into a carpet warehouse," pronounces another.

In January 2014, Al is licensed to St Thomas'. Many from the regular congregation and the wider community turn up to celebrate in a special service. Their love and support are tangible.

"I want to retire at Easter," Phil informs Al later that day, "so let's aim for a seamless handover between now and then."

Phil is true to his word and, by the time he becomes priest-in-charge, Al is already established as "the local vicar", his face familiar to children in the schools and pensioners in the care homes. He has also become proficient at chairing church leadership meetings.

Visiting St Thomas' now, it is difficult to believe it used to be a church struggling in number and on the verge of closure.

Approximately one hundred come regularly – of different ethnicities, ages, life stages, socio-economic status – and numbers continue to grow. Some come with no church background and are completely new to the Christian faith. "We run an Alpha course when we can," Al tells me, "but it's always chaotic, a bit like the lives of those in this community." Others come from other churches, already Christians and new to the area. Still others come because they want to re-engage with their faith after time away from God.

The Sunday when I attend a service at St Thomas', I receive a warm welcome and am put at ease. The worship is vibrant and the teaching is Bible-based. There is a family-friendly feel, and children of all ages are free to run around. I am told there is a thriving student ministry and a creative arts-and-crafts outreach for women. People seem to relate well to each other, but what strikes me most is the depth of unity between the original congregation members and those who have arrived more recently.

"How has this been possible?" I ask Phil and Marian, who remain active in the church even in retirement. "We prayed a lot; we still do," they tell me. "But there haven't been any fancy strategies. It's always been about building on God's grace."

Al agrees. "I've always been keenly aware of the foundations laid by those who've gone before me," he explains. "If it wasn't for God's grace, I'd have nothing to build on."

"There's just one loose end," I say. "What happened to the role that you turned down? Did it ever get filled?"

"It wasn't long later, when someone suitable came along," Al explains. "She'd already handed in her notice, in faith that God would find her a new job."

"There wasn't really any gap," Lucy adds, "and she seems like a great fit for the role."

"It's a good reminder that God's in control of the details, isn't it?" I remark, and Lucy nods.

"I love telling people this story because it's just so faith building," Lucy remarks. "Perhaps in sharing it in this way, more people will realise that God really can – and does – provide in miraculous ways."

I am inclined to agree.

The struggling remnant of this church congregation has been blessed in abundance by God's provision, and so has its community. Threatened with closure, it has stayed open. Lacking in leadership, God found them an unpaid vicar who, building on the foundations of others before him, nurtured them through some significant changes. And then he produced money out of thin air, which paid for the vicar who followed.

But it has also been because of Al and Lucy taking steps of faith. The turning down of a perfectly good job on nothing more than the instinct of God's leading. The acceptance of uncertainty in the waiting that followed. The dawning realisation that they were already exactly where God wanted them. And the utterly impeccable timings throughout.

"We were fully prepared to move many miles away," Al adds, "but God has put us in a place where we are needed, and where we can learn, right where we already were."

"What about the future?" I ask tentatively.

"There is so much potential here," Al replies enthusiastically before pausing a moment to reflect on how far they have come. "I'm sure there's a long-term viable future for St Thomas' – but it will only ever be by God's grace."

CHAPTER 8

Nothing can separate us
A boy in a hammock accident (2015)

"For I am convinced that neither death nor life,
neither angels nor demons,
neither the present nor the future,
nor any powers,
neither height nor depth,
nor anything else in all creation,
will be able to separate us from the love of God
that is in Christ Jesus our Lord."

Romans 8:38-39

This story is about Jed, who was twelve years old when he had a hammock accident. It is mostly told by his parents, Lisa and Steve, and it features his sisters, Illie and Scarlett. I have known of Lisa a while – our sisters are close friends; we also work in the same sector. At the time of the accident, I was receiving regular prayer updates through a mutual friend. It was only later when I met the family in person.

"Hi Jed!" ten-year-old Scarlett announces, standing outside the bedroom door of her brother, two years her senior, "I just want a lock of your hair." She presses her ear in to listen, her right hand poised to knock, her left hand clutching a pair of kitchen scissors. But there is no response. *Maybe he's just messing about*, she thinks as she pushes open the door.

Her voice trails off as she enters the room, and she stops still in her tracks.

Jed is dangling in his hammock, which is wound round his throat. He is facing the door, his wavy ginger hair dishevelled, face pale, eyes closed, mouth open, and a line of dribble trickling from the corner of his mouth. His legs are dragging on the floor. *Why won't he stand up?* she wonders.

"Jed, if you're messing with me, this isn't funny," she exclaims, feeling concerned. "It's not a joke."

Gently, she nudges his arm. Peering at his face, she opens one of his eyes and is met by a blank unseeing stare. Putting the scissors down on the floor, she tries to lift him, but he is too heavy for her ten-year-old frame.

Without hesitation, she heads downstairs. Standing on the bottom step, she looks out across the kitchen where her dad is having his hair cut, sitting in a sea of laundry.

"I don't want to worry you, but Jed is tangled up in his hammock," she says. "He looks kind of funny, and he isn't answering me when I talk to him."

Steve leaps out of his chair, squeezes past Scarlett, and sprints up the stairs, his athletic build striding them three at a time.

Lisa is in hot pursuit of her husband, her heart racing. "Stay here and pray," she instinctively instructs Scarlett as she bounds up the stairs behind him.

It's the following morning when I hear the news. Preparing breakfast, my phone alerts me to a text from one of my prayer partners who is a trustee for the charity that Lisa recently started leading. A short while later I receive another text, this time from my sister who is close friends with Lisa's younger sister.

The gist of both texts is the same. "Please pray urgently," they read, before describing what has happened to Jed. Sitting at the kitchen table, my hands wrapped around a mug of tea, I pray aloud, asking God to save Jed's life.

Over the course of the following weeks, I'm drawn to pray regularly for this family, even though I know them only indirectly. So I'm pleased when an opportunity arises, some while later, for me to meet them in person.

Driving along a quiet road through the beautiful village that they call home, I discover their house is an attractive period property, set back from the street by a garden largely laid to lawn and bordered by climbing roses.

Lisa and Steve give me a warm welcome, ply me with freshly brewed coffee, and invite me to join them in their spacious living room, where we sit on comfortable sofas. Both in their forties, they are kind, friendly, and make me feel at ease.

"We always enjoy meeting people who prayed for Jed," Lisa says. "It reminds us of how much impact his story has had."

"Why don't you take me back to the beginning?" I invite, not knowing how the story will unfold.

By nature, Jed is more of an introvert, energised by solitude. At school he eats alone, preferring to socialise with friends in form time. At home, after school and on the weekends, he hangs out in his room by himself, reading, writing, playing games.

For months "hammock" has been at the top of his Christmas list. Last month his wish was granted, and his brand-new colourful stripy hammock is now suspended from his bedroom ceiling, nailed into a gnarled wooden beam, an original feature of the centuries-old characterful family home.

Ever the practical joker, Jed has been intent on practising and perfecting his circus flips and acrobatics, only stopping when boredom or hunger kick in.

A few weeks into January, the Christmas decorations have come down and the family are embracing the rhythm of a new year. In the kitchen, the laundry has been draped to dry around the warmth of the range, and the scent of lavender washing powder is strong in the air.

Everyone has gathered in the kitchen where they are helping to fold freshly clean clothes and bed linen, and each child is being plied with neatly stacked piles to deposit in their bedrooms and the communal airing cupboard.

Out of the corner of his eye, Steve notices his twelve-year-old son, Jed, heading out of the kitchen, a mound of clean clothes balanced carefully between both arms. His pale face, framed with wavy ginger hair, peeks over the top of the pile, watching his step as he heads upstairs to his bedroom.

Ten minutes later, Steve strolls into the kitchen. "Please will you cut my hair?" he asks Lisa.

"Sure," she replies, "if you go and get the clippers." She has been regularly cutting Steve's hair for fifteen years now, ever since they married.

Steve rummages in the drawer and locates the clippers and a comb. Returning downstairs, grabbing a towel on the way, he finds his two daughters, fourteen-year-old Illie, and Scarlett, reading quietly in the family room, and Lisa standing behind a chair pulled out from the kitchen table, poised and ready to cut his hair.

"Jed seems quiet," he mentions to Lisa. "That's probably a good thing," she jokes. His momentary thought is quickly dismissed.

Looking up from her book, Scarlett's gaze fixes on the rhythm of the clippers. She is in thoughtful mood when she announces, "I'm going to make a time capsule!" Her imagination is running wild. "I'd like a lock of hair from everyone in the family to put in it." She leaves no room for negotiation.

Leaping up from the sofa, she unearths a pair of scissors from the cutlery drawer beneath the kitchen window and heads for the stairs. "Jed's going to be first," she declares.

"Lisa, call an ambulance," Steve yells out behind him, as he takes in the scene in front of him.

The door is open and the room is illuminated from the single central ceiling light. The curtains have not been drawn and the window reveals limited light pollution in the night sky. Jed's face is pale, grey and cold. His hammock is twisted around his neck. There is vomit on the carpet.

Grabbing Jed with his left arm, Steve lifts him up to loosen the noose-like grip of the hammock, and Lisa unwraps it from round his neck and hurries out of the room to find the phone. Waves of nausea sweep over her.

Laying Jed gently flat on his back on the floor, Steve, a qualified doctor, lets his medical training kick in. He places his index and middle fingers on Jed's neck, to the side of his windpipe, but he can feel no pulse. He listens over Jed's mouth and nose for breathing, but hears no sound and feels no breath. Without hesitation, he starts resuscitation, compressing Jed's chest and breathing into his mouth. Time is of the essence. Suspended in a surreal sense of disbelief, he is acutely aware that this is not just another unconscious patient.

He vaguely hears Lisa talking tearfully to the 999 emergency operator. He is praying wordlessly, pleading with God for the life of his only son with every compression he makes.

After four or five minutes, Jed takes a single, shuddering breath. Steve is incredulous.

Once again, he checks Jed's pulse. He feels a palpable sense of relief when he detects a weak, irregular output, so he waits a moment. His breaths are slow and laboured, no more than two a minute, so Steve does some more artificial respirations. When they gradually increase in frequency, he rolls him on to his side on the carpet, and puts him in the recovery position.

"We need an ambulance," Lisa is telling the 999 emergency operator, holding the handset close to her ear. "It's my son and it's urgent." Her cheeks are wet with tears, her voice choked.

Lisa is standing on the landing at the entrance to Jed's bedroom, gazing blankly at the resuscitation taking place on the carpet. Her mouth is mechanically answering the operator's questions.

"Have I done the right thing?" Steve is asking her. "Would he be better off if we let him go?" He pauses a moment, letting parental love and professional instinct kick in.

"Please stay on the line," the operator insists.

"I can't," Lisa informs her, "I have to pray." The operator is adamant.

"OK," relents the operator, "you can pray, but you must keep the line open. Please put the handset on speakerphone on the floor so we can still hear each other."

Lisa falls to her knees on the bedroom carpet, calling upon God to come and save Jed, in Jesus' name. She doesn't care whether the operator can hear her.

Their house is set back from the road, so Lisa asks the girls to stand outside and steer the ambulance to the correct location.

Steve takes down the hammock, leaving it in a heap on the floor, and then the paramedics arrive in a whirlwind of efficiency, filling the house with their presence and paraphernalia. A consultant in the Helicopter Emergency Medical Service (HEMS) arrives a short while later as he lives in a neighbouring village, followed closely by an Accident and Emergency consultant who has come from further afield. Scarlett points each of them to the stairs, which they leap up, two at a time, their hands crammed to capacity with kit. They dovetail together, immediately getting to work on Jed, testing vital statistics and inserting lines.

A member of the ambulance crew removes the pull-up bar from the bedroom doorframe. "It's to allow unrestricted access," he explains to Steve.

Stabilising Jed's neck takes an hour, but it feels like an eternity to Lisa as she watches, waits and prays. Every precaution is taken. Eventually, encased in a neck brace and strapped to a hard board, he is carried carefully downstairs and into the crowded kitchen.

"His Glasgow Coma Scale reading is three," the HEMS consultant pronounces after testing Jed's eyes, verbal and motor skills, to determine the severity of his brain injury. He proceeds to insert a tube through Jed's mouth and into his airway, and asks the paramedics to place him on a ventilator to assist with breathing.

Steve is the only family member with the clinical capacity to understand what this means – and his frown of consternation speaks volumes.

"It's not a good prognosis, is it?" Lisa says.

"Jed is clinically dead," he responds mechanically. "His chances of survival are slim."

It is standard procedure for the police to attend an emergency incident of this kind, and six burly uniformed policemen squeeze into the house, occupying any spare space not already occupied by the family or paramedics. "We have to rule out foul play," one of them says. He holds up his identification photo card, revealing he's from the Crime Investigation Department.

Another stands on sentry duty, stationed outside the door to Jed's bedroom. "Sorry ma'am," he says, blocking Lisa's path as she tries to enter, "this is now a potential crime scene."

"But I need to get his dressing gown, pyjamas, slippers," Lisa explains, "and things he might want when he wakes up."

The policeman is adamant. "I have orders," he tells her, refusing to move.

Lisa doesn't want a stand-off. "Please," she pleads, looking him in the eye.

Reluctantly, he makes way. "Don't touch the hammock," he instructs her curtly, as she heads for Jed's wardrobe. "We'll need to remove it as evidence." He pauses a moment. "If your son dies, ma'am, we have to rule out murder and manslaughter."

Standing in the kitchen, leaning against the sink, her back to a stack of washing up, her hands shaking, Lisa sends a text to close friends and family: "Jed got his neck caught in his hammock and wasn't breathing for at least five minutes," she types. "Breathing shallow and occasional. Ambulance here. Pray for a miracle and please get others to pray."

The text soon gets passed on and their circle of support starts to grow – amongst relatives, friends, church family, neighbours, village community, Lisa's and Steve's colleagues, teachers and pupils at Jed's school, and beyond. People they will never meet are praying; some are also fasting. Most are in the UK; many are in other nations. All of them are pleading with God to bring healing to Jed – in the name of Jesus.

With the ambulance on its way, Lisa has to think on her feet about who could look after the girls.

The village church youth group is thriving. The leader is popular and pastoral. He and his wife are in their early twenties and not long married. Every week they gather together fifty teenagers for fun, fellowship and discipleship in the Christian faith.

When Lisa calls, he and his wife are hosting a youth group meeting. About twenty-five of them are beginning to pile into a large and beautifully decorated living room in the house of a church family in the village, a wood burner lit to fend off the wintry temperature outside. Hot drinks are being brewed and handed out, and they will soon start discussing a passage from the Bible.

"Please will you come and look after the girls?" Lisa's voice is trembling as she gives the youth group leader a hasty synopsis of the situation, keen to leave her daughters in capable hands. "Would you be able to take them to the hospital too?"

Without hesitation, he asks the young people present to pray for Jed, and leaves the host family in charge while he and his wife head over to help with the girls.

The waiting ambulance draws attention and word soon spreads through the village. It doesn't take long for a small crowd of onlookers to gather in the street, silhouetted by the street lights, watching and waiting in hushed whispers. Jed, strapped motionless to the hard board, is stretchered into the back of the ambulance, the medics and paramedics squeezing in around him and the equipment, cramming it to capacity.

Steve is invited to get into a police car, with Lisa in another, and both follow in the slipstream of the ambulance, blue lights flashing, sirens blaring. Watching through the windows in wonder, vehicles pull aside ahead and flow back in behind as they weave their way through the traffic, heading for the huge hospital in the nearby city.

"This is utterly surreal," Steve ruminates, more to himself than to the policeman driving the car. "It's like the parting of the Red Sea."

A team of ten are poised inside the entrance to the Emergency Department ready to receive Jed, and Steve observes an extremely efficient procedure unfolding as the police cars park up behind the ambulance. He follows on foot behind his son as Jed is carried on his hard board through the entrance. All around him there is a hive of activity and, as a fellow medic, he is impressed with what he witnesses.

He and Lisa are ushered into a side room furnished with a few easy chairs and a bland mass-produced photograph hanging on the wall. While they are waiting, a uniformed policeman enters, notebook in one hand and pen in the other, and occupies a spare seat.

"I need to take statements from you both," he informs them in a no-nonsense tone. Both comply, and Steve draws a diagram to help explain what seems to have happened.

As the policeman leaves the room, closing the door behind him, Lisa expresses her concerns to Steve, conscious of several officers sitting in the main waiting room next door. "Are they assessing whether we're acting suspiciously?" she asks.

"Possibly," Steve says, "but I was actually thinking how strange it is, that, in this day and age, the police still use tiny notebooks and small pens to take down verbatim statements."

"Jed has an anoxic brain injury," the blonde-haired paediatric neurologist explains. Her manner is kind and gentle. "His brain was deprived of oxygen, so some of his brain cells started to die before he was resuscitated." She pauses a moment to allow her words to penetrate. "We've put him into a medically induced coma," she continues. "It will protect his brain while we monitor him."

"Is that to keep his metabolism in the middle of the normal range?" Steve enquires.

"Yes, it's routine procedure after a brain injury," the neurologist replies. "We'll keep him like that for twenty-four hours and, if there's evidence of brain damage when we do the MRI scan, we'll extend it for another twenty-four hours."

Lisa and Steve are standing side by side next to Jed's bed, flimsy white cotton curtains the only privacy provided. He lies intubated, ventilated, anaesthetised and unconscious. Tubes and lines are connecting various parts of his body to different machines and monitors. His neck is encased in a brace; his head is taped down, wedged between padded supports.

"He also has some lung damage," the neurologist says, "but that's totally treatable."

The Paediatric Intensive Care Unit is located in the hospital basement, where natural light is non-existent and the sterile smell of detergent permeates the air. Jed's bed is in the corner of a ward, the three other beds occupied by children who are noticeably younger. "It's unusual to have an older child in here," remarks one of the nurses.

Scarlett is visibly shocked when she walks onto the ward and sees her big brother lying in bed, surrounded by tubes and lines.

"Don't be afraid, girls," Lisa reassures her daughters, greeting them both with a hug before turning to thank the youth group leader and his wife for getting them there safely.

Illie is measured, containing her emotions. "It's OK, Mum," she says.

"We've made a box for Jed," Scarlett announces. "It's got sweets and treats in it." Lisa smiles, and Scarlett continues, "Lots of people are giving treats to Illie and me because Jed is ill, and we've each put a third of ours into a box for Jed, so that we all get two thirds each." Lisa feels proud of such a kind gesture.

Lisa and Steve have been given a basic, cramped room a short walk along the corridor from the ward. Two single beds have been squeezed into the space, and it still contains evidence of clinical use.

Desperate for fresh air, Lisa heads out into the darkness, late in the evening. In the middle of a deserted hospital car park, she paces and prays.

It makes a huge difference to know that, two years earlier, Jed made an independent choice to follow Jesus. His name means "beloved of Jehovah".

Heading inside, Lisa confides in Steve. "I was begging God to heal Jed, pleading with him to bring our precious boy back to us as he was before," she reveals. "As I called on the name of Jesus, I became keenly aware of God's presence, and I sensed him reminding me of his love for Jed." She pauses a moment. "Deep down, I know that if Jed dies, Jesus will wrap his arms around him and carry him home."

"Promise me I won't come back to find an empty bed," Lisa says, "with the sheets changed and Jed gone." Heart in mouth, the words come tumbling out, verbalising her worst fear. She is begging the matronly ward sister in the Paediatric Intensive Care Unit.

"I promise," she reassures her. "We'll wake you immediately if Jed deteriorates." Her demeanour is kind. "You must try and get some rest," she insists.

Sleep evades her and time seems to be passing interminably slowly so, leaving Steve slumbering, Lisa returns to Jed's bedside. She wants to be with him if the worst happens.

Shortly before midnight, Lisa sends a text to close friends and family, urging them to please keep praying. Jed, she explains, is unconscious but stable. The next twenty-four hours are critical. Her text goes far and wide, and I am one of many to receive and respond to it.

The vicar from the village church visits the hospital on Monday morning. Outside, the day is overcast. Clasped in one hand is a vial of anointing oil; in the other is a Bible. Applying a principle set out in the Biblical book of James, he prays over Jed in the name of Jesus, laying a hand on his head and anointing him with oil.

"I'm going to open the church building this evening," he tells Lisa and Steve, his spectacles framing eyes wet with tears, "for anyone who wants a place where they can come and pray for Jed."

"That would be wonderful," Lisa responds, "I'm confident prayer will influence the outcome."

"I'll email everyone in the congregation," the vicar adds, "so let's see who turns up."

Lisa is not used to being on the receiving end of such kindness. It's not just the vicar; it's the wider community. She is losing track of all the offers of practical support they have received, unable to keep up with responding. If she dwells on it for too long, she feels overwhelmed.

The doctors are discussing whether to bring Jed out of his medically induced coma. His electrocardiogram readings reveal his heart rate to be on a rollercoaster ride, spiking and dipping, failing to stabilise. The decision is made to extend his anaesthetic regime.

In the evening, a junior doctor ushers Lisa and Steve into a side room and invites them to take a seat. A moment later, the paediatric neurologist arrives, clutching Jed's MRI scan results in her hand.

"This small important area of his brain has been damaged due to oxygen deprivation," she explains, holding the results up to the light and pointing specifically. "It means it's highly likely Jed will have a disability." Lisa and Steve are sitting in silence, trying to take in what they are being told. "It's impossible to say how severe it will be until Jed wakes up," the neurologist continues, "but you need to be ready for the long haul."

Late in the evening, having been urged to get something to eat, Lisa and Steve are sitting in an Indian restaurant looking back at the hospital on the opposite side of the road. The smell of curried spices is thick in the air. Their tears are mingling with the chutneys, dripping onto their poppadoms as they pick at the food in front of them.

"How are we going to cope?" Lisa calmly asks. She is thinking through how they could convert the ground floor of the family home should Jed return home in a wheelchair.

Steve is quietly doing the same and, together, they share their ideas for how the house could be adapted to accommodate Jed's disability. As the options flow, he draws diagrams on a paper napkin to try and capture them.

"We'll make it work," she assures him.

Deep in thought, fearful of the future, waiting for their curry to be cooked, Lisa sends a text, thanking people for their overwhelming prayers and love. "A small but important area of Jed's brain has died," she types. "Apparently it could turn out to be better than the scan suggests, or a lot worse. We will continue to totally adore Jed whatever the outcome, and we continue to put our faith in our saving God."

Moments later, Steve's phone pings. It's a text from the vicar. "The church building was packed," he reads. "People kept pouring in and praying for Jed all evening." His throat constricts and he cries.

❧

There is a modern house on the top floor of the hospital, near the paediatric wards, which offers rooms where parents can get much-needed rest, comforted in knowing they are under the same roof as their children. Managed by a charity, it contains kitchens, laundry facilities and a lounge area, and is in constant use. That night, a compact but comfortable en suite bedroom becomes available for Lisa and Steve's use.

The ward sister reassures Lisa once again that she will not wake up to find Jed's bed empty; that they will wake her immediately if anything changes. But sleep does not come easily.

"Let's try to sleep in shifts," Steve suggests. "One of us can sleep until 2am and then we can swap."

While Steve gently purrs, Lisa turns to prayer. Overwhelmed by the perceptible sense of God's presence in the room with her, she falls on her knees in awe.

X-rays on Tuesday morning reveal no broken bones in Jed's neck and spine; everything is as it should be. There is a tangible sense of relief when the trauma team are consulted and confirm that his neck brace and head cushions can be removed.

"We will definitely start withdrawing the anaesthetic today," the paediatric neurologist informs Lisa and Steve, "probably this evening." Lisa's heart is in her mouth. Deep down she knows they can trust God, whatever the outcome when Jed wakes up. But the prognosis seems so clear: Jed has brain damage; disability is highly likely.

Watching their son oh-so-slowly emerge from his medically induced coma is both painful and distressing.

"How is anyone meant to prepare for such unexpected disability?" she asks Steve. "Will he wake up? Will he remain unconscious? Will he be able to breathe on his own? Will he be paralysed? Will he recognise us? Will he remember what happened? Will he know where he is? Will he be his normal self? I feel I'm wrestling with so many unanswered questions."

"We just have to keep giving our concerns to God," Steve says.

"Jed is opening his eyes slightly and coughing – but sleeping most of the time," Lisa texts. "He can sometimes squeeze our hand and move his feet if we ask. That means he can understand what we're saying, and respond! We praise God for this and are so grateful. Every day with Jed still here feels like an undeserved blessing."

In the early hours of Wednesday morning, Jed starts showing signs of discomfort and the monitor reading reveals he no longer needs his breathing tube. "Thank you," he says to the nurse after she removes it. "Would you like me to wake your mum?" she asks him. "Please don't bother her," he responds. But the nurse takes no notice.

Lisa sprints across the hospital in her socks and pyjamas, finding Jed asleep when she gets there. "I've never seen anyone arrive so quickly from the parents' house," the nurse remarks with a chuckle.

"I'm just so grateful to God that he's waking up," she replies.

Lisa's two sisters have moved into the family home to look after the girls. Both of them live in other places and have families of their own.

"Why doesn't one of you sleep in Mum and Dad's room?" Illie suggests. "Then if Scarlett wakes in the night and goes to their room, she won't find an empty bed."

Everyone agrees it's a great idea, and they create an intricate pulley system to give the girls peace of mind. Each time Scarlett has a nightmare, she pulls a string, which rings a bell. Her aunt is wakened and comes to comfort her.

The girls attend school, although it's sometimes hard to concentrate. When school is out, they visit the hospital. "Jed's gradually breathing for himself now," Steve informs them late on Tuesday afternoon, observing Scarlett noticeably relax. "He's starting to show signs of consciousness."

"I'm so relieved, Mum," Scarlett later confides. "I was really worried I'd made things worse because I touched him when I found him."

"But you were key in God rescuing him," Lisa reassures her. "If you hadn't found him when you did, he might have died."

"I'm sure Jed will be OK," Scarlett asserts, "because there are so many people praying."

Lisa doesn't want to crush her fledgling faith. "We don't know whether he'll be healed," she responds, "but it's going to be OK, even if he isn't." She pauses a moment before continuing, "God doesn't owe us a healing, but he will be with us whatever happens."

Yet Scarlett is right: there *are* so many people praying. Friends. Family. Neighbours. Colleagues. Acquaintances. People they will never meet. Some near, others far away, many in different countries.

Two of Lisa's oldest, dearest friends, neither of whom lives nearby, are even now here in the hospital. "Don't come," one of them texts, "but we're in the chapel praying. Shout if you need coffee."

A senior cleric in the Orthodox Church, originally from North Africa, calls Lisa and insists on visiting Jed. "I can't *not* come," he insists. Dressed in his priestly garments, black from head to toe, including his hair and beard, he gives Jed an icon of Jesus as the Good Shepherd carrying a lamb. "Thank you," says Jed.

Close friends of the family, who live in a different town, get in touch. A friend of theirs, a midwife, was out on a lunchtime walk with a colleague when the friend and her colleague each received Lisa's latest text. Prior to that, neither of them knew the other was a Christian.

Less than a month ago, Lisa was meditating on a quote from Saint Julian of Norwich, taking it with her into the new year: "God of all goodness, give me yourself for, if I were to have anything less, I should always be in want." It has now become her constant prayer.

When Jed no longer needs constant one-to-one nursing, he is transferred to the Paediatric High Dependency Unit. He is regaining consciousness, but is far from lucid.

At times he reacts to alarming visions, clearly confused and hallucinating. He believes he has superpowers; that he can fly and, if he holds his arms straight out ahead of him, he can shoot lasers through his fingers. He becomes agitated about protecting Lisa. "Jed, I'm your mum," she tells him. "Well, that's creepy," he muses in response, clearly not recognising her.

He keeps coming out with strange phrases. "Why are you wearing a dress?" he asks his aunt. "No, I'm too handsome," he says to his other aunt, when she requests a kiss. "Burglar! Burglar!" He shouts at his dad. "Hello," he says to the youth group leader, "prepare to die!" "Cherries, lollipops and dizzle-dazzle," he announces to nobody in particular.

The doctors struggle to distinguish between how much the drugs are talking and how much might be brain damage. "Each case is unique," the neurologist states.

At one point a uniformed policeman appears on the ward, announcing that forensics have finished with the hammock and asking whether they want it back. "No thanks," says Lisa, emphatically.

Late in the evening, Lisa sends a text from their haven in the hospital's parents' house. "Thank you for your prayers," she types, explaining Jed's progress and urging ongoing prayer. "We believe God is at work! Still early days and lots of unknowns, but the medical staff say things are going far better and quicker than they expected."

In the middle of Wednesday night, when sleep is eluding her, Lisa is sitting at a table in the parents' house, scribbling notes on scraps of paper with a Bic biro. She is planning what to include in a service of thanksgiving for Jed's life, jotting down thoughts and reflections.

Gazing out the window, the lights of the city illuminating the night sky from her vantage point on the top floor of the hospital, she is contemplating an uncertain future.

It's clear that Jed is going to survive, but it's far from clear how his brain damage is going to affect him. "Will he be permanently disabled? Will 'confused and agitated' be his new normal? Will we lose our gorgeous boy as he has always been? Or will God restore him?" she writes on a piece of paper.

As a Christian, she knows God can heal Jed. She has seen enough situations where he has done the impossible, implausible, or miraculous. But she also recognises that God doesn't always answer our prayers in the way we would want; that the Bible doesn't shy away from the reality of pain and suffering.

"I'm holding this tension in my heart," she writes. "Whatever happens, I know God's love for Jed and the family is unwavering."

Jed is very disturbed and confused, particularly at night, seeing things that are not there. He keeps trying to climb out of bed, even if the spongey sides are up, hitting out at the nurses who seek to stop his escape strategies. His solid stocky build means he can pack a painful punch at anyone who comes within striking distance.

During the day he remains agitated and distressed, seeing his parents as a threat. "You're not my parents," he says, "I don't believe you." He recognises them only intermittently.

"Is this how he's going to be now?" Steve asks.

"We think the hallucinations and confusion might be due to the swelling in his brain caused by the injury, but they could be because of the drugs that have been keeping him in a coma," the paediatric consultant explains to Lisa and Steve. "It should improve in the coming weeks, although it's difficult to say to what extent."

When his mattress is moved to the floor to create a makeshift bed, Lisa and Steve decide to take turns to stay with him during the night. They sleep in a big brown armchair adjacent to the bed, swapping over at 3am. Jed crawls around, completely disorientated, bothered by the low-level light in the ward, so Steve lies next to him. When Jed is wide awake at 5am and refusing to stay in bed, Steve receives a blow to the nose and chin, and a scratch to the cheek.

On Thursday morning, the paediatric consultant takes a fresh look at Jed's MRI scan results. "The part of his brain that's been damaged means his fine motor skills are likely to be impaired," he informs Steve and Lisa. "You need to be prepared."

As the consultant walks out of the ward, Steve grabs hold of a plain piece of paper. Jed is gifted at complex origami, a skill that requires incredible dexterity. He wants to test the consultant's assertion about Jed's fine motor skills.

"Please can you make a peace crane for me?" Steve asks.

He watches his son's fingers and thumbs folding and bending the paper, creating an aeroplane with only one wing. Jed lifts his arm and tries to lob it into the air but, instead of flying, it flops straight to the floor.

A tear trickles down Steve's cheek.

On Friday afternoon, Jed is sitting on the armchair, next to his mattress on the floor. His intravenous lines have all been removed, and he is having a drink, unassisted.

"Do I really have superpowers?" he asks Lisa. "Can I really shoot lasers?" Caught out by his unexpected lucidity, she tells him he can't. "I didn't think so," he says matter-of-factly.

Soon, Jed starts to settle. When he asks to watch a movie, all five of the family lie in his bed, staring at a small screen together. But his concentration does not last long; he fails to see any film through to the end.

"I've found you a wheelchair," a young dark-haired nurse announces, pushing it up to the edge of the bed, "so you can see beyond the walls of this ward." She has a twinkle in her eye.

Lisa watches as two nurses help Jed to stand, one on each side. He is unsteady on his feet, his sense of balance gone. They lift him up and into the wheelchair. "Thank you," he says, mimicking an Irish accent, grinning when they get the giggles. "You're getting better," remarks one of them.

"Let's take you to the restaurant," suggests Steve, wondering how they will cope if Jed comes home like this. His mind is racing ahead, thinking through the adaptations they will need to make to the house.

Being away from the ward brings new-found freedom – and fun. Jed lets his sisters take it in turns to push him in his wheelchair, and is happy for them to play practical jokes. When Steve shows him the neck brace he was wearing when he arrived at hospital, he puts it on and pulls a face, pretending to be unwell. Lisa feels overjoyed to see Jed's sense of humour and quirky personality are still intact.

"Thank you for your prayers for Jed," she types in a text on Saturday morning. "They are being answered in an amazing way. He has woken up really calm and much more lucid. He's still confused for a fair part of the time, but this is huge progress."

"I really look forward to coming into work at the moment," the young dark-haired nurse confides in Lisa, "because every day I can see the strides that Jed is taking."

"Having nursed him in the Intensive Care Unit on Monday and Tuesday nights," says another, "I can't believe that this is the same boy." She has been off work since then, she explains. "The change in him is so dramatic that I got goose-bumps when I saw him this morning."

At lunchtime, the family head to the hospital restaurant to eat a Sunday roast. Lucid and cracking jokes, Jed is determined to generate laughter.

"A lot can change in a week," Lisa remarks.

"True," says Steve, "but at least he's returning to us."

Later that afternoon, he is moved to a regular adolescent ward, freeing up his bed in the Paediatric High Dependency Unit. "We're expecting a couple of sick children," one of the nurses explains to Steve, "so we need Jed's bed."

"We are so delighted to tell you that Jed is doing amazingly, especially given it is only a week and a day since his heart stopped for between five and fifteen minutes!" Lisa types in her text, early on Monday morning. "We both think we're witnessing a miracle! I feel slightly nervous to say that as it's such early days – and we need to be able to cope emotionally if he were to go backwards. But we want to publicly acknowledge what we see our loving God doing – and he's doing something extraordinary. We give God the glory."

She presses "send", and then calls Jed's secondary school. "He's improved over the weekend," she informs the school secretary. "He's doing much better now and is more himself again."

"Do you know yet when he might be discharged from hospital?" the secretary enquires.

"Not for a while," replies Lisa. "We've been told to prepare for the long haul."

During Monday morning, Jed is put through his paces. The physiotherapist observes him in action at the gym; the occupational therapist assesses his ability to do everyday tasks; the speech and language therapist gets him talking; and the psychologist says she will wait to see him in three months' time. None of them note any abnormalities.

In the Neuro Rehabilitation Unit, the neurologist wants to test Jed's manual dexterity skills and how well his hands and fingers synchronise with his eyes. "It's because the scan showed that the damage to his brain is in the part that governs fine motor movement," he explains.

He passes Jed a piece of paper. "Please can you make a peace crane?" he asks, watching as he deftly folds it into an utterly perfect origami original.

Lisa looks at Steve with incredulity.

The neurologist finds only some minor irregularities. "His short-term memory should return fully in the next few days," he informs them, "and he will feel tired for at least a couple of weeks." He is scribbling on the top of Jed's hospital notes, the dense pile of papers held together with a huge bulldog clip. "But I won't need to see him again for at least three months," he says, handing over an outpatient's appointment card.

"Are you discharging him?" Lisa asks, unable to disguise her surprise.

"Yes, he can leave hospital this afternoon," he says. "He hasn't left us anything to offer him." He pauses a moment before continuing, "Jed has either been amazingly lucky or, if you believe in it, then a higher power has been at work."

"We go with the latter," says Steve emphatically, and Lisa nods her head in agreement.

"Thank you for being such an amazing support to our family through these challenging last eight days," Lisa types in her text. "We are overjoyed to pass on more amazing news to you . . . Jed can go home today! Woohoo! We are praising God for his grace and mercy towards us and our darling Jed, and also for putting such an incredible network of family and friends around us to support us, including many dear people whom we have never met in person. Thank you!"

"You may find you get institutionalisation culture shock," a fellow parent warns Lisa and Steve as they pack their bags and say goodbye to the place that has been home, and the people who have been family, for the past eight days.

Her words ring true when returning to the family house brings an abrupt re-entry into reality. All around them, friends, acquaintances, neighbours and colleagues have been carrying on life as normal. It feels incongruous.

Lisa's sisters' head home to each of their respective families and the girls adapt to having their parents around again, leaving the family to rest, recover and recuperate.

It's not just Jed who's tired.

Lisa is in the kitchen when she answers the phone. "I've just called the hospital for an update on Jed's progress," explains the police sergeant at the other end of the line, clearly confused, "only to discover he's been discharged."

"Yes, that's right," says Lisa. "Would you like to speak to him?" She catches him off guard.

Jed has a short conversation with the sergeant before passing the handset back to Lisa. "I don't have any more questions and the case will be closed," the sergeant says, "so all the best."

Two weeks on from the accident and Jed is back at school, initially mornings only, but building up to full days by the end of the week!

Unbeknown to Lisa, one of the Christian teachers has been forwarding her text updates to the whole staff team. "The teachers in this school would do anything for your family as a result of what you've shared in your texts," one of them confides to Lisa.

God has been using her texts to witness in ways she could never have envisaged.

Three months on from the accident and the village church is packed to capacity. Warm spring sunshine is pouring through the double doors and lighting up the stained-glass windows on either side of this ancient building. Everyone has gathered to participate in a service of thanksgiving for Jed's life. There is standing room only behind the back pews.

Sitting at the front, with his parents and sisters, is Jed. He keeps glancing over his shoulder to see who is here, utterly amazed that so many people have come in his honour.

"You will have noticed that we have chosen to have a thanksgiving service today, rather than just a party." Lisa has stepped into the pulpit at the front and is speaking into a microphone. "This is because we want to publicly acknowledge that God has been with us in this situation."

"Thank you so much for coming today," she continues. "It's a very humbling experience to be as in need of the kindness, love, care and prayers of so many others as we have been in the weeks since Jed had his accident. It has been genuinely overwhelming – in that it has almost been difficult to know how to cope with, and process, it all."

Her voice chokes, as she specifically thanks those present – relatives, friends, church family, neighbours, colleagues, local community, medical staff, acquaintances, strangers – mentioning some of them by name. "To be vulnerable before others is, perhaps, part of what makes us human," she suggests to those listening. "Being on the receiving end of so much prayer and kindness over these last three months, I can tell you, makes a huge difference."

On the back of the order of service are two photographs of Jed. One shows him the day after the accident, taped, wired and tubed; the other, taken just over a week later shows him grinning at the camera.

"We give thanks to all of you," Lisa says, "but we give thanks, above all, to our loving God." She pauses a moment to open her Bible at Romans chapter 8. "For I am convinced," she reads, "that neither death nor life, neither angels nor demons, neither the present nor the future, nor any powers, neither height nor depth, nor anything else in all creation, will be able to separate us from the love of God that is in Christ Jesus our Lord."

As one of the many who prayed for Jed during the days after his accident, meeting him now is a privilege. He is a kind and caring, warm and friendly, witty and generous young man. He clearly cares about those on the margins; the people who others might overlook, and he has a wide and supportive network around him.

"Of course I want my story to be told," Jed tells me, a twinkle in his eye. "God saved my life and I want everyone to know!"

Yes, his heart stopped, and the scan showed brain damage, but there has been no indication of any cognitive deficits, and all his subsequent checks-ups have given him the all-clear.

"We are so grateful for Jed's life," Lisa reflects. "Nothing can separate him, or us, from God's love."

CHAPTER 9

Holding onto a prophetic promise
A man with blood cancer (2017)

"Weeping may stay for the night,
but rejoicing comes in the morning."
Psalm 30:5b

This story is about a man called Henrik, and his journey with blood cancer. A lot of it is told by his wife, Inger. It also features their son Melker and daughter Harriet, who are twins. I have known of the family a while – my longstanding friend and prayer partner is godmother to Melker. During Henrik's illness, she was giving me regular prayer updates. It was only later when I met the family in person.

Henrik is sitting on the edge of a metal-framed hospital bed, his bare feet planted firmly on the floor. Wearing only a pale, patterned, open-backed gown, he leans forward, elbows on knees, hands cupping his clean-shaven chin, wondering what to expect. Fit and healthy for a man in his forties, he is awaiting the results of a mandatory preoperative blood sample, ahead of routine surgery.

He looks up as the surgeon strides purposefully towards the bed, his white coat crisp, a clipboard of papers gripped firmly in his hand. "I've just been analysing your blood test results and we're not going to be operating on you today," he announces, his eyes full of compassion, "because your blood sample has revealed you've got no immune system."

Henrik's hazel eyes widen in astonishment, and he glances through his dark-framed glasses at Inger, his wife, who is sitting in a leather armchair beside the bed. Stunned, she reaches out to hold his hand.

"Whenever there's an infection, inflammation or injury in the body," the surgeon continues kindly, "a person's white blood cells travel through the bloodstream to the site in need, where they help the immune system keep the person fighting fit." He pauses a moment to make sure Henrik is following, before continuing. "In your case, your white blood cell count is almost nil, which means your body wouldn't be able to fight if the surgery should lead to an infection."

Henrik struggles to digest such shocking news. "Why's my immune system not working?" he asks.

"It could be a type of blood cancer, like leukaemia," the surgeon explains gently, "but a specialist haematologist will need to do tests."

As his words sink in, so does an intense sense of disbelief.

Henrik and Inger, both Swedish by birth, met, married and moved to the UK nearly two decades ago. Ten years later, together with a group of others, they volunteered to "plant" a new church in the east side of the vast cosmopolitan city that they call "home".

Sent out from a large, well-known flagship church, the team's task has been to establish a new congregation in what is a socially mixed and largely deprived area. The group have worked well together, bonding over blood, sweat, tears, time and hard graft, in ministering to the community and introducing people to the Christian faith.

Early on in the life of the new church, its members' elected Henrik into a couple of voluntary leadership positions – one with legal responsibility for the church's financial affairs; the other for the repair and maintenance of the fabric of the church building and its contents – and he has embraced both roles with open arms. By night, this dominates his time. By day, he works long hours as a director at an international development bank, commuting every day between home and the commercial district in the centre of the city. Meanwhile, Inger is in charge of operations for the church. Their twins, son Melker and daughter Harriet, are preparing to take the eleven-plus exam. Suffice to say, family life is full.

When Henrik starts feeling more tired than normal, he simply blames it on busyness.

"It's just unbelievable, but we've been told that Henrik has acute myeloid leukaemia," Inger types into her phone. "Those two words, 'Henrik' and 'leukaemia', just don't go together. He's never had a sick day in his life. Please pray."

She is sitting at a small table in a café near the hospital, watching through the window as snowflakes fall, slowly and steadily, settling into a thick white carpet which covers the ground. Re-reading what she has written, she presses send, and her message goes out to a self-selecting group of friends and family. Some are local, others further afield, and many in different countries. All are Christians who care for Henrik.

One of them is my longstanding friend and prayer partner, who is one of Melker's godparents. "Perhaps we can pray together for Henrik's healing," she suggests, and I agree.

Over the ensuing months, I'm drawn to pray regularly for this family, even though I know them only indirectly. So I'm pleased when, later, I'm given the opportunity to meet them in person.

Locating their home in the dark, I find an attractive town house in a city suburb, curtains suggesting warm lighting hidden behind, and I park up outside. Inger welcomes me in, and invites me through to a spacious kitchen-diner where I find a seat at a large table.

"There are so many people who prayed for Henrik," Inger tells me. "It's always encouraging to meet them."

"Why don't you tell me what happened?" I ask.

Inger is sombre as she drives home from hospital on autopilot.

When her sister calls from Sweden, she howls down the phone. "I really hope the doctors have got the right man," she sobs, "and that the test results don't belong to someone else." She pauses to sniff. "It's just so hard when there's no tumour, no X-ray, no visible evidence, nothing – and I don't know how I'm going to tell the twins that their dad has leukaemia. It all feels so surreal."

And then she recalls an incident from five weeks ago:

It is Maundy Thursday and Inger has headed to church for a special early evening service. Entering through big red double doors, the church is light and airy. Wooden chairs have replaced pews. Colourful bunting strings a zigzag line back and forth, criss-crossing the ceiling between the bright white painted balconies on either side of the building. A large, empty wooden cross leans back against the altar.

In memory of Jesus' last supper with his disciples on the original Maundy Thursday, the congregation take Holy Communion, sharing bread and wine together. The service is quiet and reflective, and Inger is deep in thought as the proceedings conclude. Looking up from her seat, she notices a middle-aged woman approaching. Tears are trickling down her cheeks, bringing with them streaks of the vivid bright blue eyeshadow that cakes her eyelids.

"Inger," the woman greets her breathlessly in a strong inner-city accent, "I've just felt prompted to pray for your family." She pauses a moment, hesitating. Inger, as someone in a paid position on the church staff, recognises her as a member of the congregation, but they have never spoken.

Unable to hold back the words that are bubbling beneath the surface, the weeping woman suddenly exclaims, "Such a hard day is coming. So hard!" Her eyes are full of compassion; her tone kind. She has Inger's full attention. "But you must hold on," she continues, "because a day of joy is coming."

Inger's back straightens in her seat, her heart racing and panic rising as she tries to digest such a shocking pronouncement.

Thanking the women, she seeks out a colleague who knows her, and asks his advice. "How can I know if it's authentic?" she asks him. "How can I test it?"

"She's a genuine Christian with a recognised prophetic gifting," he assures her gently, "so don't dismiss what she's said, but do pray into it and ask God to show you whether it's of him."

"Perhaps it's a warning, sent in advance to guide and encourage us?" Inger muses, deciding to heed his advice.

"It could be," he says, nodding.

Five weeks on, it now makes sense.

In the three days since the devastating discovery that Henrik's immune system has disappeared, he has been prodded, probed and poked in the bid to secure a diagnosis. Like a caged bird, desperate to escape, he pleads to be allowed a brief reprieve from hospital, and reluctantly the haematologist concedes. She, too, is in her forties with children of a similar age to Melker and Harriet, so her empathy is strong, but she is also aware of the dangers. "Going home is at your own risk," she declares, signing the release form with a flourish, "but you'll need to come in each morning for meds and bloods." She smiles as she shakes Henrik's hand. "Enjoy the freedom while you have it," she encourages him.

The timing is perfect. It is a public holiday weekend; the sun is shining and the sky is an iridescent blue. The eleven-year-old twins watch in wonder as their dad stands in the hallway of their home and, looking into the mirror on the wall by the front door, pulls a facemask over his nose, mouth and chin, and then puts on gloves.

"Why are you doing that?" asks Harriet.

Henrik's voice is muffled as he replies, "It's to stop me getting an infection, which might make me more poorly," he explains, his eyes twinkling at her from behind his glasses as he peers over the top of the mask.

Harriet gets the giggles. "You look funny," she pronounces.

Keeping the children informed, using simple and reassuring language, is important to Inger, and she has already made their school aware of the situation. "Better safe than sorry," she says, catching Henrik's eye and bundling the children out of the door.

Heading to the Royal Park not far from home, they meander together along tree-lined paths. Henrik and Inger hold hands; the children chase each other as they head towards the playground and boating lake, stopping in their tracks only when they catch a glimpse of a red deer in the distance. People are out in force, peeling off layers of clothing, enjoying the sunshine and sweeping views across the river to the city's cathedral and beyond.

After the bank holiday, Henrik is admitted to hospital for a month. "It feels as though I'm standing at a harbour, looking out to sea," he says to Inger, lying in his hospital bed and leaning back against the pillows propped up against the headboard. "Tomorrow, I will board a boat, bob on the waves, and embark on a voyage into the unknown."

"We'll all be watching from the shoreline, willing you to be well," she reassures him gently, squeezing his hand and smiling supportively, "and Jesus will be with you in the boat."

Acutely aware of his sterile environment, he sleeps fitfully and wakes to the faint smell of antibacterial cleaning fluid and the clinking of breakfast crockery being wheeled into the ward. When Inger arrives later in the morning, her positivity shifts the atmosphere. "Let's find the hospital chapel and commit this whole medical process to the Lord," she suggests.

Back in bed, a nurse of portly proportions pops her head around the privacy curtain which guards his bed. "Are you ready?" she asks cheerily, rolling in a wheelchair to take Henrik down to the operating theatre. "I certainly am," he responds.

During the procedure, he watches in wonder as a consultant inserts the extended catheter into a vein in his left arm. "It's called a PICC line," she informs him. "It's perfect for patients like you, requiring intensive chemotherapy over many months."

"I hope it won't take many months," Henrik replies with a smile, looking down at the line entering his arm.

Back in his room, it is hooked up to an intravenous drip. Every day, twice a day, the chemotherapy is injected into his system. Within days, his bone marrow is suppressed and, despite optimistic predictions, it fails to regenerate. Instead of developing red blood cells to carry oxygen, white blood cells to fight infections, and platelets to help with blood clotting, the stem cells in his bone marrow are decimated and all his blood levels start to decline.

"Your only option is two blood transfusions," the consultant haematologist explains clinically, "one to increase your red blood cells; the other to increase your platelets."

"Inger," Henrik whispers to his wife, "the image of a small boat on open seas seems more real than ever now, don't you think?" She nods her agreement.

Henrik's chronic tension headaches caused by work-related stress, disappear with the enforced rest. But in their place his temperature soars, nausea sets in and so does a virulent fever. One moment he is shivering, the next he is sweating profusely. "As you have no immune system of your own, we have to treat this extremely seriously," the consultant advises. "Our absolute priority is working out the source of the infection that's causing this."

"Please ask God to protect Henrik," Inger urges the prayer support group, "and to give wisdom to the doctors."

Melker and Harriet are rapidly approaching the end of primary education. Both are bright children and, earlier this year, they successfully passed the eleven-plus exam, securing places at a popular secondary school. As a family, they have committed to relocate to the school's catchment area, a suburb in the south-west of the city. It will mean leaving the church and community that they have grown to love, but they know it is the right next step for them.

Inger is holding her breath. The people wanting to buy their house have had to back out, and the landlord of their potential new rental property has changed his mind about letting it out.

"Please pray I find the right home for our family," Inger asks the prayer support group, acutely aware of the decision-making responsibility she is currently carrying solo.

"If we can find a donor who is a perfect match, then we will give you a stem cell transplant after your second cycle of chemotherapy," the haematologist informs Henrik. She seems optimistic it will be possible. "Meanwhile, your white blood cell count is completely static, so there's nothing we can do."

His fever ebbs and flows, and the medical team keep changing tack with the antibiotics as the bacteria show resistance and his body battles to fight the unknown source of infection.

"I feel like I'm being driven along one of those endless, straight, desert roads through the USA," he confides in Inger, "where the scenery stays the same for days at a time."

"Let's pray that your time in the desert isn't a day longer than needed," Inger replies.

It becomes the little things that break the monotony. Whenever Henrik craves a change of scene, Inger pushes him out of the ward in a wheelchair, and they pause by a window to watch the clouds scud past in the sky. Every evening, they nurture their tradition of "family time" when the twins call Henrik on Skype and they talk together about their day, Harriet always excited, Melker more matter-of-fact. Each Sunday, Henrik listens in to an online church service, keen for Christian community from afar; if one of the hospital chaplains is willing to provide bedside Holy Communion, even better.

"I'm only just holding onto my hairline," he jokes with the children as they present him with a farmer-style tweed flat cap to cover his scalp. "We chose it ourselves," Harriet declares with a grin.

Inger is accustomed to her husband travelling away on business, but having him in hospital is entirely different. Henrik normally handles the family finances, but now this, and other household tasks, are falling to her to manage.

When she receives a call from the letting agent, she is delighted. "The landlord of the house you like has decided to offer an acceptable compromise," he tells her. "You and Henrik should get ready to sign the contract."

"I'm praying that the finalising of the paperwork falls on a day when Henrik is well enough to join me," she tells him, feeling grateful to God for this turn of events.

The sky is swollen, leaden and grey, torrential rain is clattering onto the hospital roof, thunder is rumbling in the distance, and lightning keeps cutting zigzags through the clouds. It is meant to be mid-summer, but the weather is not obliging.

Virulent fevers are spiking through Henrik's body, emulating the storm outside. Two bone marrow biopsies in less than two days have left him weakened. "It's the only way we can work out why your white blood cell count is still so low," the consultant informs him.

Henrik feels dreadful, but he makes a conscious decision to be upbeat and positive, and to keep praying and trusting in God.

When the biopsy results are revealed, Henrik is devastated. His body has taken an enormous battering, but the first round of chemotherapy has spectacularly failed; a second round will start tomorrow using a different drug. "I don't know whether I'll be able to face another month in hospital," he confides in Inger. "All the waiting and uncertainty is just so difficult."

He has now developed a nasty chesty cough which, compounded by the fever, keeps him awake at night. "We believe you have a fungal infection in your lungs," the consultant advises him, "so we'll need to do a CT scan and a bronchoscopy to investigate." He pauses a moment, before continuing. "You may even have a superbug, given how long your fever has been raging."

Harriet holds out hope that Henrik will be home for Father's Day. In faith that her prayers will be answered affirmatively, the night before she lovingly bakes a chocolate cake. Flour and sugar stickily cover almost every surface of the family kitchen; assorted used utensils are randomly stacked in and around the sink; and an appetising aroma fills the air as the cake rises in the oven.

There is excitement when Harriet draws the curtains and finds sunshine pouring through her bedroom window. Leaping out of bed, she skips downstairs two at a time, and races into the kitchen where Inger is standing at the counter, pouring cereal into a breakfast bowl.

"Please can we make a Father's Day picnic?" she asks her mum enthusiastically. "We can collect Dad from hospital and take him to the park with us." Not wanting to curb her eagerness, Inger responds positively. "A picnic is a lovely idea, but I can't make any promises that your dad will be well enough to eat it," she cautions.

When they arrive at the hospital, Henrik is hooked up to an intravenous drip, so they settle into seats crammed to capacity along each wall of the waiting area. A pile of out-of-date celebrity gossip magazines are stacked on a low-level wooden table in the middle of the room. Once he is finally free, weak, weary and unable to carry his own body weight, Inger pushes him in his wheelchair to a corner of the hospital café, where they unpack their picnic onto a newly disinfected table.

It is not what Harriet had envisaged, but it is enough. "We love you, Dad," she tells him with a grin as she unwraps the cake she has baked. "Happy Father's Day!"

Henrik responds with a wan smile. When he looks in the mirror, he sees a skin-covered skeleton, looking close to death. He feels dreadful.

Sitting at a table in the window of a café near home, Inger and an older lady from church are catching up over coffee, and watching people walking past along the pavement outside. Suddenly, the older lady waves, the doorbell tinkles, Inger looks up, and in walks an elegantly dressed woman in her twenties, her hair swept up in a stylish chignon.

"This is my niece," the older lady explains, introducing her to Inger, and pulling an extra chair up to the table. The conversation meanders and then, "We'd love to buy a house in this area," the niece reveals, "but it's hard to find something suitable."

Inger's ears open. "How many bedrooms do you want? What sort of style home are you after? What's your price bracket?" she asks.

The niece's answers describe Inger's and Henrik's family home. "We still don't have a buyer for our house," Inger informs her. She pauses a moment, "Would you like to come and view it?"

Within a week the niece makes an offer, which Inger and Henrik accept, thanking God for his provision.

"Do you understand how seriously ill your husband is?" the consultant asks Inger, looking her in the eye with compassion and kindness. They are standing out of earshot, near the door to Henrik's hospital room. "I'm afraid you really need to prepare for the worst," he continues, his tone serious. "You also need to prime the children."

Inger struggles to absorb what she is hearing. She knows the likelihood of death is ever present. In the two months since Henrik's diagnosis, she has seen several patients arrive in an ambulance and leave in a hearse. It is little wonder that there are no shared wards. How would morale be maintained on such a slim survival rate?

Practically, they prepare for the worst, openly discussing death, writing wills, putting funeral plans in place. But spiritually, they prepare for the best, choosing to hold onto God's prophetic promise given to them ahead of time.

"I'm asking God to give you a future beyond this illness," Inger confides in Henrik. "He warned us a hard time was coming, but he also encouraged us it would be followed by joy, so I keep reminding him of that promise."

"Is Dad going to get better?" Melker asks, his eyes welling up with tears.

"My heart tells me he's going to make it, darling," Inger reassures him, reaching out to hold him close, "but I could be wrong."

Inger is methodically packing up the house, room by room, drawer by drawer, item by item. Some spark joy; others sadness. She sorts and sifts, sitting in a sea of bubble-wrap and boxes, recalling times when the twins were little. Memories emerge in unexpected objects – meshing together in touch, sight and smell – each one catching her off guard.

It's more difficult than she expected to do this on her own, and she frequently feels tearful.

Henrik is a loyal employee who has given many years' service to the bank. When he fails to return to work after the routine surgery, his deputy steps up to become acting director in his place. The bank's health insurance policy kicks in, and he remains on the pay roll, receiving a reduced but regular salary. It is enough to cover the family's outgoings each month.

"I feel so grateful for a supportive employer," Henrik confides in Inger.

"Me too," she replies. "It's such a relief not to have any serious financial concerns."

"Good news!" Inger cannot contain her elation as she types a message for their prayer support group, "Henrik has been fever-free for three days, and his white blood cell count is normal! For the first time in two months, they are letting him come home! We are elated!"

Henrik is delighted. He yearns for release from the confines of his hospital room – even if only momentary. Harriet squeals with delight when Inger leads him by the hand through the front door, Melker greets him with a grin, and suddenly it is the smallest and simplest things that matter. Sharing family food at the kitchen table. Tucking the children into bed with a book. Falling asleep in Inger's arms. Attending the celebration ceremony to mark the twins' last day at primary school. Re-enacting the Father's Day picnic, this time in the park. Swimming when he feels strong enough.

"Is there any chance I might be well enough to travel to Sweden?" Henrik tentatively asks his medical team.

Normally, they fly as a family to visit their Swedish relatives each summer. But this year, the twins are due to travel, accompanied by their grandparents, while Inger and Henrik stay behind to move house. The day the children are driven to the airport is particularly poignant; they will never return to the only home they have ever known.

A fortnight later, Henrik waits while two doctors discuss his case and double-check his white blood cell count. "Given your immune system has returned to near normal, I think we can clear you to fly," one of them says. "What matters most is that you regain weight and muscle strength, ready for a stem cell transplant, so make sure you use the time to rest." The following day, they fly.

When Harriet wakes to discover her dad asleep in bed – in his parents' house in Sweden – she throws herself on him in delight. Melker is more muted. "Are you really meant to be here?" he asks with incredulity. "I sure am," Henrik reassures him. "I wouldn't be here if the doctors hadn't let me come, and I plan to make the most of it."

"Up to twenty per cent of patients do not survive a stem cell transplant," Inger reads, "and there's only a fifty per cent chance of survival after the first few months." The statistics are sobering. The stakes are high, the side effects significant, and the likelihood of rejection substantial. It would be easy to panic, but she turns instead to prayer, and the seed of an idea starts to germinate.

"What would happen if I call a day of prayer and fasting for you, before your transplant?" she asks Henrik. "Be bold," he says, encouraging her to go for it. Before doubt can set in, she issues an invitation to their prayer support group. "You can fast from anything and pray from anywhere," she types, "but we will host an open house for anyone local who wants to join us."

My prayer partner and I are amongst more than one hundred people dotted around the world who join in prayer for Henrik on the day that Inger sets aside. We are full of faith for God to do great things. Expectations are exceeded, not just with us, as God's presence is made manifest amongst many of those praying.

"I feel as though I'm in safe harbour having just undertaken a dangerous voyage on the open sea," Henrik confides in Inger, "but I also feel equipped to venture out in the boat again."

"Your white blood cell count is good and your temperature is perfect, but it's best to go into a stem cell transplant with as few cancerous cells as possible," the haematologist advises Henrik and, once again, an intravenous drip starts depositing chemotherapy drugs into his system. He and Inger pray in the hospital room, asking God to make it a "fear-free zone", and they feel a tangible sense of peace.

But then he spikes a fever, his temperature soars, his body is wracked with shivers and shakes, and it becomes a waiting game, a battle against the odds. For the following fortnight, Inger's messages to the prayer support group echo the peaks and troughs of an emotional rollercoaster ride.

And then, "Total surprise! Henrik turned up on the doorstep tonight! The doctors have let him come home! His fever has gone. His white blood cell count has gone up. He'll be here now until his stem cell transplant next month. Thank you for your amazing faithfulness in praying."

By the time an international donor organ registry reveals an almost perfect stem cell match, the twins have started secondary school; the nights are drawing in; and golden-brown leaves are falling from the trees to create a crunchy outdoor carpet, which Henrik kicks through on his daily walks in the nearby park.

Ahead of the stem cell transplant, Henrik is hospitalised for a further round of chemotherapy. "It's to prepare your body by stopping your bone marrow producing new blood cells," the haematologist explains.

"Oh God," Henrik prays, Inger beside him, "I know there are risks, probabilities and percentages that lie ahead, but I also know, with utter certainty, that I am your beloved child and you hold me in your hands. Thank you for giving me hope and peace. Please protect me now, in Jesus' name."

"I'm amazed at how well you look," one of the nurses remarks with a smile.

"I've got many people praying for me," Henrik explains.

The stem cell donor is a young German man who, in preparation, is given medication which causes severe bone pain. "What self-sacrifice," Inger remarks, "to go through that for a stranger." The donated blood is centrifuged to separate it into its component parts, and the white blood cells are immediately couriered, by air, to Britain, all seven million of them.

The transplant procedure involves a simple blood transfusion, but Inger is praying. She knows it might look simple, but it could become complicated. With all the faith she can muster, she asks God to make the new stem cells safely graft.

"Today is Day Zero," she writes to the prayer support group. "A new beginning; a new blood type; eventually, a new immune system. But first we have to watch and wait for one hundred days. Please keep praying!"

Expectations are raised, only to be dashed when Henrik develops an indescribably sore throat. "Your mouth is covered in white spots and ulcers," the consultant states soberly, peering into Henrik's throat with a miniscule mirror. "It's an infection, so it's treatable with antibiotics," she continues, jotting down notes on her clipboard. "But it's an entirely normal reaction to the transplant, and it shows the stem cells are trying to graft, so I'll just need to monitor it."

"Mum," Melker says thoughtfully, "when will Dad next need to go back into hospital?"

They are eating breakfast, the sun streaming through the window, carving long shadows across the table. Henrik came home five days ago as soon as his white blood cell count started to show signs of recovery, but his frame is skeletal, his appetite has disappeared, and all he wants to do is sleep.

"Hopefully never!" Inger replies with a smile, her optimistic outlook thinly veiling an acute awareness that this is unfamiliar territory. "We just have to watch and wait for one hundred days, to see whether his body accepts the new stem cells and develops a new immune system."

Unfortunately, she speaks too soon.

Within hours, Henrik's skin and eyes erupt in painful itchy rashes; his throat remains unutterably sore; and waves of nausea bring surges of retching and diarrhoea that leave his abdomen in agony. Food, water and immuno-suppressant medication keep being vomited up soon after swallowing; preventing dehydration becomes of paramount concern. A bucket is never far from his side; it is being used more frequently than anyone would want.

"These symptoms are common with bone marrow transplant patients," the haematologist explains when Inger asks for advice. "It's called graft-versus-host disease, or GVHD, because there's a battle going on between the donor's cells which are trying to embed and Henrik's cells which are trying to fight back."

In the long weeks that follow, Henrik is in and out of hospital, back and forth to the bathroom, up and down in his emotions. Inger struggles to see him become a shadow of his former self, but she keeps turning her concerns into prayers, calling on God for healing, in Jesus' name. She also turns to Christian worship music as an antidote to discouragement, and the lyrics shift her focus onto Jesus.

It's more of a struggle for Henrik, especially when he starts to lose his hearing. He has been deaf in his left ear since birth, but any audible range in his right ear seems to slowly disappear.

"I can hardly hear you," he confides in Inger, choking back the tears. "I'm at such a low ebb, I don't know how I'm going to continue."

"We're not going to pretend it's easy," Inger tells the prayer support group. "We're both worn out, and Henrik still has such a long way to go. But we know it's not our situation so much as our experience of God's presence which makes the difference. The Bible tells us nothing can separate us from the love of God, so we both have no fear of the future."

Several significant annual celebrations fall during the one hundred days, and each one seems particularly poignant this year. Thanksgiving sees them gather around the kitchen table, their faces illuminated by flickering candlelight as they tuck into roast turkey and all the traditional American trimmings. "I'm thankful that we can be together as a family," Harriet announces. "I'm thankful that Dad is still here," adds Melker. Henrik's birthday is more muted than usual. "I really don't feel like celebrating," he confesses as he blows out the candles on his cake. Christmas comes and goes, stripped back to its bare bones for once. The New Year slips in quietly, a new calendar announcing the arrival of January. "Last year was bitter-sweet," reflects Inger. "It's taught us that there's no place God will lead us where he won't also sustain us, and we take his faithfulness with us into the coming year."

With each successive bone marrow biopsy, five in total, one every twenty days, there are invisible signs of positive progress: Henrik's blood cells are increasingly produced by the donor's bone marrow; his white blood cell count is consistently good; and he develops a brand-new immune system, which independently learns to recognise and fight cancerous cells. The leukaemia heads into remission, and he is incrementally weaned off the immuno-suppressants, which cause the hideous side effects to slowly start subsiding.

When he reaches the one-hundred-day milestone mark, his recovery is still a work in progress, his restoration far from complete. "But you're now a bone marrow transplant survivor," a middle-aged nurse informs him, a twinkle in her eye.

The occupational health doctor, based at the bank where Henrik works, keeps in regular contact. "We want to see you fighting fit and back at work as soon as possible," she reassures him, when she calls for an update on progress.

She has to follow strict protocol, completing paperwork each time Henrik's return date gets postponed. She does not want to worry him, but his test results are concerning.

"It's so frustrating," he confides in Inger, "I want to be well enough to return to work."

"Because of GVHD, you're not absorbing nutrients properly, which is why, no matter what you eat, you're losing weight," the haematologist explains. Henrik has come into her bright white clinic for a regular check-up appointment. It smells faintly of furniture polish and he is sitting on a soft-cushioned, hard-backed chair in the centre of the room. The single lightbulb in the ceiling shines in defiance at the winter gloom outside. "There's only one type of treatment which won't negatively impact your long-term prognosis," she tells him, "but it's not currently funded by the NHS." She pauses a moment to check Henrik is following her before continuing, "It would mean weekly injections for up to two years, but it's had good results."

"Could we ask the NHS to fund it for me?" Henrik asks, but the consultant's face says no before she even opens her mouth.

"Sadly not," she says. "It's a huge sum of money, and only six leukaemia patients have ever received it at this hospital, and very few globally."

"Maybe I can ask the bank's health insurance company to fund it then instead?" Henrik suggests.

"It's definitely worth a try," the consultant concedes.

What follows is a waiting game as days turn into weeks and then months. "I feel forgotten," Henrik sighs.

"Sometimes delays are God-ordained," Inger reminds him. "Let's keep claiming his prophetic promise that a day of joy will come, and let's pray for God to get the glory while we wait."

And then an email arrives. The insurance company have agreed to fund eighty per cent of the cost of the treatment for an initial ten-week course. Henrik is ecstatic.

At the beginning of Lent, the family's new church announces a three-day food fast. Located not far from where they now live in the south-west of the city, they are slowly starting to get involved and make friends.

"What amazing timing to have this opportunity, right here, right now!" Inger declares. "We all need God to bring breakthrough."

On the final evening, Henrik agrees to join her at the church where thirty people have gathered together. The building is light and airy, the stained-glass window above the altar beautiful, even against the backdrop of the night sky. Wooden chairs have replaced pews and, this evening, they are set out in a circle. The atmosphere is expectant. Almost all those present have been fasting for the previous three days.

"Please can we pray for you?" a smartly dressed middle-aged woman asks Henrik, and he gladly accepts. Before he knows it, he is enveloped by kind and caring Christians standing around him, some of whom lay hands on him for healing as they pray powerfully aloud, pleading with God to banish the cancer from his blood, in the mighty name of Jesus.

As their petitions gradually peter out, the middle-aged woman starts to prophesy with mind-blowing accuracy, addressing the very heart of Inger's prayers for Henrik, which none but God would have known. "A special peace has lingered with us since," Inger writes to the prayer support group. "All I can say is that fasting is grossly underrated, and God is so faithful when we make the smallest gestures towards him."

When a letter arrives from the bank, Henrik sits on the bottom step of the stairs in the hallway to rip open the envelope, but the last thing he expects is notification of a pay rise – and a bonus! "I've not actually set foot in the office for eleven months," he exclaims, visibly shocked. "It's crazy!"

"Perhaps people have been praying for our finances?" Inger suggests, deeply encouraged. "They might have heard about the cost of the treatment and the twenty per cent shortfall in funding that the insurance company aren't willing to cover."

There is a sense of awe at God's ability to add up the sums, even as she types a message to their prayer support group. "Thank you so much for praying, whoever you are. The cost of Henrik's treatment is now fully covered. This is something that only God could have done!"

Twenty years, to the day, since Henrik and Inger married, the family find themselves standing on the open-air observation deck of a supertall skyscraper in the centre of the city's commercial district. "Wow, Mum, look at the view!" Harriet exclaims, summing up everyone's thoughts.

Henrik is weak and skeletal. He can barely walk more than a few minutes before exhaustion overwhelms him. As they wander amongst the city's skyscrapers, the twins constantly craning their necks upwards to look towards the peaks of the buildings framed against the blue backdrop of the sky, Henrik is seeking out benches, low-lying brick walls, bus shelters, anywhere that will enable him to stop, sit and rest.

His grit, determination, willpower and positivity carry him through each day. They also enable him to travel to Sweden for Easter – even when, the evening before they are due to fly, he starts turning yellow and the doctors discover his liver is inflamed and infected. "I'll just have to secure some medical support while I'm there," he announces to Inger, pragmatically, as they head for the airport.

The medication for his liver proves to be a blessing and, while he is away, he becomes progressively stronger, his appetite returns to near normal, and he starts to regain weight. "You're like a new man!" declares Inger, unable to disguise her delight.

It is a momentous milestone when Henrik reaches the first anniversary of his leukaemia diagnosis. "It has been the worst twelve months of my life, yet also the best," he writes to the prayer support group. "I would not wish what my body has gone through on *anyone*, but I would want *everyone* to experience the love of God, and his people, in the same way that I have."

Facing into the second year, the haematologist warns him that he is at high risk of relapse. But Henrik's faith digs deep. "Whatever happens, I am a beloved child of God, and I hold onto that every single day," he writes. "I am also, by his grace, still in a fear-free zone. We have been lifted before God on the upraised hands of hundreds of people who have been praying, and there has not been a day when we have not profoundly felt that. No words can express my gratitude. Thank you."

"Until your new immune system slows down to normal, you won't be ready to return to work," the haematologist advises Henrik. "At the moment, it's utterly overactive."

His line manager at the bank and a nurse from the occupational health team have come to the house for a meeting to talk about the future. Dressed in suits, they sit in comfortable armchairs in the living room, clasping mugs of coffee in their hands, looking out of the big bay window at a grey and leaden sky. Henrik is conscious that this is a collision between two of his worlds.

His boss is a big man whose frame fills the chair. "Our health insurance company is deciding whether to continue paying your salary and other benefits," he states, leaning forward to emphasise the point. Henrik feels apprehensive, even though he knows him to be a compassionate man.

"We've read your latest medical records," states the nurse with a smile, "and we have to think about what's best for your team, as well as for you." She pauses a moment, looks down at her notes and then continues, "Although you're still pretty poorly, we've decided to keep your job open, at least until the autumn."

Henrik audibly breathes a sigh of relief. "You've been so incredibly kind to me," he declares, choking back tears. "You've really gone above and beyond the call of duty, and I can't thank you enough."

"When you're ready, we think you should return part-time for a while, and be based from home," his line manager continues, "until you're able to cope full-time in the office."

As he closes the front door behind them, he turns to embrace Inger. "God has been so faithful to us," he whispers into her ear. "He really does work out all things for good."

When time permits, house-hunting continues in earnest. Their rented accommodation is only temporary and they are keen to buy now that they know the area. When they find the perfect property within spitting distance of the twins' school, and their offer is accepted, Inger feels blessed beyond measure.

"God's been so good to us," she confides in Henrik, the day she collects the keys to let the renovators and decorators get to work. "I'm just praying that we can steward the house well."

Henrik is getting weaker.

He summons all his energy to swing his swollen legs to the side of the bed, angry stretch marks revealing where fluid is being retained. He sits, sometimes up to half an hour at a time, willing the nausea to subside and the relentless muscle pain to cease, before mustering sufficient strength to leverage himself up to go to the loo. To make matters worse, his hearing has inexplicably deteriorated; he can now only hear if someone is standing straight in front of him.

When he starts to spike a fever and his temperature soars, Inger manoeuvres him down the stairs and into the car, and drives him straight to hospital where he is instantly readmitted. Emergency blood tests reveal extremely high indicators of inflammation and an underactive thyroid.

"There may be a link between your expensive treatment and the impact it's having on your thyroid," a consultant endocrinologist explains, "but it's a bit too soon to tell, so we'll have to monitor it." She jots down notes on her pile of papers, clearly excited to have such an unusual medical case to tackle.

Once again, Henrik finds himself lying in a hospital gown, propped up by pillows, as an intravenous drip pumps him with intermittent doses of drugs, and his inflammation markers soar.

Harriet hesitates when she sees him that evening. "I thought you were getting better, Dad," she reveals, trying not to cry, "but you look so pale and weak, and your face is a sort of sickly yellow."

"Let's lay hands on him and ask Jesus to come and heal him," Inger suggests gently, hating seeing her daughter so visibly upset.

Melker needs no persuading. "Oh God, in Jesus' name, please heal my dad, please make him better," he prays, standing on the same side of the hospital bed as the drip. "We want him at home, not in hospital." Harriet quickly joins in. "Please help Dad feel your presence, God," she prays, "so that he knows he's not alone."

Lying in bed that night, Inger cries out in prayer, battling with disappointment. "Oh God, I can't keep going on like this," she informs him, her voice choked with tears. "Is Henrik going to make it? Is it just going to be me and the children moving into the new house?" She pauses to blow her nose into a tissue. "I'm struggling to see the day of joy that you promised. Please help me hold on. Please strengthen and sustain me with the same mighty power that rose Jesus from the dead."

As her prayer draws to a natural close, the indescribable peace of God's presence fills the room, and she falls into a deep and dreamless sleep.

Although Henrik is released from hospital, his condition remains critical. "Only God can help me now," he confides in Inger, acutely aware that he may not have long left to live.

On Sunday morning, despite his frail condition, he attends the church service where people greet him warmly and gather around to pray. That afternoon, for the first time in many months, he is pain-free.

But it does not last long, and the chronic incessant pain soon returns.

"We can't be sure, but we believe you may have an auto-immune disease," the endocrinologist informs Henrik. "So your new immune system may be attacking your thyroid and liver and, because your haemoglobin levels have fallen so dramatically, it may also be attacking your red blood cells."

There is a palpable sense of relief that, at last, there is a diagnosis, even if only theoretical. But it is quickly followed by a wave of despondency: none of the doctors know how to treat this.

For the second time since embarking on this journey, Inger feels prompted by the Holy Spirit to call for united prayer and fasting for Henrik's healing. "I've never seen him so low," she types, inviting their prayer support group to participate. "If you have it in your heart to pray for him, and to fast if you can, then please join with us on Wednesday evening, so we are all interceding at the same time."

As twenty-five Christian friends and family squeeze into Henrik's and Inger's front room, my prayer partner and I are meeting to pray at my house. Marching round and round the low wooden coffee table, which sits on the carpet in the centre of my living room, I pray out loud, Pentecostal style, petitioning God to heal Henrik. I know that Jesus can do it; I've seen him do it for other people. Faith is rising as I cry out to him to do it, tonight, for Henrik – and my prayer partner, sitting on the sofa, echoes my prayers, tears streaming down her face.

All over the world, people are praying, proclaiming Scriptures, and pleading with God to bring breakthrough, in a phenomenal outpouring of love and support. Henrik is anointed with oil by his vicar. There is a sense of anticipation and expectation.

Yet there is no instantaneous miracle, no dramatic healing, no extraordinary occurrence. To the naked eye, nothing happens.

But Henrik and Inger have a tangible sense of God's love, presence and peace. "I think we just need to wait and watch," she whispers to Henrik, as they head to bed that night. "It says in the Bible that the Lord will fight for us, and we need only to be still. I think that's what we need to do."

When Henrik wakes the following morning, his pain has completely disappeared.

He stretches out under the duvet, first one leg, then the other, followed by both arms. "Is this real?" he asks Inger, his voice trembling.

He throws back the duvet. His legs are no longer swollen. His muscles have stopped cramping. The relentless sense of exhaustion has evaporated. Absolutely no part of his body is in agony. He cannot believe it.

Inger is sitting bolt upright in bed, dressed only in her nightie, mouth wide open in wonder at what she is watching unfold before her. "What's happened?" she asks, knowing the answer even before the question is fully formed.

"Maybe God's healed me?" Henrik suggests. He is cautiously optimistic, but the past fifteen months have involved such a rollercoaster ride that, at the back of his mind, he can sense a niggling doubt:

"Let's get a professional medical opinion, just in case it's only a temporary reprieve," he tells Inger, tentatively standing up, and then smiling down at her, steady on his feet. "I'm curious to find out what the consultant will say."

"I don't understand it," the haematologist pronounces, sitting in a swivel chair in her clinic, clearly confused. "Your blood test results show your haemoglobin levels are normal, your inflammation markers are normal, and your liver is functioning as it should be."

She brings up a graph on the computer screen and turns the monitor to an angle which enables Henrik and Inger to have an optimal view. They bend forward in their seats to peer at what looks like a mountain on the screen in front of them.

"What's happened to you, Henrik?" she asks incredulously.

"We gathered our Christian friends and family together to pray for healing," Henrik calmly informs her, "and they joined in from all over the world." He cannot stop smiling.

"Oh!" she declares. "That's good!"

When Henrik meets the endocrinologist, she reacts in a similar way. It seems that none of his medical team can make sense of what's happened.

Suddenly, the summer takes on a new sense of purpose and, with it, unbounded joy.

Moving out of their rented accommodation into the house they have purchased, Inger delights in Henrik's involvement in unpacking boxes and deciding which possessions to put where. "I'm so glad to have you back!" she tells him.

As the family settle into their annual holiday in Sweden, Inger updates their prayer support group. "We want to thank the Lord – and encourage you to keep asking God for the impossible. Henrik's healing is a miracle. Thank you all for praying, and thanks be to God for his goodness to us."

The day that Henrik returns to work is a significant milestone. It's been more than five hundred days since he last set foot in the bank. Starting part-time from home and building up to full-time in the office, he embarks on a staggered return.

Almost every day, God opens up opportunities for Henrik to share his Christian faith with colleagues, old and new. "Jesus has healed me," he informs them, surprised at his own boldness. Some of his co-workers respond cynically, questioning whether his healing is for real. Others reveal that they, too, are Christians. Many of them cry, moved by all that he has gone through.

"I never used to speak about my faith at work," he tells me, "but now I am fearless in proclaiming what God has done and how I've been healed."

Nearly two years on from his healing, Henrik is back at the hospital for a routine check. Waiting in the clinic is a new consultant, a dark-haired, middle-aged man.

"I've just been reading your medical notes," he says, "yet seeing you in the flesh, I can't believe you've had a stem cell transplant."

"I have," says Henrik calmly, "it's in my file."

"But you can't have," the consultant continues, clearly puzzled. "Stem cell transplants usually leave skin in a mess, but your skin is perfect."

"That's because God healed me," Henrik tells him. There is a look of awe in the consultant's eyes.

"When I look back at all that has happened, there are so many moments that stand out for which I am thankful," Inger writes. "But maybe more than anything, this precious prayer support group. How you have prayed and cheered us on through thick and thin. We will never forget how you poured yourselves into prayer for Henrik to make it to the other side. We are so thankful."

As one of the many people who prayed for Henrik, it is a delight to meet him. He comes across as gentle, kind and humble – and genuinely amazed at how many have been impacted by his healing.

"I'm grateful for the gift of life," Henrik tells me. "Every day I cultivate an attitude of gratitude, thanking God for the things that previously I might have taken for granted."

"I still feel profoundly grateful for the prophetic promise God gave us," Inger tells me. "He told us that a hard day was coming, so we were prepared, but he also told us that a day of joy would follow." She pauses a moment before continuing, "When I wasn't sure how to pray, it gave my prayers direction. I knew that, if God was going to turn this around, we needed to ask him for joy. Without that, I'd have found it hard to hold on."

CHAPTER 10

Release from a prison of darkness
A teenager ill with ME (2018)

"Daughter, your faith has made you well."
Mark 5:34

This story is about Anna, the daughter of my friends Chris and Gillian. It tells of how she journeyed with ME while she was a teenager. It also features her brother Matthew. I met Chris and Gillian and their wider family when we were in our twenties, and we have been friends ever since.

Solo on stage, fifteen-year-old Anna is performing a complex modern dance routine, the spotlight highlighting her every move before the sizeable festival audience. Graceful and elegant, her long blonde hair swept up in a chignon, her body flows in rhythm with the music, recalling the moves she's been rehearsing for weeks.

Suddenly, she freezes mid-flow, her memory empty.

Unable to recall the remainder of the routine, she momentarily pauses, and then continues impromptu, her improvisation obvious only to those who have choreographed the dance. As the music fades, she takes a bow, her head giddy, unable to digest the applause. The curtain closes and she walks off stage, where she promptly projectile vomits out of the backstage door.

"That's not like Anna," Gillian muses, watching from the audience. "She normally remembers her routines like clockwork." She represses her anxiety. "Something must be really wrong."

When Anna's parents meet, they are working on a hospital ship anchored off the west coast of Africa. Chris, as the ship's photographer, is larger than life, hugely creative and full of vitality. Gillian, one of the ship's nurses, has a big heart and speaks with a gentle Northern Irish lilt. Both are blonde-haired and, at the time, in their twenties.

They have just returned home to the UK from honeymoon when we are introduced at a mutual American friend's Thanksgiving dinner, and we quickly become part of the same friendship group, connected to two lively churches, all of us young adults. Chris and Gillian have a gift of hospitality, and we regularly gather for food in their home.

By the time Anna comes along, I am working as a Legal Aid solicitor, and lodging with her granny in a beautiful converted barn on the outer edge of a popular market town in the south of England. Over the years that follow, I move away and watch, mostly from afar, as Chris and Gillian raise Anna, and then her brother Matthew, in the Christian faith, through weekly involvement in their local church and annual input from a summer Christian conference.

Anna's family settle near the sea so her parents can pursue their passion for sailing. When she starts secondary school, she has to commute a considerable distance on public transport.

Some pupils resent Anna for her popular, confident, fun-loving nature. Jealous and insecure, they begin to bully her, their imaginations limitless. As well as being regularly pushed and kicked, on one occasion she's forcibly locked inside a changing room locker; on another, she's hung by her school shirt on a cloakroom peg. They post hateful comments on social media and verbally harass her, frequently using innuendo. They mock her for being slow and stupid, failing to factor in her dyslexia.

Dance becomes Anna's outlet. It's the only way she can cope with the constant underlying stress.

Her parents are desperate for their daughter. "Why do they hate me so much?" she sobs. "It's like I'm trapped in a prison, and I can't face it anymore. Please don't make me go to school."

"Why are you not answering our prayers, God?" They ask as they intercede together on Anna's behalf. "When is it going to stop?"

With heavy hearts and no easy answers, her parents plead with the school to intervene. They lodge complaints of mistreatment and intimidation against the ringleaders. They cite specific examples. They gather evidence in support. But the headteacher, Anna's form tutor, and other key staff members, can't seem to stop the bullies.

Nothing of substance changes. Chris and Gillian feel powerless.

"You need to nurture your talent," Anna's modern dance teacher tells her. "I can coach and support you, but you also need to play your part and put in the practice."

"If you keep going as you have been, then you'll go far," her ballet teacher discloses. "You've got a natural aptitude and flair."

Spurred on by this encouragement, Anna needs no reminding. Chris becomes her chief chauffeur, faithfully ferrying her to and from lessons and rehearsals, at least four times a week, proudly watching while she runs through her routines. He also supports her when she successfully auditions for the lead character in the school play, keen to enable her to grow her gifting.

Conversations in the car cover every conceivable topic, and Anna enjoys the outlet it gives her to chat with her dad. "If I didn't have dance," she confides in him, "I wouldn't be able to handle school."

The bullies, unbeaten and undeterred, show Anna no mercy or compassion, not even when the headteacher rebukes their behaviour.

By the summer term, approaching the midway marker of Anna's two years of end-of-school exam studies, the situation has become critical and a change of school is the only option. Chris and Gillian, fully aware of the ramifications during such a crucial academic year, find a new one, nearer home, prepared to take their daughter. There is just one condition: she will need to drop down an academic year and restart her first end-of-school exam year afresh.

Anna is absolutely delighted. There is a lightness in her spirit as she throws herself into the new school. Friendly and vivacious, she soon finds friends who are supportive and encouraging. Her social life takes off, and she starts dating one of the most admired boys in her year.

"What a contrast to this time last year!" she remarks. The relief is palpable.

The nights are drawing in and the leaves are falling from the trees, covering the ground in a thick crunchy golden carpet. It is during this season that the symptoms start.

Anna is fifteen, embarking afresh on the first of her two end-of-school exam years. With the stress of her old school now behind her, she is fit, healthy and happy. Her new school suits her, and life is on the up.

A few months into the autumn term, she starts feeling fuzzy-headed and fatigued. One moment, she's concentrating on a teacher and the interactive white board at the front of the classroom; the next, she has floating black dots blurring her vision. Walking requires real effort and she keeps feeling hot and shivery. Her throat is permanently painful; swallowing is agony and it hurts to talk.

"You have tonsillitis," her family doctor tells her. "You need to rest and drink plenty of fluids."

Anna tries her best to rest, but the symptoms seem to get worse, not better. Returning to her family doctor, this time the diagnosis is different. "You have swelling in the glands on the side of your neck," she informs Anna as she presses the affected area gently, her hands cold to touch. "I'm going to have to take a blood test to confirm this, but I think you've got a glandular fever." She pauses a moment before continuing, "If that's the case, then it's little wonder that you feel so exhausted, but there's nothing I can give you as it's caused by a virus."

When the results of the blood test come back positive, Anna feels relieved. At least she now knows what's wrong with her.

"How do you think I got glandular fever?" she asks Gillian, but then she recalls how she's shared water bottles at school and at dance classes. "Perhaps that's how it's happened?" suggests Gillian.

During the depths of winter, and into the following spring, Anna's symptoms evolve and advance. The veins in her skin keep coming to the surface and she discovers inexplicable bruising on her torso and back. Every muscle in her body aches with pain. When she stands up, she feels dizzy. When she lies down, she struggles to sleep. Worst of all, she is coughing up blood.

With a sense of panic, she desperately searches the Internet for answers, wondering whether she might have leukaemia. It's hard to fend off the rising sense of dread – and the constant tiredness.

One warm spring evening, Anna's boyfriend escorts her to a solo dance lesson. They are holding hands, walking down the road, heading for the rehearsal hall, when severe pain suddenly grips her chest and spreads through her body. She collapses onto the pavement, coughing up blood on the side of the street.

"What should I do, Anna?" he asks her, panicking at what's unfolding in front of him.

"Go and get my dance teacher," she instructs him.

"But I can't leave you," he says, his eyes betraying how frightened he feels.

Helping her up, she leans her weight upon him, and he carries her to the class. Not long later, midway through her one-to-one lesson, she once again falls to the floor.

When she opens her eyes, her vision is disturbingly blurred, but she can just about make out that she's lying in a hospital bed. She's immediately aware of the pain in her chest reasserting itself, and she screams in agony. Her boyfriend is sitting on an armchair beside the bed, gently holding her hand. He's clearly been crying. A doctor, dressed in a crisp white coat, is standing at the end of the bed taking notes.

"You were utterly unresponsive," her boyfriend explains, his voice choked, his face betraying his relief that she's come round. "I helped lift you into your mum's car and she drove us here."

"It came out of nowhere and happened so fast," she explains to the doctor, and he nods sagely. "It feels like a shot of toxic poison's been injected into my entire body."

Anna is active in a twenty-strong dance troupe. They practice for hours on end, several times a week, none of them happy until their sequence is perfectly synchronised, every limb and sinew moving in harmony with the melody of the music. Their friendships are deep; they depend on each other to deliver the whole.

In the week leading up to the semi-finals of a local dance competition, Anna is exhausted and Gillian takes her to the family doctor.

"I don't want to let the group down," she explains, "but I've not got enough stamina to do the show."

The family doctor is pastoral, practical and pragmatic. "Regular doses of an isotonic energy drink should do the trick," she advises, recognising that Anna's energy levels are severely depleted.

When the group win the semi-finals, Anna reluctantly pulls out of the finals. Her ability and aspiration are undiminished, but her energy and endurance have vanished. "I feel I'm falling over a cliff edge," she tells Gillian in tears, "but I just can't carry on."

Overnight, Anna stops dancing.

Anna loathes routine, but her symptoms foist it upon her, and every day is the same.

Early in the morning, Gillian knocks on the door and comes into her bedroom. "Morning, Anna!" she pronounces cheerfully in her Northern Irish inflection, opening the curtains to let as much light through the window as possible, and leaning over the bed to listen for her shallow, laboured breathing.

Anna wakes up, fully aware of her mum's presence in the room, but unable to acknowledge it in any way. Her body is completely paralysed, rooted to where it has moulded its shape on the mattress during the night. Her eyelids feel like lead weights and remain firmly shut. Her lips are swollen and dry, so she does not attempt to speak.

Her phone is too heavy to hold. So is pen and paper. A glass of water is out of the question. Her mum has to hold it to her mouth so she can sip it through a straw.

On average, it takes an hour to get out of bed and upright, but she cannot coordinate her body. Her muscles go into spasm and she appears to be drunk. In a stupor, she leans on Gillian who leads her downstairs to the living room. "Please don't stress me," she requests as she regularly wrestles with the inner turmoil of being powerless to get her body to do what she wants. Lying on the sofa, she turns cold and comatose.

Deep down, she is terrified. "What's wrong with me?" she keeps asking. "God, if you're there, do something," she prays.

Chris and Anna are wandering around the supermarket, filling a trolley with groceries, ticking off items from a shopping list. It's been a beautiful spring day, the sun shining, the trees laden with pink and white blossom. Gillian has asked them to get a few items before they head home for dinner.

Loading their shopping bags at the checkout, Anna suddenly announces, "Dad, I don't feel too good." Her face is pale. Handing over cash to pay the assistant, Chris grabs the bags in one hand and offers the other to Anna. "Let's get you home," he says.

Strapped by her seatbelt into the passenger seat, less than two minutes into the ten-minute journey, Anna loses consciousness.

"Gillian, please pick up the phone," Chris pleads, willing her to answer. He has pulled up and parked on the pavement while he works out what to do. Home is ten minutes in one direction, and the hospital twenty minutes the other way. There's a click as the ringing submits to voicemail. "Anna's out cold," he says, panic rising as he leaves his message.

Deciding to head for home, he sweeps the car up to the front door, leaps out, opens the door, and yells up the stairs for Matthew. "I need you to help me lift your sister out of the car and onto the sofa," he informs him when his son's tousled blonde mop of hair appears on the landing, peering over the banister, jolted out of his laid-back reverie.

It's nearly two hours before Anna wakes up.

She's learning to heed the warning signs, and her loved ones are learning how to respond, but the increasing frequency of her fainting is frightening her.

Anna's family doctor refers her to a paediatrician at the nearest hospital. One by one, a series of medical tests eliminate any suggestion of problems with her heart, lungs, thyroid and nervous system. They confirm that she does not have angina, diabetes or epilepsy.

The day she's due to have an MRI scan on her brain, Anna creates a bucket list. If her life is being cut short by some mysterious disease, she wants to make sure she achieves a few things first. *Have a dance masterclass with a famous ballerina. Legally buy my first alcoholic drink. Cut all my hair off. Live in Africa. Find my soul mate,* she writes. There's no limit to her imagination.

Sitting next to her parents in the hospital waiting room, surrounded by sick people, she gazes out the huge sash window at a beautiful late spring day. "Oh God, I don't want to be sick," she prays aloud as she takes in the clear blue sky. "I just want to know what's wrong with me. Please will you show the doctors?" Her parents join her in saying, "Amen."

Her name is called and she's ushered into a small warm room, lacking in natural daylight. Paperwork complete, she's invited to lie motionless on a motorised bed while the radiographer disappears into a different room. Her voice echoes over the intercom, and the bed slides Anna slowly, head first, into the cylindrical MRI scanner. Barely daring to breathe, she listens to the machine's loud tapping noises. Terrified of the unknowns, she prays fervently, thanking God that he is in control.

Invited for an appointment to collect her test results and talk about her sleep patterns, Anna heads to the hospital with her parents on a sunny day. School is about to finish for the long summer holiday; the days are long and light. They are greeted warmly by the consultant paediatrician.

"I've made a note of all Anna's symptoms," Gillian explains, rifling through her handbag balanced on her lap, producing a piece of paper and flourishing it aloft. The consultant listens patiently as Gillian reads out a long list of ailments, citing specific examples. "Whatever is wrong with Anna," she states emphatically as she reaches the end, "I feel sure it's been caused by the intense stress of recent years at school."

"I don't want to scare you all," the consultant says kindly, "but from what you're telling me, I think your daughter has ME."

Her words are greeted by a stunned silence. Chris and Gillian turn to Anna, eyes wide in astonishment. "Why has no one mentioned this before?" she asks.

"I need you to know this though," the consultant continues, "I've seen other girls of the same sort of age as Anna, who are unable to even get out of bed. So the fact Anna's here is amazing." She pauses a moment, and turns to smile at Anna, looking her straight in the eye. "I suggest I refer you to the specialist hospital for paediatric ME. It's one of the best in the world."

When Anna realises their relationship has no future, she breaks up with her boyfriend, but he sadly takes to social media to vent his hurt. Both of them are popular people, prominent in their peer group, and many mutual friends offer opinions without taking time to hear both sides of the story.

It takes all the emotional energy that Anna can muster to hold her head high in the face of unkind comments and unfounded verbal harassment. "This is a private matter," she decides, "I don't want to denigrate him in public." But it soon starts to have an adverse effect on her.

Within a month, Anna has inadvertently become socially isolated. On the one hand, she's been freed from the relationship; on the other, she's been trapped by its ramifications. "What's the point in going out?" she asks her parents.

As the nights start to draw in and the autumnal nip in the air becomes more evident, a lack of motivation to get up and out of the house combines with constant fatigue, and Anna spends increasing amounts of time lying in bed, unable to move.

On a dull and drizzly day in November, Chris and Gillian drive through an unfamiliar city and park outside the specialist hospital for paediatric ME.

Anna looks around her. The waiting room is deserted. Three walls, devoid of decoration, are lined with plastic-covered sofas, one of which contains large floor-to-ceiling windows looking out over the car park. It feels sterile and intimidating.

A friendly middle-aged man, an Australian accent evident in his voice, invites them into his consulting room. He keeps cracking jokes as he jots down notes, while Anna and her parents describe her symptoms. The atmosphere is relaxed; his laugher is contagious.

"We were booked into a guest house last night," Gillian explains, "and I suggested we could walk to a nearby restaurant for dinner because we'd been so long in the car." She looks at her daughter before continuing, "But Anna was in such chronic pain that she couldn't even walk those five minutes."

"I can see that various tests have eliminated potential possibilities," the consultant remarks, scrolling down the computer screen on his desk. "ME can only be diagnosed by a process of exclusion. But listening to you now, and based on my experience, I have no doubt at all that Anna has it."

"Finally, I have an official diagnosis!" Anna says.

"We are running a research programme into teenage ME," he announces. "Would you like to take part?" he asks, turning in his swivel chair to direct his question to Anna.

"What does it involve?" she asks.

"We'll put you on a structured exercise programme with the aim of gradually increasing how long you spend doing activities that raise your heart rate, such as swimming or walking," he explains. "It's called Graded Exercise Therapy, or GET, and it's bespoke to you and your physical capabilities."

Anna nods hesitantly.

A kind, smiling, middle-aged physiotherapist ushers them into a sparsely furnished room, save for some gym equipment along one wall. "Take a seat, Anna," she invites, indicating a chair in the middle of the floor, and measuring her pulse. "Please can you stand up and sit down until you feel tired," she requests, "and I will time you." Anna duly obliges, and then she asks her to walk back and forth across the room. "Please stop when it feels uncomfortable," she reassures her, "and I will check your heart rate."

Chris and Gillian admire their daughter's tenacity, conscious of the toll that these tests will take. "She's going to hate having an activity tracker," Gillian says to Chris, watching Anna's reluctance while it's fitted to her wrist. "It's wireless-enabled," explains the physiotherapist, "so it will measure all your personal fitness metrics." Anna nods, knowing what this means. "Every six weeks, you and I will need to have a video call to set some goals, and I will analyse the data that the tracker submits," she says. "Over time, I'm sure you'll start to see progress."

Gillian opens the curtains to let in the drab grey light of a dull damp day. Sitting in her flannel pyjamas at the end of Anna's bed, feet firmly on the floor, tears slowly start trickling down her cheeks. "Lord Jesus," she prays, "how many more times will I come in to wake her, only for her to not know I'm here?"

Fear is never far away. Lying in bed, awake in the night, aware of their daughter asleep in the adjoining room, Gillian's and Chris's conversations keep returning to the unknowns that lie ahead.

"What if Anna never improves?" Chris muses. "How will we get her through her end-of-school exams?"

"How will the house need to be adapted to cope with a wheelchair?" Gillian frets. "Are we going to have to be her carers for decades to come?"

Mindful of an old school friend who was diagnosed with ME in her early teens and, thirty years on, is still living with the condition, she is terrified that this is the future that seems to be unfolding for Anna too.

Anna is doggedly determined, refusing to be part of the ninety-five per cent of ME sufferers who get depression. Every day she relies on the power of positivity to see her through, pushing down the pain and trauma of what's happening to her. She simply builds on her natural propensity for optimism, adopting an upbeat attitude to life.

Her bedroom becomes home to a hired sun lamp and dry sauna tent, both recommended by the specialist consultant and quickly integrated into her long and laborious morning routine. She's instructed to sit inside the tin foil tent, her head protruding from the top, while she waits for her body to sweat out its toxins. But Gillian frequently opens the tent doors, heat bursting out in a blast, to find her daughter lying motionless on the carpet, curled up in the foetal position.

"It's awful," Anna sobs. "I can't force my body to sweat. It just won't do it." It seems that positivity is sometimes not enough.

Anna detests the activity tracker with a vengeance. It monitors her every move – both day and night – daily transmitting her personal data to the researchers at the specialist hospital.

"I feel like an offender who's been released on bail," she moans to her mum. "It constantly reminds me I'm ill."

"You must follow the routine that the specialist consultant has set," Gillian chides. "Otherwise you won't get better."

"But it's been imposed on me," Anna laments. "I didn't have any say."

If she completes her quota of steps before the day is out, she lets her friends lift her into a shopping trolley in an attempt to defy the tracker into the evening. Alas, when she's being bounced down winding paths to parties on the beaches near her home, every jolt of the wonky wheels continues to be recorded. She becomes accustomed to it getting annoyed with her – and she mutes its alarm.

"I just want to be a normal teenager," she confides in her dad. "I want to fit in, so people like me." Chris understands, well aware of how much she was disliked in her previous school.

Influenced by her peers, she starts to drink regularly, staying up all hours. Gillian has to call the parents of Anna's contemporaries, requesting invitations for Matthew too. "He needs to look after his sister," she explains, aware that it's forcing her son to grow up sooner than might be advisable, but feeling she has no choice.

Matthew frequently comes to his sister's defence when she's accused of faking her illness.

"She just goes to parties and gets wasted," they claim. "Why can't she come to school?"

"You need to understand that she does nothing, quite literally, all week," he clarifies. "She expends all her energy at weekends."

When the physiotherapist checks in every six weeks, Anna creates excuses. "I'll just have to be strict with you," she tells her disapprovingly, "I've got to be firm to be kind."

Anna knows she's deceiving those who are trying to help her. She's also deceiving herself. Her resentment of her ME intensifies.

Gillian has to give up her job to care for Anna, and the family learn to survive on Chris's fluctuating income. Writing her resignation letter to the local doctor's surgery is a difficult decision, but she knows she cannot carry on as their practice nurse – not with Anna so sick and unable to manage more than two to three hours at school at a time. She can just about fit in a dog walk each morning before she has to bring Anna home from school.

The research regime forbids any sleep during the daytime so, although desperately tired, Anna has to constantly fight off fatigue, and it feels like a losing battle. Too weak and ill to go to school, she falls further and further behind. "I'm never going to pass my end-of-school exams," she discloses to her mum. "I've missed too many classes and not done the coursework."

It is early spring, the clocks have just gone forward, and the tips of lilac-coloured crocuses are pushing through the garden beds, when the headteacher comes to the house to discuss Anna's situation. Making himself comfortable on the sofa, his hands cupped around a steaming mug of tea, he asks about Anna's progress.

"I think you're going to have to pull out of school," he informs her ruefully. "Even if you were to get better tomorrow, you'll never be able to catch up."

"Is that actually an option?" Chris asks. "What happens if she doesn't complete her end-of-school exams? Aren't they the foundation for so many things?"

The headteacher is kind and compassionate. "My sister has ME," he reveals supportively, "so I understand what it involves." He pauses a moment and then makes a suggestion. "How about you stay at school, but take a role in the office instead of the classroom?"

Anna is excited by his generous offer and seizes the opportunity. On the days she can muster up enough energy, she works two to three hours, supporting the school secretary, taking phone calls, completing spreadsheets, filing paperwork.

"How many others of my age get work experience like this?" She remarks to Gillian.

Occasionally Anna will offer up a token gesture prayer, but God is mostly a distant memory. She doesn't doubt his existence, but she finds it easier to rely on the power of positivity than prayer.

She knows her granny is praying for her daily, but she's oblivious to the prayers of many others – aunts, uncles, cousins, and family friends like me. When Chris and Gillian come with Matthew for a fleeting visit, I am shocked to learn of Anna's deterioration and, together, we sit in my living room and cry out to God for her healing. I also ask him to supernaturally sustain them in their role as her carers.

When her dad gives her a copy of the "Footprints" poem, a spiritual meditation by an unknown author, she is moved by the words she reads. Slowly it dawns on her: "God is with me and carrying me, even when he feels far away."

"You need to join us for the school prom," urge Anna's school friends. "It wouldn't be the same without you." She knows it will be exhausting, but she doesn't want to miss out.

On a sunny mid-summer's day, dressed in a stunning figure-hugging, floor-length, sparkly sequined red dress, her long blonde hair hanging in loose curls around her shoulders, her make-up done to perfection, Anna is ready for the prom. Her beau for the evening – a tall, dark and handsome friend from school – looks dapper in his smart suit and matching red tie.

Chris takes photographs as they leave the house, capturing the moment for posterity. "Anna is going to prom!" he posts on social media. "The end of a journey and the start of another. God is faithful and our daughter is beautiful."

She loves being part of her class again for one last time – even with the inevitable bittersweet goodbyes. This academic year hasn't ended as she would have wanted, but she's happy to see it out in style.

Anna is reluctant, but her parents persuade her to come to the summer Christian conference which the family have attended almost every year since she was a child.

The venue, a large agricultural showground, has been transformed. The main field lies submerged in a colourful sea of tents and caravans, stretching out in every direction, surrounding an assortment of bright white marquees and circus-style tents in the centre. Christians from churches across the country have gathered together to collectively worship in song, study the Bible and find fellowship with one another.

Lying on the grass near the exit of the youth venue, gazing up at the ceiling of a vast red-and-yellow tent, Anna can smell sweaty feet in close proximity. "Don't tread on me," she pleads, as they step round her. A band of musicians are singing about Jesus' love and she's trying to focus on the tune without taking in the words. "I don't want to be here," she rants at God. "I don't want to join in. I don't want to worship you. I don't even know if you're there anymore."

Suddenly, she senses God speaking. "Anna, you need to give me another chance," he whispers. "You need to start again with me and, this time, don't run away."

"Is that really you, God?" she asks, wondering whether she's imagined it. A feeling of warmth washes over her and, dredging up distant childhood memories, she recognises it to be the Holy Spirit. Slowly surrendering, a balm comes over the pain in her body, and the tears trickle down her cheeks and onto the grass by her head.

⁕

"Hey Anna!" Matthew is nudging his sister, urging her to sit up. "Have you seen the good-looking worship leader up on the stage?" He's pointing at a dark-haired young man, aged no more than twenty, dressed in a cream hoodie and confidently strumming away on lead guitar.

It's a couple of days since Anna's encounter with the Holy Spirit and her response is firm. "I don't want to be distracted by boys, Matt," she informs him nonchalantly. But she struggles to concentrate, acutely aware of the young man's whereabouts. When newfound friends introduce them, she is secretly delighted and, within weeks, they are dating.

He is kind, courteous and respectful, and it's an immensely restorative relationship. Despite the distance between their home towns, they see each other on alternate weekends. With her Christian faith rekindled into life, and his already deep-rooted, they encourage each other in ways she had never imagined possible. Before she knows it, her prayer life ignites from a spark into a flame, and she wants to talk about Jesus with anyone willing to listen. Her friendships start to change, and the desire to party disappears. She is attentive to the changes, embracing them wholeheartedly.

Anna's ME stabilises during the summer. The pain is mostly manageable and the power of prayer has replaced positivity. For the first time since her diagnosis, she experiences an inexplicable joy. "Lord Jesus, please heal me," becomes her daily prayer.

"This is what you have to do if I faint," she explains to her boyfriend. When it happens they are in a taxi, heading for his house with some friends. She recognises the warning sign thirty seconds before it happens, and then she faints.

When she wakes up, she's lying on her boyfriend's bed, unable to move. "I carried you out of the car and up the stairs," he informs her, tears trickling down his cheeks. "I've been praying the whole time you've been unconscious."

His younger brother is sitting on a chair near the door, clearly frightened by what he's witnessed. "Please don't freak out," Anna reassures him. "This is just part of my illness." He walks up to the bed and, at an awkward angle, bends over to give her a hug.

As the end of the summer approaches, Anna starts waving friends off to dance school. "My life is running on a parallel track to everyone else's," she confides in her mum, "and they are all speeding ahead." She sits on her bed and cries. Her ME has taken a turn for the worse, and she's using a wheelchair when the pain makes walking unbearable.

"You could always study fashion and textiles," a friend suggests. "You don't need any end-of-school exams for some of the courses available." Anna is unenthusiastic. "What else would I do instead though?" she concedes. "ME has robbed me of my dream of dancing."

The course gives her a regular routine and a vehicle for recovery when she has the energy to get into college. But her heart's not in it.

College is located near the centre of town, and her lectures are scattered sparsely throughout the week, freeing Anna to head onto the streets whenever her timetable allows. Asking God who he wants her to find, she's delighted when she discovers them, seizing each opportunity to share her newly ignited faith in Jesus. Her gift of evangelism is growing.

On one occasion, she stumbles upon a bedraggled, bearded, homeless man, sleeping in a cardboard box at the entrance to a shopping mall. "Would you like me to pray for you?" she asks. "Yes please," he replies. Over several short meetings she shares her faith in Jesus with him. But later he dies and she is devastated.

"I don't know whether he got right with God before it was too late," she confides in her mum. "You played your part," Gillian reassures her. "You just have to trust him to God now."

It's late spring, the branches of the trees are burgeoning with delicate blossom, and bluebells have burst into bloom in every shady spot. Anna is staying with her paternal grandparents at their beautiful converted barn, where I used to live as a lodger, and I've been invited for lunch.

Clasping our mugs of tea while the meal is being prepared, Anna and I sit on soft chairs next to an old oak dresser, looking out at the immaculate lawns and flower-filled beds of her granny's prizewinning garden, through the floor to ceiling window of the living area. She looks remarkably well, given the reports I've heard of her deteriorating health in the last year or so.

"Last week, a friend of mine went to a national Christian women's conference," she tells me. "She felt God prompt her to film a small section of one of the talks, not knowing what the speaker was going to say." She grins excitedly and pulls her phone from her pocket to show me.

As the film clip plays, I can see a dark-haired woman standing behind a pulpit on a stage, a bright blue strobe light beaming over her head. She communicates with authority; her accent is Australian: "I speak this over the people who are ill, who have got a diagnosis over them. The Word of God, the Bible, says that you will be nourished; you will come through this ordeal without a scratch; you will be healed."

We simultaneously raise our gaze from the phone screen and look at each other. "How amazing is that?" says Anna.

"She recorded it, not knowing what the speaker was about to say, but simply as an act of obedience to what she felt God prompting, and she knew it was for me." She pauses a moment to catch her breath. "I really believe God's going to heal me," she states simply.

"Maybe that's God giving you a promise ahead of time," I suggest, "so you can hold on for what's coming."

"I already know it's happening," she volunteers, "because I had my final appointment at the specialist hospital last month, and the consultant said there were some noticeable improvements."

As our conversation continues, "Would you like me to pray with you?" I ask, gesturing to indicate the present moment.

"Yes please," she responds and, claiming authority in Christ, I place my hands on her and command the ME to go, in the name of Jesus.

"Thank you!" she says delightedly.

As Anna reaches the end of the academic year, she's had enough. "I'm not going back to college after the summer break," she announces to her parents. "I want to be on fire for God!"

God soon opens up a paid position for her as a young photographer friend's assistant. Sitting in bed, her laptop balanced carefully on her knees, she manages his email inbox, spreadsheets and photographic filing. When she's not working, and energy permitting, she's out on the streets, one or two hours at a time, praying for people and sharing the good news of Jesus.

"I'm happier working than studying," she tells her mum.

Gillian's sister and brother-in-law are living in Southern Africa. Attached to a missionary hospital, he's in charge of all the medical equipment while she looks after their children and uses her nursing training to support local health clinics. This summer, the whole family will be visiting for a few weeks. Vaccinations have been completed. Flights have been booked. Travel insurance has been secured, but no company will cover Anna for her ME. She knows she's taking a risk in going.

Their rustic guesthouse, with its whitewashed walls and red-tiled roof, nestles on the tree-lined shore of a lake. A handful of fishing boats have just headed off for a fresh catch. The sun is starting to rise in the morning sky and there's a gentle hum as people prepare for the day ahead. Last week was for visiting orphanages and feeding centres; this week is for relaxing.

Sitting around the breakfast table on the veranda, Chris kicks off his flip-flops and runs onto the beach. "Let's run in," he shouts out behind him, and Gillian and Matthew leap up and follow without hesitation.

Anna has woken feeling weak but, determined not to miss out, she summons up strength and wades into waist-deep water. Oblivious to the others splashing in the waves further out, she senses the sand solid beneath her feet. The waves around her stop; the surface of the lake is as smooth as glass. Immersed in the moment, she stretches out her palms to touch the water in front of her, warm in the morning sunlight. Looking down, she notices glitter sparkling in the sand at her feet.

It's then that she hears God's audible voice: "I'm healing you," he tells her gently. Speechless, she looks up, wondering whether she was the only one to hear it.

Heading out of the water, she flops onto her seat at the veranda table, picks up her pen and writes in her journal in capital letters: "GOD IS HEALING ME!" She knows she's speaking faith into the spiritual realm.

As she sits and stares across the water, in awe at what just happened, she recalls an incident from her childhood. She was eight years old at the time, when she had a picture of Africa in her mind's eye, and she could see God pointing to this country that she's in right now.

Did he know, even then, that she would encounter him when she came here?

"Dad, I've decided I want to be baptised," Anna announces one Wednesday evening in early autumn. "I want it to be in the sea, at my favourite beach, with you and the youth pastor doing the dunking." Her mind is made up, and time is of the essence as the nights are drawing in.

She extends the invitation far and wide, her excitement evident.

"Why are you so happy?" her maternal grandma asks when she calls from Northern Ireland.

"I'm getting baptised on Sunday!" Anna replies enthusiastically.

"Can we come?" her grandma enquires. "You sound different."

"Of course!" Anna responds, feeling guilty for not inviting them.

"We'll book our flights tonight," her grandma declares excitedly.

"But they aren't Christians," she says to Gillian, "so I hope they won't feel awkward."

It is a beautiful sunny Sunday afternoon, and the sea is reflecting the blue of a cloudless sky. Rusty red leaves are starting to fall to the ground in the woodland leading down to the beach. Anna is standing on a vast stretch of golden sand, her back to the sea, watching as more than one hundred relatives, friends and acquaintances snake their way along the footpaths and gather on the shoreline.

Her body might be sick, but her spirit is bursting with courage, and she is bold in confessing her Christian faith to the waiting crowd. "I am getting baptised as an act of faith and obedience," she declares. "Jesus died on the cross to defeat sin and pain and sickness. When I go down into the water in baptism, I will identify with his burial and, when I come up out of the water, I will identify with his resurrection from the dead." She commands attention as she speaks, authority in her voice.

With Chris on her right and the youth pastor on her left, all of them barefooted, dressed only in t-shirts and shorts, they wade gingerly into the sea. "Anna, we baptise you in the name of the Father, the Son, and the Holy Spirit," Chris declares as he and the youth pastor lower her carefully into the water. Lifting her out, she's beaming. Eager to pray for her, people quickly gather round as she steps out of the waves.

Never has God's presence felt so tangible.

"I've heard you're a dancer," the youth pastor's wife says casually to Anna at the end of a Sunday morning service, sunshine pouring through the windows at the back of the church building.

It catches her completely off-guard. "Who told you that?" she replies. "It's been nearly two years since I last danced, and I'm not sure I'd have the confidence to dance again, even if I was pain-free."

"Why don't you try?" she suggests. "We've got a church project coming up, which needs dancers."

"I don't know," says Anna reluctantly. "I'm so out of practice."

"You won't know unless you give it a go," she replies. "Maybe someone could film you?"

And so it is that one sunny summer's evening, with Christian worship music blasting out at full volume on a deserted country lane, the Holy Spirit comes upon Anna and she does the impossible. She dances non-stop for two hours while a videographer friend captures it on film.

When Anna and her boyfriend split up in the autumn, she's utterly heartbroken. Both of them, independently, are sensing God calling them in different directions, he into music and her into mission. For weeks, she cries herself to sleep.

"Why don't you apply for a Christian discipleship training year?" suggests one of her cousins. "If your heart's in global mission, you should just go!"

None is more surprised than Anna when, a short while later, her application is accepted. She's been completely candid about the way ME limits her life, and how she daily manages it. She's also been upfront about her lack of formal qualifications. Neither, it seems, has phased the course provider.

In a few months' time, early next year, Anna will be heading to Southern Africa.

At church one sunny Sunday morning, a young South African man strikes up conversation with Anna.

"Why don't you come and see the boat we're working on?" he suggests, introducing his friend and co-worker, another South African of the same age. "It's docked in the shipyard at the moment because of complications which have caused delays."

"We're preparing it to sail to Papua New Guinea," interjects the other. "You'd be more than welcome to come hang out with us."

During the day, Anna works as a photographer's assistant. Each evening, she can be found on the boat, out on deck if dry or inside the cabin if raining. Her spirit soars when she's with her new-found friends as they sing, pray and share their faith with the crew of the boat.

One starlit evening as the nights are drawing in, wrapped in hoodies, the power cuts and they huddle inside the cabin, aglow with flickering little candle lights. Outside, just beyond the marina, the vast expanse of the ocean lies still beneath the pitch-black sky. One of the Papuan New Guineans starts to sing a beautiful worship song in his mother tongue. Others join, in English.

They have just prayed, in Jesus' name, for a crew member's cataracts to go, whose sight has been restored, and a visitor to the boat whose broken wrist has been healed, when one of the South Africans turns to Anna. "Would you like us to pray for your healing too?" he asks.

Anna is unsure. She mostly manages the constant chronic pain these days, although she's conscious that her legs and arms are agony this evening. "OK," she says tentatively.

"In Jesus' name, we command the ME to go, and all the pain with it," one of the South Africans says as he speaks out a simple authoritative prayer. "Yes," says the other, laying his left hand on her head, "may Anna be healed in Jesus' name."

Eyes closed, she sits cross-legged on the cabin floor, permitting their words to penetrate. Aware of God's presence with her, she feels a searing heat soaring through every inch of her body, and she starts to laugh. An incredible sense of peace washes over her, and she spontaneously starts to sing a worship song to Jesus, which the others soon join, in pitch-perfect harmony.

Later, as the South Africans steer her to shore in a tiny dinghy, she senses God whispering to her gently, "Anna, you need to declare your healing now, in Jesus' name." Cautiously, she calls out, "Guys, please stop the boat." The dinghy comes to an abrupt halt in the middle of the marina, the engine cuts off, and a serene stillness covers the water.

"IN JESUS' NAME," she shouts at the top of her lungs, "I AM HEALED!" And then she watches in wonder as the darkness dissipates, scattering over the surface of the sea.

As soon as she lands on shore, she runs to the waiting car. The engine is purring; Chris is dozing in the driver's seat. "Dad, I've got some good news," she pronounces excitedly, unable to contain her unadulterated joy. Stirring from slumber, Chris winds down the window. "God has healed me!" she squeals. "That's great," he says cautiously. "It's really late, Anna. Let's get home."

For the first time in three years, Anna experiences deep, restorative sleep. She wakes early, feeling refreshed and free from pain. Leaping out of bed, she charges downstairs two at a time.

"What are you doing up?" her dad asks, staring at her, wide-eyed in disbelief as she stands in the kitchen doorway while he opens the fridge door to pull out the milk to pour into his coffee mug.

"Are you OK, love?" her mum enquires as she tips breakfast cereal out of the packet and into her bowl at the table.

"God has healed me!" Anna declares excitedly, running out the door into the garden, where she proceeds to sing and dance, back and forth across the lawn.

Gillian looks at Chris in utter astonishment. "Have our prayers really been answered?" she asks.

From that day on, Anna never has a symptom of ME again.

When Anna arrives in Southern Africa, ready to start her Christian discipleship training year, all the students are invited to share the stories of how they have ended up there. When it's Anna's turn, there's a sense of amazement.

"We were expecting you to get here exhausted and in pain," the course leader exclaims, "but you're quite the opposite."

"I've got three years' worth of adrenalin stored up and waiting to come out," Anna announces, as she dances her way around the compound that will be her new home for the next few months. She barely sits still, constantly running and jumping for joy in worship, sharing her story at every opportunity.

"I don't get how you can radiate so much energy, always running around, all day, every day, with such a huge, beautiful smile," one of her fellow students reveals. "It wasn't until I heard your story that I realised how restricting your illness had been, and how much gratitude and joy have come through your healing."

"How are you feeling, Anna?" Her family doctor is soft-spoken and kind.

Anna and Gillian have come to the surgery because they want medical verification of her healing. She breaks into a broad grin as she explains what's happened, giving all the glory to God.

"What an amazing story!" the doctor declares. "I can't believe you're the same person who I saw when I used to come to your house and find you languishing in bed, with a little piece of toast beside you. It's been such a long journey, but what a complete and utter transformation!"

She's clearly stuck for superlatives, the shock in her voice evident.

"I'm keen to know," she says, "have you got back to dancing since your recovery?"

"I don't dance competitively anymore," Anna explains, "I just dance to worship the Lord who healed me, sometimes for an hour or two at a time. Everyone's noticed the difference."

The conversation continues, and then: "It's so unusual to see any improvement with ME, let alone a complete healing. You're a totally different young woman! You've been so sick, but now you're so full of energy and life, in a way that I never expected to see." She pauses a moment to find the right words, "I don't say this lightly Anna, but it's genuinely miraculous. I'm absolutely thrilled for you, despite how difficult it's been, and I can tell you now that I've never had a conversation like this with a patient, in all the twenty-five years I've been practising medicine."

She's choking back tears, and Anna cannot stop smiling.

Anna's zeal for life is infectious. Catching up with her now, it's clear that she's not just been healed, but liberated and released from a prison of pain.

"God spoke to me so clearly," she tells me. "He said, 'Daughter, your faith has healed you,' and I believe that to be true." She pauses for a moment to reflect. "It's not that my healing was conditional on having enough faith," she says, "but he told me clearly that he would heal me, and I had to hold onto what he was saying, even when it seemed impossible."

If doubts ever bubble to the surface, Anna starts to dance. "I'm so in awe of what he's done and how he's healed me, that words feel inadequate," she explains, "so I express my thanks to him in dance."

Everywhere she goes, opportunities arise to share her story and, through it, her faith in Jesus. "I want everyone to hear how God has healed me," she says excitedly, "because I know he wants to heal other people too."

Acknowledgements

Saying thank you is important, and I have a lot of people to thank.

My heartfelt thanks go to everyone who entrusted me with their stories, and the other named people who had key roles to play in those stories. You have all combined to make this book what it is. Thank you to everyone who provided me with the raw materials for the stories, some of which were deeply personal. I so appreciate your vulnerability and trust. Thank you to the medical and other professionals who provided verification.

Thank you to the many friends who, in the immediate aftermath of my car accident, urged me to write down all the details of what happened, just in case I might, one day, decide to include them in a book: Rachel Southall, Jenny and Steve Rees, Julia and Doug Hammond, Di Bamber, Ian Horne, Elaine Bond, and Lorien Megaw. Your foresight yielded dividends.

Thank you to the Costa Rican, the Australian and the South African, whose public prophetic words kick-started me into writing for public consumption and not just privately. God used you to speak to me, and it directly led to the birthing of this book. (I have explained more in the Introduction.)

Thank you to Elvin and Jackie Turner for your creativity in coming up with the title that glues this book together, and Sheridan Voysey for helping me strengthen the subtitle. Thank you to Martyn Sandford and Harford Smith for your generous provision of homes in beautiful locations, enabling me to write so much of this book during my sabbatical.

Thank you to all my family, friends and colleagues who have journeyed with me, cheered me on and encouraged me to keep going over all the years of writing one-day-a-week while juggling a full-time job in the other four-days-a-week. Thank you to Dad, Mum, Adrian, Ruth, Pippa, Matt, Katy, Lily, Sam, Barney, Luke, Amy and Abigail for your constant encouragement, prayers and support. Thank you to my great friend, Mary Oakes, for not allowing me to give up and walk away, and for plying me with cups of tea when I needed them. Thank you to Liz Pienaar and Claire Mortimer for being there through thick and thin, and undergirding this book with your prayers. Thank you to Kate Coleman for being such a brilliant mentor, and for your unwavering championing of me as an author. Thank you to Astrid Foxen and Alice Philip for coaching me so well. Thank you to Helen Gaw, Sarah Onduko and Paul Cook for our various inspiring conversations about faith-based writing.

Thank you to some of my most loyal blog subscribers for championing my writing and encouraging me to write this book, especially Anna Shaw, Janet May and Joy Margetts. Thank you to Kay Miles for all your creative marketing ideas; Paul Bell for helping me build a brilliant website from which to promote and sell this book; and the talented John Cairns for all the author photos. Thank you to my new-found friends at the Association of Christian Writers for all your peer support through the various steps of the publishing journey. It makes such a difference to know you have been there before me.

Thank you to everyone in my publishing team: Malcolm Down for your belief in the book from the moment we first discussed it, your calm reassurance whenever there have been hiccups, and your unwavering assistance at every step of the process. Sheila Jacobs for your commissioning editorial review of my initial book manuscript, and your suggestions for improvement, which greatly strengthened it. Louise Stenhouse for your sharp editor's eye, your editorial suggestions, and weeding out all my excess commas. Sarah Grace for conceptualising, and Esther Kotecha for designing, a front cover that both catches the eye and conveys the metaphor behind the title in equal measure. And all my endorsers who took time to read and review the book, despite your busy schedules.

Finally, but most importantly, my heartfelt thanks go to Jesus, without whom this book would not exist.

Making contact

You can keep in touch with Joanna at joannawatson.co.uk

Further help

Explore faith, life and meaning: alpha.org

Be equipped and inspired to pray: 24-7prayer.com/prayer-course

Further reading

Why testimony stories matter:

Richard Gamble, *Remember: Revealing the Eternal Power of Answered Prayer* (SPCK, 2018)

Miracles:

C.S. Lewis, *Miracles: A Preliminary Study*

Lee Strobel, *The Case For Miracles: A Journalist Investigates Evidence for the Supernatural* (Zondervan, 2018)

Rachel Hickson, *Supernatural Breakthrough: The Heartcry for Change* (New Wine Ministries, 2007)

Prayer:

Pete Greig, *How to Pray: A Simple Guide For Normal People* (Hodder & Stoughton, 2017)

Jack Deere, *Surprised by the Voice of God* (Zondervan, 1996)

Rachel Hickson, *Supernatural Communication: The Privilege of Prayer* (New Wine Ministries, 2006)

When God seems silent:

Pete Greig, *God On Mute: Engaging the Silence of Unanswered Prayer* (Kingsway, 2007)

Joni Eareckson Tada, *Where's My Miracle?* (Rose Publishing, 2015)

Healing:

Francis MacNutt, *Healing* (Hodder & Stoughton, 1989)

Derek Prince, *Invisible Barriers to Healing: Six Common Barriers to Healing and How to Overcome Them* (Audio CD or MP3)

Suffering:

C.S. Lewis, *The Problem of Pain*

Philip Yancey, *Where Is God When It Hurts?* (Zondervan, 1997)

Amy Orr-Ewing, *Where Is God In All the Suffering?* (The Good Book Company, 2006)

Sharon Dirckx, *Why: Looking At God, Evil and Suffering* (IVP, 2013)

About the author

Joanna Watson is an inspirational British Christian author and speaker, whose passion is to see ordinary people encountering God in extraordinary ways.

Light through the Cracks is birthed out of her experience of surviving a dramatic car accident that could have left her dead or paralysed, during which she witnessed first-hand how God breaks in when life turns tough.

She blogs regularly, sharing stories and reflections that follow the same theme as this book. She also keeps a private prayer journal, recording her observations about how God is at work in the world, whether or not we are aware. She often speaks on the themes covered by *Light through the Cracks*, including faith, hope and miracles.

When not writing, preaching or teaching, Joanna can be found leading a large team for Tearfund, a Christian relief and development organisation. Her work and other travels have taken her to more than 50 countries over the past 20 years.

She lives in Oxfordshire in the UK, where she enjoys being with her family and friends.

You can connect with Joanna at joannawatson.co.uk